D1484084

IRISH SETTERS
TODAY

Eve Gardner

Howell Book House

New York

Copyright © 1998
Ringpress Books, PO Box 8, Lydney,
Gloucestershire GL15 6YD, United Kingdom.

HOWELL BOOK HOUSE
A Simon & Schuster / Macmillan Company
1633 Broadway
New York, NY 10019

MACMILLAN is a registered trademark of Macmillan, Inc.

Library of Congress Cataloging-in-Publication Data
Gardner, Eve.
    Irish setters today / Eve Gardner
         p. cm.
    ISBN 0-87605-147-6
    1. Irish setters.   I. Title.
SF429.I7G35   1998
636.752'6--dc21   98-11600
                                             CIP

Manufactured in Singapore

10 9 8 7 6 5 4 3 2 1

CONTENTS

This book is dedicated to the memory
of a very special Irish Setter
CHAMPION CARNBARGUS CASHMERE
13.3.1985 - 11.7.1997

*A*CKNOWLEDGEMENTS

Many people have helped with this project by freely giving me information and advice. I am particularly indebted to Sybil Lennox, Jean Leighton-Boyce and Peter and Julie James for their time and patience and for allowing me access to their photographic treasures. My thanks also to the photographers for their permission to reproduce their work. They are acknowledged under their photographs.

Mary Gurney kindly agreed to let Sh. Ch. Caspians The Music Man of Danaway be used as a model for the trimming photographs and Jean Ryan in America allowed her Am. Ch. Sametsuz Ard-Righ to be trimmed the "British" way. Many thanks to them and to Angela Begg for her excellent drawings which she completed despite ill health.

I am indebted to the following for collecting overseas information and photographs for me: Australia, Helene Gration; Belgium, Jean Struyf de Groof; Holland, Henk ten Klooster; Ireland, Trudy Walsh; New Zealand, Gayle Sheridan; Sweden, Madeleine Bäckman. Without their help I could not have managed.

To Simon Jones, BVSc., MRCVS I offer my thanks for his time and for the benefit of his wisdom on the Health Chapter.

Finally I am particularly grateful to Rita Bryden for her dedication to the task of reading my manuscript and for keeping a watchful eye on the contents.

Note on titles: Overseas dogs can carry a number of titles that are won at one show on one day: these titles have been omitted. Titles such as Champion and Show Champion have been used as notified by the dogs' owners.

Title page photograph: Carnbargus Courage, Carnbargus Caleche, Sh. Ch. Carnbargus Continuity, Ch. Carnbargus Cashmere.

INTRODUCTION

Writing about one's favourite breed is not only a pleasure, but also a daunting task, as there are so many sides to these wonderful dogs, Irish Setters. Their great physical beauty has given them a reputation for being decorative but empty-headed, and lacking any serious side. After all, it is hard to believe that such a glamorous red-head could also possess a brain, be biddable, and have the ability, when given the opportunity, to do a decent day's work in the field. Do not allow yourself to be misled: Irish Setters can be highly intelligent and are quite capable of fulfilling a multitude of roles in modern life.

However, there is no denying that the breed has a reputation for being wilful and often rather wild. Much of this is quite undeserved and is frequently due to an owner's lack of understanding of what makes the Irish Setter tick. They are supposed to be high-spirited and full of fun, but this natural exuberance has to be kept in check, in just the same way that lively, bright children have to be controlled with a kind, but firm hand. Therefore, it is of great importance to establish a routine as early as possible and to make sure that an Irish Setter learns about his place in life. Yes, Irish Setters can be infuriating when they decide not to hear or see you. Having a good time can often be much more important to them than returning to a frustrated owner, but Irish Setters know very well when they have offended and will do their best to ingratiate themselves back into their owner's good books.

The Irish Setter is still valued as a working gundog.

Photo: Colette Tuite.

THE GUNDOG

In the field Irish Setters are really in their natural element, and the breed has an enthusiastic following, not only at field trials, but also as a working gundog. Whatever Irish Setters are bred for, be it as a companion or as a show dog, the origins of the breed must never be forgotten and only those of us who have been fortunate enough to see Irish Setters working on the moors and in other open spaces can really fully appreciate them.

Some years ago a very famous breeder of Labrador Retrievers told me that she had not come across an Irish Setter that could not be trained to work as a gundog. She had never bred a litter of Irish, but had taken them in as young adults, usually when they were in need of a home. Most of them had been allowed to get into some sort of trouble by their previous owners, but after careful, corrective training and education, together with patience and understanding, they could be turned into sensible gundogs. The majority of the dogs had been bred entirely from show stock, proving that the basic working instincts are, fortunately, still well preserved within the breed. She did not have the same experience with any of the other varieties of Setters.

THE TOWN DOG

With this background the Irish Setter should, ideally, live as a country dog and have plenty of room to enjoy free gallops to let off steam. Unfortunately, their owners' circumstances do not always make this possible, but the breed is extremely adaptable and Irish Setters are quite capable of living happy lives in towns and cities. However, it is up to their owners to work out, *before* they acquire an Irish Setter, how they are going to provide the exercise their dog will undoubtedly need. If you are not prepared to make the time available, maybe you should consider a less demanding breed.

I owned my first Irish Setter when I lived in a

Irish Setters are popular as show dogs. Sh. Ch. Goldings Hella and her mother Sh. Ch. Goldings Heike have both gained their titles in the show ring.

flat in London. Great efforts were made to ensure that she had daily walks and frequent outings to the local parks. I do not think she was deprived in any way, but it was never forgotten that she was a sporting dog.

THE FAMILY DOG

Irish Setters make wonderful companions and great family dogs. They are devoted to their families and like to join in all their activities, and to be excluded is considered a punishment! Children are their particular favourites, and it is quite amazing to watch the lively, even boisterous Irish turn into a gentle fool when meeting small children and babies.

On the whole, they are blessed with excellent temperaments and kindly natures. They are safe

The superb temperament of the Irish Setter makes them ideal as family dogs.

Photo: Ryan, USA.

with children, whom they tend to regard as their own property, though children must be taught not to tease or torment the dog, but to respect their pet. In the evening, when the family settles down, Irish Setters will appreciate nothing more than a place on a favourite settee or in an armchair, preferably by the fire. But more than anything, they just want to be with you!

THE SHOW DOG

Irish Setters are very popular as show dogs, not only in the UK, but in the USA, Australia and New Zealand. They also enjoy great popularity in the show ring in many European countries and the sport is on the increase in former eastern block countries such as Hungary, where shows had already been popular under the communist regime.

In the UK, the Irish Setter has achieved huge success in the show ring. Three Irish Setters have won the ultimate prize, Best in Show at Crufts, in 1981, 1993 and again in 1995, and another was Reserve Best in Show in 1983. This is a great achievement, particularly so when one considers that the Kennel Club registrations for the breed have been quite stable over recent years, and that they average about 1500 to 2000 per annum. This is quite a change from the height of popularity in the 1970s and early 1980s, when registration figures in excess of 5000 per year were not uncommon. A very high percentage of Irish Setters find their way into the show ring, and the breed often provides one of the top entries at Championship shows. Such entries are achieved despite the fact that the breed does not even appear in the top twenty most popular breeds registered at the Kennel Club.

ABOVE: Brayville Regal Lady of Corribeg: There is no need to worry about enthusiasm – Irish Setters love agility! Photo: Bill Bunce.

RIGHT: International Champion Coppersheen Alacrity is a trained Search Dog in Switzerland. Photo: Kind permission KYNOS-Verlag, Germany. Taken from: 'Rasse-Portrait Setter', by Hilde Schwoyer.

THE VERSATILE DOG

During recent years Agility has become a popular sport. There is no need to worry about a lack of enthusiasm in the breed as Irish Setters cheerfully enter into the competition! As far as Obedience is concerned, there have been a few successes, but this is not really the Irish Setter's strongest subject. Even if they put on a brilliant performance one day, the next time they could well be bored by the repetition and decide against the whole idea!

Irish Setters have joined the ranks of Therapy Dogs, and their visits to the Homes for the Elderly are eagerly awaited by the residents. They also visit schools for disadvantaged children, and it is hard to tell who enjoys the visits more. Their cheerful, lively presence gives so much pleasure to the children who might otherwise not have the opportunity of close contact with a dog – especially not one as charming and responsive as an Irish Setter.

Their great beauty has provided Irish Setters with some quite unexpected careers. They have featured in advertisements promoting the most diverse range of products on television and in magazines. The lovely chestnut-coloured coat adds glamour to even the most beautiful human model. Above all, they always look as if they are enjoying themselves, and give the impression that they are having a wonderful time. However, the Breed's most famous starring role came in the film *Big Red,* which must have been seen by millions all over the world.

If all this seems a very long way from the breed's origins in Ireland, it only proves just what a versatile and adaptable breed the Irish Setter has become.

1 ORIGINS AND DEVELOPMENT

The Irish Setter is, reputedly, an ancient breed, with its early history lost in the Irish mists of time. Many theories have been put forward concerning the earliest ancestors, but in the absence of any records they must remain just that. It is believed by some that even before the arrival of Christianity, Ireland had its own bird dogs, and there were 'sitting' or 'setting' dogs in existence long before they acquired the name of 'Setter'. Spaniels, undoubtedly, had a major role to play in the development of the breed – the most likely type being the larger land spaniels. The origins of such spaniels have also been open to some debate but, according to Mr W.J. Rasbridge, the breed's senior historian, and others, they originated in Spain and took their name from that country.

What is clear is that the dogs were used by wild fowlers, who were either hawking or netting to provide food for their cooking pots. When working with a hawk, a dog would hunt and search for game. Once birds had been located, the dog would flush them into the air and then the fowler would release the hawk to bring down the bird and make a kill. When working with the net, the dog would be sent to locate the birds and, once

game had been scented, the dog would adopt a certain stance, with one foreleg raised, which indicated, or 'indexed', to the handler where the game was to be found. On command, the dog would then crawl closer to the birds on his belly, allowing the hunter to get into position to throw his net over the birds and his dog. A dog that was capable of quietly locating game, and then creeping towards it without alarming the birds, must have been of great value and, sooner or later, dogs with the same ability would have been bred together to improve such special talents in their offspring.

DAWN OF THE BREED

Probably the first reference to a "Setter" in literature can be found in a work by Dr. Caius *De Canibus Britannicis,* first published in 1570 and in the revised version, with the main text in English, which was published in 1576. In his book Dr Caius lists the different types of British dogs and the work for which they were used. In this context, the word "Setter" appears as an approximate translation from the Latin: "The Dogge called the Setter, in Latine, Index: Another sort of Dogges be there, serviceable for fowling, making no noise either with foote or with tongue, whiles they follow the game. They attend diligently upon theyr Master and frame their conditions to such beckes, motions and gestures, as it shall please him to exhibite and make, either going forward, drawing backeward, inclining to the right hand, or yealding toward the left. When he hath founde the byrde, he keepeth sure and fast silence, he stayeth his steppes and wil proceede no further, and with a close, covert, watching eye, layeth his belly to the grounde and so creepeth forward like a worme. When he approaches neere to the place where the birde is, he layes him downe, and with a marcke of his pawes, betrayeth the place of the byrdes last abode, whereby it is supposed that this kind of dogge is calles Index, Setter, being in deede a name most consonant and agreeable to his quality."

It would be a mistake to assume that the term "Setter" referred to a particular breed in the way we understand it now, and the most likely type of dog to be involved was a large land spaniel. However, the description of how the dogs performed their work can easily be recognized by anyone who has been fortunate enough to see Setters at work. The assumption that Dr Caius was probably describing a "setting spaniel" seems to be confirmed by Surflet and Markham when they write in *The Country Farme* published in 1616: "There is also another sort of land spannyels which are called Setters."

EARLY HISTORY
The development of the shotgun in the 17th century was to put an end to netting, but falconry with Setters has survived and still has a following to-day, although now it is practised as a sport rather than as a serious method of hunting for game. The Spanish Pointer showed itself to be particularly adaptable to the new work with the gun and it is believed that, through cross-breeding, its

blood has also contributed to the creation of the Setter. What is clear is that by the early 18th century a dog called 'Setter' had come into existence, and that Ireland had its own variety. The Irish considered their variety of Setter to be better suited to their much rougher terrain and weather conditions, and their particular breed started to prosper. In 1804 *The Shooting Directory* by R.B. Thornhill contained a reference to red and white Setters which confirmed the high regard in which the "Irish" Setter was being held by sportsmen: "There is no country in Europe that can boast of finer Setters than Ireland."

Landed families in Ireland took a particular pride in their own strains of dogs and kept records of their breeding. The de Freyne family of French Park, for example, had started to keep a stud book as early as 1793 and it was continued until 1879. The de Freynes had come to Ireland from France, and it seems quite likely that they had brought their own Epagneuls with them which could well have contributed to their particular strain of Setter. Other strains at the time were owned by Lord Clancarty, Lord Dillon, the Marquis of Waterford, Sir George Gore and the Rev. Robert O'Callaghan's family – the Earls of Lismore, among others.

A STANDARD
In a reference to the colour of the "setting spaniells" Dr Caius had written in 1570: "The most part of their skynnes are white, and if they are marcked with any spottes, they are commonly red, and somewhat great therewithall." If this description has any bearing on the development of the Irish Setter, it seems correct to assume that it was selective breeding that very gradually changed white-and-red to predominantly red-and-white. By the end of the 18th century self-coloured reds were also starting

to be reared, instead of being destroyed as undesirable. In 1845 Youatt was able to write that "Irish sportsmen are a little too prejudiced with regard to particular colours. Their dogs are either very red, or red and white, or lemon coloured, or white patched with deep chestnut."

Gradually, the self-reds began to outnumber the red and whites, though they remained popular mainly with the shooting fraternity. Up to that time the Irish Setter had been purely a working gundog, but it seems that the selective breeding for a wholly red coat was for a very different reason – appearance. This, in turn, brought about a change of attitude to and use of the Irish Setter and by 1859 the first dog show was held, in Newcastle upon Tyne in England, with the entry restricted to Pointers and

Setters. Exhibiting Irish Setters caught on and an increasing number of dog shows gave owners the opportunity to compare the physical attributes of their animals. However, there were wide differences in the appearance of the dogs and some uncertainty as to what was true Irish Setter type.

The first field trial followed, in 1865, where owners could test the working ability of their dogs by letting them compete against each other in the field. The first Irish Setter to win an award at a field trial was the dog Plunket, born in 1868, when he won a second place at the Shrewsbury Trials in May 1870. Showing and trialling required a much more uniform animal and, therefore, a standard by which the dogs could be judged. The Irish Red Setter Club was founded in Dublin in 1882 and a Standard for the breed was drawn up and approved on March 29th 1886. It was based on a scale of points for the head, body and coat and feather, but the scale of points was later dropped. Apart from some minor changes, this Standard is still in

"Setters." Published in 1831 in 'The New Sporting Magazine'.

use to-day and will be discussed in a later chapter.

The Scale of Points of the Irish Red Setter, as approved by the Irish Red Setter Club in Dublin on March 29th 1886, read as follows:

Head	10 points
Eyes	6 points
Ears	4 points
Neck	4 points
Body	20 points
Hind Legs and Feet	10 points
Fore Legs and Feet	10 points
Tail	4 points
Coat and Feather	10 points
Colour	8 points
Size, Style and General App.	14 points
	100 points

THE EARLY 2OTH CENTURY

Breeders continued to mix the working and show strains well into the early years of the 20th century, but the social and economic changes brought about, more than anything, by the First World War, led to a decline in the popularity of the working Irish Setter. However, show stock continued to make progress and influential stud dogs of that time have left their mark on the breed.

Young Phil, whelped in 1900, was the sire of at least nine CC winners, and his influence has been such that he features, albeit way back, in all the important modern pedigrees. Mr Rasbridge described him as "perhaps the greatest stud influence of the century". Another stud dog of lasting importance was Gorse of Auburn whelped in 1917, a dog praised for his sweet head, dark eyes and lovely expression. He had a large number of winning offspring to his credit, not only on the bench, but also in the field. In 1924 Mrs Florence Nagle bought his son, Ben d'Or, as a companion to a lonely Wolfhound. Ben's dam, Ruby Mahoney, was by the dual-purpose sire Ch. Terry of Boyne, and Ben had the honour to win the only CC Mrs Nagle gained in the Breed. She must have been pleased with Ben as she bought three others of the same breeding. One of them, Sheilin d'Or, was the first Irish Setter to win the Champion Stake in 1927 and her owner rated her as the best of her 17 Field Trial Champions.

THE RHEOLAS

Mrs Ingle Bepler's Rheola Kennel had emerged from the First World War not only as a dominant force but as the premier show kennel, and her stock would go on to

FT Ch. Sulhamstead Sheilin D'Or. From a painting by Cecil Aldin. By kind permission of the Kennel Club and the estate of the late Cecil Aldin.

Rheola Bryn with five of his children. Pictured left to right: Ch. Shaun of Matsonhouse, Miss Thorne-Baker with Ch. Shamus of Ballyshannon, Mrs Ingle Bepler with Bryn, Ch. Biddy of Gadeland, Rebecca of Redshoot, and Mistyn.
Taken from Mrs Darley's scrapbook. By kind permission of the Irish Setter Association, England.

provide the foundation for many other successful kennels in the future. In 1908 she, together with others, had founded the Irish Setter Association, England, to break the stranglehold of "the Irishmen" who were dominating the Irish Setter show scene at that time with their Irish-bred dogs. Feeling against them ran so high that membership of the new Association was restricted, for more than twenty years, to residents of England, Scotland and Wales. However, Mrs Ingle Bepler, in her capacity as the secretary of a rival club, did not hesitate to adopt the Standard of the Breed that had been drawn up by the Dublin Irish Red Setter Club!

The Rheola Kennel had been started in the early 1890s by Mrs Ingle Bepler before she was married, when she was Miss Ingle Ball. She described her foundation bitches as follows: "From the three bitches, Lady Honora, Ch. Winifred and Ch. Carrig Maid, all bought by me as puppies, the 'Rheola' strain was evolved. Each owned Ch. Palmerston as a common ancestor, Lady Honora being from Ch. Aveline (known as

'The Beautiful'), Ch. Winifred from Sullivan, a grand worker and sire of many Field Trial winners, and Ch. Carrig Maid was descended from those wonderful bitches, the Geraldines."

Her deliberate choice of stock descended from Ch. Palmerston is of some interest and had been suggested to her by the Rev. Robert O'Callaghan when he lived at Brandeston village in Suffolk, and where she had been a frequent visitor as a girl. Facts

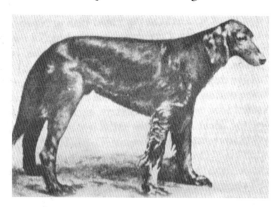

Palmerston.

Champion Norna: The winner of 18 CCs and dam of seven CC winners. Her brood bitch record stood for more than forty years.

concerning Palmerston's breeding and date of birth cannot be guaranteed, but he was owned by Mr Cecil Moore, a solicitor of Omagh, County Tyrone, where he kept a kennel of working Irish Setters. He was a founder member of the Dublin Irish Red Setter Club and had been highly influential in drafting the Standard of the Breed. Palmerston turned out to be a poor worker and passed into the hands of Mr T. Hilliard in 1874 when he was already getting on in years. Accounts of how this transfer came about are varied, but it was in Hilliard's ownership that Palmerston became a successful show dog in 1875. However, and much more importantly, he also began his great career as a highly influential stud dog in Hilliard's hands. By 1934 Mr Rasbridge had worked out "that there were five tail male lines starting with Palmerston, Muskerry, 'Frisco, Peaceful Times and Ravenhill Phil" – which means that there were five direct male lines of descent.

However, Mrs Ingle Bepler told him that Palmerston was also the direct ancestor of Muskerry, which then reduced the lines to four. Furthermore, if the lines behind Ch.

Peaceful Times and Ravenhill Phil could be extended far enough back, it is almost certain that they, too, would link up with either Palmerston or 'Frisco. This would leave the Breed with just two male foundation sires. This makes Palmerston's influence enormous, as it would be difficult to find an Irish Setter anywhere in the world that does not go back to him on many lines. His distinctive white head markings have been described by several writers and vary from "a slight snip of white on the nose" to "a small white blaze on his forehead". One of the judges described the mark as "a thin thread of white running down the foreface" and, to this day, any white head-markings, whatever their shape or size, tend to be referred to as a "Palmerston snip".

With such a background, Mrs Ingle Bepler could say, with some justification, that her kennel had been built on "firm foundations" and, with a reference to type, that "Rheola dogs could be 'spotted' in a show without the aid of a catalogue." She had imported a dog of pure English bloodlines from Holland, Ch. Clancarty Rhu, whelped in 1901 and known there as Castor. His daughter, Show Champion Ypsilanti, still features, way back, in many modern pedigrees; especially behind the Wendovers. When mated to Ch. Carrig Maid in 1906, Clancarty Rhu became the sire of Ch. Rheola Toby, who in turn became the double great-grandfather of the important Show Champion Rheola Bryn, who was not shown until he was four years old. The two matings between Rheola Bryn and Rheola Mallie produced Irish Setters that were not only responsible for a high proportion of the top winners and producers of their time, but were also thought to have been largely responsible for the spread of the gene for PRA throughout the breed.

Mrs Ingle Bepler always considered Bryn's dam Sh. Ch. Rheola Didona to have been her best bitch, but many would have argued that Ch. Norna, a Didona daughter by Loc Garmain Barney, had been the better of the two. Norna was sold as a puppy to Mr P.H. Holme but was later bought back by Mrs Ingle Bepler, only to be sold again, this time to Mrs M. Ogden of the famous Borrowdale Irish Setters. Norna won a total of 18 CCs and produced seven CC winners – a brood bitch record that was to stand for more than forty years.

THE BOYNES

The Boyne Kennel of Mr J.A. Carbery, of Drogheda in Ireland, at one time held a position of almost equal importance to that of the Rheolas, lasting from the early 1900s until well into the 1930s. According to Mr Gilbert Leighton-Boyce it would be "unwise to take the direct male line behind Ch. Barney of Boyne further back than his grandsire Beltra", but Barney proved himself as a dual-purpose sire. Not only did the Field Trial Champion Sulhamstead Token d'Or come from him, but also Champion Hundridge Mary of Boyne. Stories abound concerning the breeding of some of the Boynes, including how Bloodhound and Flatcoated Retriever blood were introduced. A possible Bloodhound connection could certainly account for bloat being present in the Irish Setter!

Mr Carbery's Boyne Kennel provided the foundation stock for many of the emerging kennels, in the UK as well as in the USA, in much the same way that the Rheolas did, but some of the most successful results were achieved through a combination of the bloodlines from both their kennels. Ch. Gadeland Neula of Boyne, owned by Mrs E. Baker, was to have considerable influence on the breed through her litters by Sh. Ch. Rheola Bryn and by Bryn's son, the famous show dog Sh. Ch. Shamus of Ballyshannon, owned by Miss Thorne-Baker, and she can be found behind most of the present-day show stock in the UK. Although the Boyne kennel was primarily a show kennel, Mr Carbery never lost his interest in field trials and aimed, in his breeding, at a dual-purpose Irish Setter.

EARLY AMERICAN IMPORTS

Irish Setters that were to make names for themselves in America started to be imported from Ireland and England from the 1870s onwards. Probably the first import of note was Plunket, a winner at shows and field trails in England, and his owner, the Reverend J. Cuming Macdona, became, in 1874, the first Englishman to judge at a dog show in the USA. Plunket was born in Ireland in 1868 and was line-bred to Birtwhistle's Tim. Three of his children followed him to the USA where only imported Irish Setters and their progeny could be registered as Irish Setters in the National American Kennel Club Stud Book. 'American' or 'Native Setters' were registered in a separate section as 'Cross Bred' and

'Other Setters'. The imported Irish Setters set a new standard for quality and type and they and their progeny were given separate classes at shows.

In 1875 Charles H. Turner imported Sullivan's Rose, Erin and Frisk and the great Elcho. He was born in May 1874 and became the first American Irish Setter bench Champion. However, his importance to the breed came through his progeny which excelled on the bench and in the field. In 1877 Dr William Jarvis of New Hampshire acquired Ch. Elcho and mated him to his imported Rose, a Palmerston daughter, and to Noreen, also descended from Palmerston. Both matings were repeated many times, providing America with some excellent foundation stock to build on. The best, by far, was Ch. Elcho Jnr. (out of Noreen) who had a tremendous show career which was remarkable not only for its success, but also for its length, running from 1882 to 1891 without him ever being beaten.

TRANSATLANTIC EXCHANGES
After Dr Jarvis had discovered the nick – the successful combination of the Palmerston and Elcho lines in America – he recommended it to the Reverend O'Callaghan who adopted it wholeheartedly and confined his breeding to those lines. In turn, O'Callaghan exported Ch. Winnie II and Desmond II to Charles T. Thompson of the Chestnut Hill Kennels in Philadelphia. They were the same way bred as Ch. Aveline "the beautiful" and Ch. Shandon II (by Frisco, a Ch. Elcho grandson ex Grouse II, a Palmerston daughter). In fact, the same lines also provided the foundation stock for Mrs Ingle Bepler's Rheolas. Coleraine, a Ch. Aveline daughter by her own brother, Fingal III, followed her relations to the USA and her brother Ch. Finglas was exported in 1891. He gained his title on the bench and

won at field trials. A successful sire, his name appears way back in the pedigrees of most American-bred Irish Setters.

In the 1890s three of Muskerry's sons were imported, which further deepened the Palmerston/Elcho lines. One of the dogs, Signal, was particularly suited to Ch. Finglas' daughters and left his mark on the breed.

The last two decades of the 19th century saw an increase in the popularity of the Irish Setter right across America, leading to a Breed Club being established. The Irish Setter Club of America was founded in 1891, but according to its first Secretary, Michael Flynn, the Irish Setter Club of the USA had been founded in 1886 and was renamed the Irish Setter Club of America in 1891.

Influential kennels started to come to the fore, producing important dogs such as Ch. Ben Law, born in 1896, the founder of the Law strain. He and his six Champion sons all had leading roles to play in the development of the Irish Setter in America. Joseph and Thomas Wall founded their Lismore Kennels, and their Ch. Lismore Freedom sired six Champions as well as the great brood bitch, Craigie Lea Mona.

Imports from Ireland and England continued to arrive and in 1914 Mrs Ingle Bepler sent out Rheola Clanderrick, by Ch. Clancarty Rhu ex Rheola Ronda. He quickly gained his title and became a widely used stud dog whose influence was to last for many years.

THE 1920s AND 1930s
Following the end of the first World War, Irish Setters in the USA started to enjoy a similar growth in popularity to their cousins in the UK, but the working Irish Setter lost ground in favour of the show dog. The 1920s were remarkable for the large number of imported dogs, in particular those from

the Boyne Kennels. Eng. Ch. Terry of Boyne went to the Woodbine Kennels in Missouri and a large number of his offspring were to follow him to his new country. However, none of them were to have the influence of Higgins' Paddy of Boyne. Imported in 1923 by William W. Higgins, his highly successful matings with Craigie Lea Mona have assured him of his place in Irish Setter history. From their four litters came six Champions that were to influence the development of the breed in the USA. One of them, Ch. Higgins' Red Pat, born in 1924, was a great showman and did much to popularise Irish Setters. However, his full brother, Ch. Higgins' Red Coat, born in 1927, became the sire of 30 bench Champions.

His most influential sons proved to be Ch. Milson O'Boy, Ch. Kinvarra Son of Red Coat and Ch. Redwood Russet of Harvale. Milson O'Boy enjoyed a spectacular show career from 1933 to 1938. He was owned by Mrs Cheever Porter and handled by Harry Hartnett who acquired the Milson Kennels in 1930. Many already well-established kennels owed their greatest success to O'Boy and his progeny, among them Fred Nielson and the Rosecroft Irish Setters, and Mr and Mrs Knight and their Knightscroft Kennel which had been started in 1932. O'Boy also contributed to the success of the Caldene Kennels, owned by Dr Jay W. Calhoon, who acquired the Milson dogs in 1944.

Another breeder who benefited greatly from Ch. Higgins' Red Coat's prepotency was Lee Schoen who had established his famous Kinvarra Kennel in 1932. He mated his imported bitch Borrowdale Yseult of Kinvarra to Ch. Kinvarra Son of Red Coat to produce Ch. Kinvarra Craig. In 1936 Lee Schoen imported Ch. Kinvarra Mollie of Gadeland on behalf of Ted Eldredge, who was then aged only fourteen, and Mollie

became the foundation for the equally famous Tirvelda Kennels, which produced more than 100 Champions. Lee Schoen had retained the right to select the sire for Mollie's first litter as well as the right to keep the best puppy for himself. Mollie was mated to Craig, and Ch. Kinvarra Kermit – one of the all-time great Irish Setters – was born. Kermit sired 29 Champions, and there is not a kennel of note in America that does not go back to him. Mrs Joyce Nilsen's Thenderin Kennel has produced over 200 Champions and was founded by a Kermit daughter, Ch. Kinvarra Portia, the dam of twelve Champions, making her one of the breed's leading brood bitches.

CH. HARTSBOURNE SALLYANN
From time to time Lee Schoen and Ted Eldredge continued to import stock from England and their clever blending of the imported Irish Setters with American-bred stock was reflected in the enormous success both their kennels enjoyed. However, none of the later imports proved to be as influential as Hartsbourne Sallyann, who was bred by Mrs Eileen Walker and imported by Ted Eldredge in 1957. Sallyann quickly gained her title and was mated to Ch. Kinvarra Malone, descended from Mollie of Gadeland, and all the subsequent Tirveldas go back to two important bitches of that breeding, Ch. Tirvelda Sybil and Ch. Tirvelda Nutbrown Sherry. With 23 Champion offspring to her name, Nutbrown Sherry had the honour of becoming the top brood bitch. From one litter alone came 11 Champions, including Ch. Tirvelda Michaelson, one of the most influential sires in the breed. In time, the strength of the lines developed to such a degree that most American kennels of note were influenced by Tirvelda breeding.

2 *PRA AND RECONSTRUCTION*

During the early 1920s Mr H.E. Whitwell founded the numerically strong Ardagh kennels. At first, the very best dogs that money could buy were acquired, such as Ch. Ravenhill Phil and Ch. Delaware Kate who went on to become an International Champion, gaining her titles in England, Ireland, Canada and in the USA. In the hands of Mrs Dorothy Whitwell the kennel produced numerous home-bred champions, including Champions Factor, Forrester and Flower of Ardagh. The mating of Factor and Flower was to have a lasting influence on the breed as it is behind Hartsbourne Shaun and his son Branscombe Robyn. The same combination produced Favour of Ardagh, the foundation for Mrs Mary Darling's Boisdale line.

TWO GREAT KENNELS

The late 1920s saw the emergence of the first of the two great kennels which were to have the most profound influence on the breed, Mrs E.K. Walker's Hartsbourne Kennel. Her kennel was founded by the bitch Val (Rheola Bryn ex Rheola Mallie) whelped in 1926. When mated to the successful sire Loc Garmain Barney (Gorse of Auburn ex Portsdown Patricia by Ch. Brian of Boyne) she produced the first

Ch. Hartsbourne Jade: The first Hartsbourne Champion (Loc Garmain Barney – Val, the foundation bitch).

Hartsbourne Champion, Jade, a big winner and excellent worker, and also Jade's litter sister Jewel. When mated to Rheola Benedict (a younger brother of Val) Jewel became the dam of Ch. Hartsbourne Vanity, the winner of 15 CCs and one of the few Irish Setters of that time to win Best in Show at Championship shows, including at Cheltenham in 1934, after having been made Best Bitch at the Kennel Club Show in 1932.

Vanity gained her qualifier at the Scottish Field Trials and Gilbert Leighton-Boyce recalls in his book *Irish Setters* (1973) that he had seen her when he was very young and remembers that "Vanity had a white foot" and that "her stifles or hocks or both were less bent than they

ABOVE: Ch. Hartsbourne Vanity: The winner of 15 CCs, Best in Show Cheltenham 1934 and Best Bitch at the Kennel Club Show 1932.

RIGHT: Show Champion Sugar of Wendover: The model for the famous Beswick sculpture.

ought to have been." He goes on to describe Vanity's granddaughter, Ch. Hartsbourne Veracity, as a "gorgeous creature", but still declared his preference for Vanity. From the outset, Mrs Walker set an incredibly high standard of physical beauty in her Irish Setters which she was to maintain throughout her long career in the breed. The other great kennel to come to the fore a little later was the Wendover Kennel, owned by Mr and Mrs L.C. James, based largely on Boyne lines. Mr James had acquired his first Irish Setter to counter the black Labrador his bride had brought into their marriage. Gay Lady was whelped on November 25th 1929 and was bred by Mrs F. Golding by Loc Garmain Don ex Moira MacFin, but she had no role to play in the development of the Wendovers. After attending his first Championship show at Birmingham in December 1930, Mr James soon realized that Gay Lady was not good enough to do much winning, so Bessie of Gadeland, whelped in 1928, was acquired from Miss Wells. Bessie had been bred by Mrs E.M. Baker and was a

daughter of Ch. Gadeland Neula of Boyne by Rheola Bryn – a familiar and successful combination!

From Bessie came Ch. Wendover Biddy and, via another daughter, Maureen of Wendover, the famous Show Champion Sugar of Wendover, considered by many to have been the best of the pre-war Wendovers, and whose beauty has been immortalised in the much sought-after Beswick sculpture. Another purchase from Mr Carbery was Wendover of Boyne (Ch. Barney of Boyne ex Sh. Ch. Florrie of Boyne). Mated to Robin Hood of Gadeland, she produced Rona of Wendover, the dam of the CC-winning Wag of Wendover, who in turn sired Sh. Ch. Raycroft Mediator who was to play a leading role in the post-war reconstruction.

The Hartsbournes and Wendovers had already enjoyed great success before the turmoils of the Second World War and before the ravages of PRA, but their greatest achievements were yet to come in rather more peaceful times.

THE 1930S

The 1930s saw a tremendous growth in the popularity of the Irish Setter as a pet dog and companion, and several kennels with lasting influence started to come to the fore. Joe Braddon, later to become successful in many other breeds and a famous judge, established his "of Ide" Kennel, having scored Stud Book entries as early as 1931. Two of his big winners, Ch. Nutbrown Sorrel and Nutbrown Sherry, were bred by Miss Manuelle from her bitch Nutbrown Tessa. Other famous Irish Setters to be housed in his kennels were Marksman of Ide (Rheola Benedict ex Solemnity of Ide), Ch. Wendover Biddy and her son Danilo of the Downs (by Pandaris of Elmford) and Moyra of Halcana. In the late thirties Rachel Lamb founded her Raycroft Kennel which, after the war, went on to enjoy great success. Some other breeders who were starting out at that time and whose interest was to survive the Second World War, were Mrs Jean Clarke whose 'Brynmount' prefix later passed to a younger relative in the USA, Mrs Flora Banks 'Casamia', Mr Jack Whittaker 'Gaelge' and Miss M.E. Martino, later Mrs Stokes, with her 'Marrona' Irish Setters. With hindsight, the 1920s and early 1930s were a remarkable time for the Breed as the combination of the Rheola and Boyne lines further deepened the development of the Irish Setter as a show dog and as a pet.

THE FIGHT AGAINST PRA

However, the 1930s also produced the first cases of 'night blindness', the condition more correctly known as Progressive Retinal Atrophy. Breeders observed their Irish Setters colliding with objects, especially during twilight hours and at night, which led to the description 'night blindness'. The condition is progressive and inevitably leads to eventual blindness in both eyes. Mr Rasbridge had first encountered the condition in a young puppy as early as 1931.

He wrote: "Before it was six months old I discovered that as darkness fell, so did its powers of vision and willingness to venture away from the house." His vet could not help him to find an explanation of why this puppy could not see an object until it had collided with it, but the fact that the puppy had been the result of a brother and sister mating led him to wonder if the condition could be hereditary.

At that time most breeders did not know anything about hereditary defects and the condition was blamed on various reasons, including a virus infection. However, Mr Rasbridge's studies of pedigrees confirmed his suspicion that PRA was inherited and caused by a simple autosomal recessive gene. Unfortunately for the breed, many of the Rheolas turned out to be carriers; most tragically, one of them was Rheola Benedict (Rheola Bryn ex Rheola Mallie), probably the most widely-used and successful stud dog of the 1930s. In their search for the ever more perfect show dog, breeders had distributed PRA throughout a large number of lines of Irish Setters.

Many breeders must have been fully aware of what was happening to their Irish Setters, but chose to ignore the symptoms of blindness in their stock. In fact, blind animals were still being bred from. If Mr Rasbridge's earlier warnings that 'night blindness' was a hereditary condition had been taken more seriously by some breeders who still persisted in using the heavily implicated blood-lines simply because they were fashionable, the problem might not have developed on the scale that it did, but by 1940 no breeder could use ignorance as an excuse for what was going on.

With the outbreak of the Second World War the National Championship shows came to an end and only the smaller, more localised shows continued. Irish Setter litters were still being bred, but on a reduced scale and with breeders availing themselves much more of local dogs.

Mrs Ingle Bepler and other leading breeders refused to accept that their dogs were tainted by PRA and buried their heads in the sand. In 1944 Mr Rasbridge, supported by concerned breeders, made his views clear, and a series of articles in *Our Dogs* drew attention to the perilous state in which the breed found itself. In 1945 the Kennel Club decided that a dog which was "totally blind or suffering from nightblindness" was liable to be disqualified.

By 1946 Mr Rasbridge had succeeded Mrs Ingle Bepler as the Secretary of the Irish Setter Association, England, and he was able to persuade the majority of members to sign a statement that they would *not* breed from Irish Setters which suffered from PRA or from any proven carriers. He also led a deputation to the Kennel Club which requested that the registrations for Irish Setters should be tightened up. It was decided that no Irish Setter could be registered or transferred unless a declaration had been signed which stated that neither the parents or grandparents were actively afflicted with the disease, that neither of the parents was known to have produced a case of the disease and that the dog to be registered had not produced a case of the disease.

Mr Rasbridge advocated that test-mating, to identify carriers and clear animals, was the only way forward. Irish Setters can carry the autosomal recessive gene and possess normal vision, but when mated to another carrier, the resulting litter will contain at least one case or several cases of PRA. If a suspected carrier is mated to a blind Irish Setter and the resulting litter does not contain any blind puppies, the animal will have been cleared. Based on some complicated, statistical calculations Mr Rasbridge had established that a minimum of six puppies from test-matings had to be reared to an age of 10 to 12 weeks before an accurate diagnosis could be undertaken. (In later years the period was increased to six months.) This

particular type of PRA or Rod Cone Dysplasia (RCD1) is unique to the Irish Setter and, fortunately, made an early diagnosis possible.

Such measures were not universally popular, especially when Champions and other well-known Irish Setters had to be discarded after failing their test-matings. Most intelligent breeders availed themselves of the test-mated stock and gradually the situation improved. However, human error cannot be discounted and, whether deliberately or by chance, suspect Setters slipped through the net and continued to remain a danger for following generations.

FOUR PILLARS OF THE BREED

The first phase of the reconstruction, after the breed had been decimated by PRA, was largely based on four clear stud dogs – Show Champion Raycroft Mediator, born October 22nd 1939 and the first male Show Champion after the war, Branscombe Robyn, born April 1st 1941, Beau of Wendover, born February 17th 1942 and Brynmount Redgaynes Mars, born March 12th 1944. As more test-mated Irish Setters were cleared, their lines became available to the breed, but the enormous influence of those four dogs cannot be underestimated as all sired large numbers of puppies in a breed with a much reduced genetic base and numbers.

THE RAYCROFTS

Several of the kennels that had already been started before the war now really came to the fore. Among them was Miss Rachel Lamb's Raycroft Kennel which had been founded in 1936. Her Sh. Ch. Raycroft Mediator, born in 1939, by Wag of Wendover, was one of the four clear dogs and went on to sire seven title holders and a further CC winner. His daughter Ch. Raycroft Rena, in turn, produced three Show Champions, and another one of his daughters, Raycroft Meg, provided the foundation for Miss Lennox's Brackenfield

Sh. Ch. Raycroft Mediator.

Branscombe Robyn.

Beau of Wendover.

Brynmount Redgaynes Mars.

Kennels. Over the succeeding years, Rachel Lamb, later Mrs Rae Furness, made up 16 title holders including several full Champions, Ch. Raycroft Gay Girl and her daughter Ch. Gay Lass being amongst them.

Other breeders and exhibitors successfully campaigned Raycroft-bred stock. Mrs V. Hill, later Mrs Banks, made up a Rena son, Sh. Ch. Raycroft Huntsman, by Sh. Ch. Hartsbourne Tobias, born in 1951, and later, Miss Thorne-Baker showed the Group Winner Sh. Ch. Raycroft Chorus Girl, born in 1965, by Sh. Ch. Call Boy. Her dam, Sh. Ch. Raycroft Tammie, was bred by Mr J. Whittaker who made up her

litter sister Sh. Ch. Gaelge Gisena. Several of the big winners were exported, among them the sire of Tammie and Gisena, Sh. Ch. Raycroft Hoobram Rich Corona. He was the winner of 11 CCs and a successful and influential sire in the UK before his departure to Pakistan. Sh. Ch. Raycroft Call Boy, whelped in 1963, was the winner of 17 CCs and three Gundog Groups before he was exported to Japan. The last of the Raycroft Irish Setter Show Champions, Bosun, whelped in 1973, was a direct descendant of Mediator, born more than 30 years earlier. Over the years, Rae Furness did not restrict herself to using only

Sh. Ch. Raycroft Callboy: Winner of 17 CCs and three Gundog Groups. Photo: Anne Roslin-Williams.

Wendover or only Hartsbourne lines, but availed herself of the best stud dogs both kennels had to offer. Nor did Rae Furness limit her interest to Irish Setters but bred and exhibited several other breeds with great success, and, at the time of her death in 1993, her Raycroft Clumber Spaniels had become the dominant force in that breed.

THE RETURN OF OTHER PRE-WAR KENNELS

Joe Braddon, another Irish Setter breeder from the pre-war years, continued with his interest in the breed with an Irish import Sh. Ch. Ronor Rena of Ide. After test-mating, he put her to Branscombe Robyn and produced Sh. Ch. Copelia of Ide and Mr Whittaker's Ch. Gaelge Copperplate of Ide among many other winners. Like Rae Furness, Joe Braddon did not limit his interest to Irish Setters, but campaigned several other breeds to the top, becoming one of the most famous all-rounder judges on the way.

Mr Whittaker built up a strong line based on Ch. Copperplate and produced a string of beautiful Show Champion bitches. A Copperplate son, Ch. Gaelge Ardrew Pride, born in 1950, not only gained his Qualifying Certificate in the Field but, through his grandson Sh. Ch. Raycroft Hoobram Rich

Corona, has had a lasting influence.

Mrs D. Cucksey, Maydorwill, played an important role in the action against PRA by giving her whole-hearted support to Mr Rasbridge's campaign. Through her use of mainly test-mated stock, she produced a number of Show Champions including Mr and Mrs T.J. Harper's Sh. Ch. Bodewell Beginagen, born in 1953. The Maydorwills can now be found behind the Cornevons and some of the Sowerhills.

Mrs M.E. Stokes also had to make a new start with her Marrona Irish Setters, based on a clear Wendover bitch by Beau of Wendover which she mated to Mr Rasbridge's Watendlath Joao O'Pandy. A dog from this mating, Marrona Milesian, features behind her Sh. Ch. Marrona Meriel who won Best of Breed at Crufts in 1974.

Mrs Nagel's Sulhamstead Kennel continued to flourish but now in joint ownership with Miss M. Clark, who had become her partner in 1951. Her active involvement with Irish Setters ended with the retirement of her trainer George Abbot in 1964 after having achieved the incredible record of 17 Field Trial Champions. However, just like Rae Furness and Joe Braddon, she continued with enormous success in her original breed, the Irish Wolfhound.

3 GREAT KENNELS

After the end of the Second World War the Hartsbournes and Wendovers came to dominate the Irish Setter scene in much the same way that the Rheolas and the Boynes had done after the First World War. As mentioned earlier, both kennels had already enjoyed great success before the war, but both had been affected by PRA in their stock and they had to rebuild their lines through test-matings and through the introduction of other clear stock.

THE HARTSBOURNES

Before the war Mrs Walker had bred and owned some outstanding Irish Setters, but of the 32 CC winners owned or bred by her, 28 came after the war. Hartsbourne Maeve would, undoubtedly, have gained her title if war had not intervened, but her importance to the post-war Hartsbournes came from the link she provided between her grandmother, the great Ch. Vanity, to her own grandson Hartsbourne Masterstroke, the sire of the important Sh. Ch. Hartsbourne Tobias. Tobias was whelped in 1947, out of Hartsbourne Flame, and ranks as one of the great sires in the breed with a tally of seven Show Champions, three Champions and another certificate winner. Mrs Walker had imported his dam Hartsbourne Flame from

Ireland, bred by Miss Kiernan and a litter sister to Irish Ch. Derrycarne Martini. Flame had the legendary 'shower of hail' coat which was described by Mr Gilbert Leighton-Boyce as "a set of little white dots, hardly visible, scattered all over her body".

Five of Tobias' title-holders came from the two matings to his kennel-mate Ch. Hartsbourne Popsy, who was born in 1948. During that year Mrs Walker had imported an American dog, Hartsbourne Senor of Shadowood, who only sired this one litter. He was mated to Maeve's grand-daughter Poppet to produce Ch. Popsy. A great show bitch, she won a total of 22 CCs and qualified in the field at the Kennel Club's Spring Trials for Setters and Pointers in 1952. This was an enormous achievement for a bitch in the days when rather fewer sets of CCs were available than there are to-day.

She also managed to fit in two litters by her kennel-mate Tobias, and the Tobias/Popsy brood were to dominate the show scene for some considerable time, with many of them going on to produce more winners in their turn. One of their offspring, Sh. Ch. Hartsbourne Brilliant, was exported to the USA after he had already sired three full Champions in the UK, including the litter-

Hartsbourne Flame: The legendary 'shower of hail' coat.

Champion Hartsbourne Popsy: Winner of 22 CCs.

mates Ch. Hartsbourne Penny and Sybil Lennox's Ch. Brackenfield Hartsbourne Bronze. Another litter brother and sister joined Ted Eldredge's famous Tirvelda Kennels in the USA. Penny won four CCs and qualified for her Champion title at the ISAE Setter and Pointer Trial in July 1959.

At Bath Championship Show in May 1958 Mrs Walker won a first CC with her latest import from the USA, American Champion Erinhaven Dennis Muldoon. He quickly also gained his Show Champion title in the UK and was used at stud by many as a welcome outcross. Unfortunately, in 1962 he became involved with the re-appearance of PRA, at a time when only very few cases of the disease were known of in Britain. Through successful test-matings, two of his sons were cleared.

Sh. Ch. Hartsbourne Honeysuckle, whelped in 1954, won four CCs and produced three Show Champions in her three litters. Her most important daughter, Sh. Ch. Hartsbourne Zinnia, won six CCs and was exported to the USA in 1966 to join the Tirvelda Kennels. However, she did not leave the UK before she had whelped an important litter by Hartsbourne Comet which contained Sh. Ch. Hartsbourne Astra, owned by Val Albertis, and Sh. Ch. Hartsbourne Starlight. When Mrs Walker was asked which of her Irish Setters she considered to have been her best, she replied that Starlight had been her 'most beautiful'. Starlight was mated to Carnbargus Hartsbourne O'Brady who gained his title in 1971. Mrs Walker died on May 19th 1970 during a visit to the USA where she had been staying with her great friend Lee Schoen, the owner of the famous Kinvarra Irish Setters. Starlight's litter was born at roughly the same time that her owner died, and contained the last Hartsbourne title-holder bred by Mrs Walker, Sh. Ch. Carnbargus Hartsbourne Mattie, as well as the CC-winner Heathcliffe Hartsbourne Suzette.

Mrs Walker was a highly talented artist and had trained as a sculptor, which might explain her constant search for physical perfection in her dogs. According to her wishes, most of the remaining Hartsbournes, including Starlight, as well as the prefix, passed to Sybil Lennox who

Sh. Ch. Hartsbourne Starlight: CC and BOB at Bath 1971.

still keeps the name alive, alongside her own Brackenfield prefix.

THE BRACKENFIELDS

Miss Lennox started her Brackenfield Kennel in 1946 with a Mediator daughter, Raycroft Meg. Her breeder, Rachel Lamb, later Mrs Furness, and Sybil Lennox had met when they were at school in Matlock – Rachel as a boarder and Sybil as a day girl. Both remained resident in Derbyshire, the Raycrofts near Chesterfield, and the Brackenfields still live only a short distance from what used to be the old school. In her first litter, born in 1948, by Sh. Ch. Storm of Casamia (by Beau of Wendover), Meg produced Sh. Ch. Brackenfield Romulus of Casamia, but probably more importantly the two bitches Brackenfield Pandora and Smallbridge Poppy. Pandora was mated to Sh. Ch. Hartsbourne Tobias and whelped Sh. Ch. Brackenfield Primula. This was the first litter to be based on the Hartsbourne/Brackenfield mix which proved to be of great benefit to both kennels. Sybil had first met Mrs Walker at Alfreton Agricultural Show in 1946 and their friendship continued until Mrs Walker's death. Incidentally, Sh. Ch. Raycroft Mediator won Best in Show that day at Alfreton!

Smallbridge Poppy, in turn, was mated to Brynmount Redgaynes Mars, and that litter contained Ch. Brackenfield Poppy, the winner of three CCs, who gained her Qualifying Certificate in 1955. In 1959 she was mated to the American import Sh. Ch. Erinhaven Dennis Muldoon and produced Brackenfield

Raycroft Meg: Foundation bitch of the Brackenfields.

Dandelion who, after the PRA scare in 1962, was successfully test-mated. He turned out to be a prepotent stud dog and sired six CC winners, including Sh. Ch. Brackenfield May, the winner of nine CCs and also Best Gundog at City of Birmingham in 1964. Mrs Page's Dandelion daughter, Orichalc Freyja, was also test-mated and was clear of PRA, and her son Ch. Brackenfield Orichalc Juniper, whelped in 1965, the winner of 4 CCs, gained his Qualifier in 1970.

He was by Ch. Brackenfield Hartsbourne Bronze who had come to Matlock from Mrs Walker aged seven and a half weeks in exchange for an older pet puppy. Sybil may not have planned to acquire Bronze, but never regretted it as he turned out to be a highly successful stud dog. He gained his title in 1956 and qualified in the field in 1957 at the ISAE Setter and Pointer Club's July Trials. Both Bronze and his son Juniper were trained and handled for

Four Brackenfield title holders with Miss Sybil Lennox, 1965. Pictured left to right: Sh. Ch. Brackenfield Lozell Whisper, Ch. Brackenfield Hartsbourne Bronze, Sh. Ch. Brackenfield May and Sh. Ch. Brackenfield Fern.

their qualifiers by Mrs Auriol Mason, who gained a Certificate of Merit at field trials and a Stud Book number with a Bronze daughter, Acornbank Biddy.

Another successful union with Hartsbourne blood came via Sh. Ch. Brackenfield Lozell Whisper, a Bronze daughter. She was the pick of a litter, bred by Mrs G.F. Hollington, and was kept by Miss Lennox on the advice of Mrs Walker and Lee Schoen. When Whisper was mated to Ch. Juniper she produced Sh. Ch. Brackenfield Tertius, the sire of of four Show Champions and four other CC winners. His litter sister, Brackenfield Cathy, provided the foundation for my Carnbargus Irish Setters, and another Whisper daughter, Brackenfield Wistful, by Hartsbourne Comet, became the foundation bitch for Jimmy Johnston's Allsquare Kennel in Scotland. From the two matings of Wistful and Dandelion came Sh. Ch. Flame of Allsquare and Champion Laurie of Allsquare, who qualified at the Scottish Field Trials in 1975 and spent her life as a working gundog. They were very closely bred, but Sh. Ch. Allsquare Mickey Finn, the winner of seven CCs, was the product of a partial outcross between Sh. Ch. Allsquare Flame and Sh. Ch. Cornevon Lovebird.

Other kennels that were built on a Hartsbourne/Brackenfield blend were Ron and Margaret's Cordwell's Ronettas. Their bitch, Brackenfield Holly, in her litter by Bronze, not only produced their own Sh. Ch. Brackenfield Elm, but also Brackenfield Iris, the foundation bitch of the famous Cornevons. Betty Worth made up her Dandelion son Sh. Ch. Heathcliffe Jason, whelped in 1961, and won a CC with Suzette, a Hartsbourne O'Brady/Starlight daughter. When mated back to her grandsire Hartsbourne Comet, she became the dam of Sh. Ch. Heathcliffe Joanna, who gained her title in 1973. Another successful breeder using the same bloodlines was Val Albertis who started her Greenglades Kennel with Sh. Ch.

Hartsbourne Astra, a Starlight litter sister.

One of the Hartsbournes to come to Sybil Lennox after Mrs Walker's death was Hartsbourne Trident. He gained his title in her hands and provided Show Champions for two long-established breeders: Brendower Brown Sugar for Brenda Howe and Barnsforde Winston for Mr and Mrs A. Dodman. When Sybil later repeated the mating of Sh. Ch. Tertius and Hartsbourne Velvet, she bred Sh. Ch. Hartsbourne Periwinkle, the winner of seven CCs and considered by many to have been one of the best. After more than fifty years, Sybil is still actively involved in breeding and showing Irish Setters. Her most recent Show Champion, Hartsbourne Snapdragon, was born in 1988. She is credited with having owned or bred 15 title-holders, three of them going on to gain their qualifiers and becoming Champions.

THE WENDOVERS

Like so many others, the Wendover Kennels owned by Mr and Mrs L.C. James, also had to undergo a reconstruction which was based on their own PRA test-mated stock and other clear lines, but this was not achieved without heartbreak. When Mrs Foot's Beorcham Kennel was dispersed, Beorcham Miss Bracken was acquired, together with two of her sons and a daughter, Sh. Ch. Beorcham Bryony of Wendover. Bryony had a brilliant career winning 12 CCs, and was only beaten once in breed classes at the LKA in 1947. The judge on that occasion was Joe Braddon who preferred Wendover Dinah for the CC, and Bryony had to settle for the Res. CC.

Miss Bracken had been test-mated and cleared, but one of her sons, Blazonson, sired some puppies that were afflicted by PRA. The investigation which followed showed that instead of being by Sh. Ch. Beorcham Blazon, as had been assumed, the litter containing Bryony, Blazonson and Beorcham Blases of

Wendover had probably been sired by one of two carriers that had been in the Beorcham Kennel at the time of the mating. Bryony was test-mated and found to be a carrier, but the other brother, Blases, was cleared and continued to be used at stud. Mr and Mrs James made all the facts known and the carriers went to pet homes.

At the outbreak of war Wag of Wendover had won one CC, but as the sire of Sh. Ch. Raycroft Mediator, one of the four clear dogs, his influence was of great importance and has become a lasting one. The Wendovers were further strengthened by importing Beau of Wendover, by Kerry of Wendover, who had been sent to live in Ireland at the outbreak of hostilities. As one of the 'four clear dogs', he produced out of Wendover Robina (a Beorcham Blases of Wendover daughter) Ch. Wendover Beggar, whelped in 1951. Beggar won 10 CCs and gained his Field Trial Qualifier in 1955 at the ISAE's/Setter and Pointer Club's July Trials. He has left his mark on the breed with nine Show Champions and a further two CC winners, but most importantly, many of them went on to be just as prepotent as their sire.

Two of his outstanding daughters, Show Champions Wendover Kelly and Katie, out of Wendover Lola, were born in 1958, and a repeat mating in 1961 produced Sh. Ch. Wendover Vagabond. All three have had a profound influence on the development of the breed by providing the foundation stock for many new and successful kennels such as the Heron's Caskeys Irish Setters. Wendover Lola, by Mr Rasbridge's Sh. Ch. Watendlath Kevin O'Pandy ex Sh. Ch. Wendover Roberta, had further influence through her litter by Watendlath Joao O'Pandy which produced, in 1956, Ch. Wendover Romance, the foundation bitch of Judy Russell's Ballywestow Kennel. Joao O'Pandy was by Wantendlath Double Top who had been acquired by Mr Rasbridge at the

Wendover Bracken: Test-mated clear of PRA and the link between the pre-war and post-war Wendovers. Photo: Fall.

Ch. Wendover Beggar: The sire of nine Show Champions. Photo: Thurse.

time of the dispersal of the Beorcham Kennels, and this Watendlath/Wendover combination has proved to be highly influential – not only in the UK, but worldwide.

Sh. Ch. Kelly made her mark by producing, in her litter to Watendlath Joao O'Pandy, the brothers Wendover Game and Wendover Gary of Acres, and when her litter sister Sh. Ch. Katie was mated to Gary, she had the honour of whelping the famous litter mates Sh. Ch. Wendover Nancy and Sh. Ch. Wendover Gentleman. Gary only sired this litter before his departure to New Zealand where he soon became a Champion. Whelped in 1962, both Nancy and Gentleman were sold as puppies, but were bought back later. Nancy won 14 CCs, Gentleman won 19 CCs and was Best in

Wendover Lorna, born 5 February, 1995. Bred by Mr and Mrs Peter James.

Photo: Prangle

Show at the Southern Counties Canine Association in 1969. Gentleman had made his first appearance at a Championship show in Bath in 1967. He won the CC under Mrs Mary Darling, but Hartsbourne Freesia, by Brackenfield Dandelion, was Best of Breed on that day. As a stud dog, he established the then breed record for first generation CC-winning progeny with a total of 17, of which 11 gained their titles.

One of his litters, bred by June Coates, out of Musbury Melisande of Twoacres, contained four Show Champions and a dual CC winner. This litter has proved to be of importance, not only through Sh. Ch. Twoacres Troilus, but also through his litter sisters Show Champions Teresa and Traviata, who provided the foundation for two successful kennels, Shelagh Vant's Barleydales and Jean Quinn's Wickenberry Irish Setters respectively. Another Gentleman son, Sh. Ch. Wendover Colas, helped to establish the Gurney's Danaway Kennel. However, some already well-established kennels, such as Miss Hunt's Sowerhills and Mrs Anderson's Andanas, also benefited greatly from his influence.

Quite apart from his highly successful show career and his role as a leading stud dog, Gentleman also possessed a perfect temperament and was a favourite house-dog. Mr and Mrs James decided right from the beginning of the Wendover line, that a correct temperament was of the utmost importance in their Irish Setters and, therefore, it can be said that Gentleman fulfilled all the criteria for their ideal dog.

Wendover Game, Gary's litter brother, went to Mrs Jarosz of the Joanma's Irish Setters after he had won one CC. He gained a second CC and was probably unlucky not to have gained his title. However, he more than made up for this by becoming a highly successful stud dog. Among his famous offspring are illustrious names such as the litter mates Show Champions Cornevon Prince Charming and Cinderella and Sh. Ch. Scotswood Barabbas. Their widespread influence will become clear in the review of present-day kennels in a later chapter.

A long line of Show Champions continued to

be bred by Mr and Mrs James, including Sh. Ch. Wendover Jeeves. When he won his first CC in 1974, Jeeves became the 26th challenge certificate winner to have been bred in the Wendover Kennels, the 23rd since the war. He went on to win four CCs, but his lasting importance has come through his sons, the brothers Sh. Ch. Sowerhill Sahib, the sire of Sh. Ch. Kerryfair Night Fever, and Sh. Ch. Sowerhill Satyr of Fearnley, the one-time breed record holder.

After the death of Mr L.C. James, better known as 'Jimmy', on December 17th 1981, and after Mrs 'Jay' James had retired from active involvement with the kennel, their son Peter and his wife Julie took over and have kept a famous tradition alive. Right from the outset, Labrador Retrievers have always been a part of the Wendover Kennels and several gained their titles, as did some outstanding Beagles. History seems to have repeated itself, as Julie James is an enthusiastic Labrador owner! Since taking over, Peter has made up two more Wendover bitches: Sh. Ch. Maid Marion and Sh. Ch. Country Girl, making it a total of 34 individual CC winners to have been bred by the James'.

MIXING AND BLENDING

During the many years when the Hartsbournes and Wendovers were at the height of their power and influence, it had been possible roughly to divide Irish Setters into those that were descended from either one or the other kennel, as their creators had carefully avoided the mixing of their quite distinctive lines. However, other breeders have not shown such reservation and have mixed and blended the unique achievements of the twokennels to great effect.

THE CORNEVONS

One breeder who used this mix with huge success was Janice Gibson, later Mrs Janice Roberts, whose Cornevon Kennel headed the

Janice Roberts with Sh. Ch. Cornevon Primrose, holder of the brood bitch record with 10 British CC winners.   Photo: Kingsley Michael.

breed for a considerable time. Her first dog, Cornevon Coppernob (by Maydorwill Happy Lad ex Maydorwill Soubrett), was bought as a pet in 1958, but Miss Gibson was encouraged to show him. She followed the advice and, as she put it, "was bitten by the bug". Her foundation bitch, Brackenfield Iris, came into her possession when aged two and in need of a home. This daughter of Ch. Brackenfield Hartsbourne Bronze ex Brackenfield Holly was mated to Coppernob and produced Sh. Ch. Cornevon Snowstorm, the first of a long line of Cornevon Show Champions. However, much more importantly, this litter also contained the bitch Cornevon Snowbunting. A great brood bitch, she was mated to Wendover Game and whelped the successful litter mates Sh. Ch. Cornevon Prince Charming and Sh. Ch. Cinderella. From Snowbunting's next litter by Sh. Ch. Scotswood Barabbas born in 1968 came Sh. Ch. Violet and the influential Sh. Ch.

31

Sh. Ch. Cornevon Lovebird.
Bred by Janice Roberts, owned by Alister Watt.
Photo: Rab Munro.

Primrose. An outstanding bitch who, during her long show career spanning some six years, won 17 CCs, all under different judges.

However, her greatest claim to fame has come through her many winning children. She produced a total of 10 CC winners, of which four became Show Champions, thereby replacing Ch. Norna as the holder of the brood bitch record for first-generation CC-winners. Primrose's first litter by her half-brother Prince Charming contained two title holders, the bitch Sh. Ch. Cornevon Love Story and the important stud dog Sh. Ch. Cornevon Lovebird, the winner of 15 CCs and the founder of Mr A. Watt's Shenanagin line. In Primrose's second litter, by Sh. Ch. Twoacres Troilus, who was himself the product of a Brackenfield/Wendover mix, came Sh. Ch. Cornevon Stargem the winner of nine CCs and the sire of two Show Champions. From a repeat mating came Cornevon Tamarind who was exported to New Zealand, but not before she had a litter by Wynjill Country Woodland. Their daughter, Cornevon Spring Melody, had the honour of becoming the mother of the great sire Sh. Ch. Kerryfair Night Fever.

A second litter from Primrose and Prince Charming contained Sh. Ch. Cornevon Westerhuys Dream, who gained his title in the UK before his departure to Holland, together with Sh. Ch. Cornevon Westerhuys Cloggy.

Both were owned in partnership with Mrs Willy Duynkerke, and had already made their mark in the UK before going on to their new home in the Netherlands, especially through Cloggy's litter by Sh. Ch. Cornevon Lovebird. Two sons from that litter won CCs, and a daughter, Westerhuy's Dutch Spirit, went on to produce two litters of importance to Sh. Ch. Wendover Colas. Primrose's litter sister Sh. Ch. Violet won 3 CCs and was mated to Sh. Ch. Cornevon Snowstorm. Their daughter, Sh. Ch. Cornevon Woodsprite, whelped in 1972, gained her title in the hands of Jill Bacon, later Mrs Holley, who had started her Wynjill Kennel with another Cornevon bitch, Tranquil.

Janice Roberts, Roberts-Oldham after her re-marriage, is credited with having bred 28 CC-winners, of which 16 went on to gain their titles, the last being Sh. Ch. Honeypie of Cornevon, born in December 1982, by Free Spirit of Danaway, a Sh. Ch. Wendover Colas/Westerhuy's Dutch Spirit son. Honeypie, who was bred by Janice in partnership with her husband Ian Oldham, won her title in the hands of Magi Henderson. Apart from providing many young kennels with foundation stock in the UK, Cornevons also formed the basis for many successful kennels all over the world, but especially in the Netherlands and in Belgium. Essentially, Janice always maintained a very small kennel, and her dogs lived in the house as her companions because she firmly believed that Irish Setters were quite unsuited to live as kennel dogs. Her untimely death at the age of only 47 was a tragedy, but the impact of her Cornevon line is proving to be a lasting one. Recently, Janice's sister, Penny Jeffries, was granted a separate interest in the Cornevon prefix and has acquired a bitch puppy bred from Cornevon lines. This should ensure that the famous prefix will continue.

4 *CHOOSING YOUR IRISH SETTER*

The ownership of a dog, any dog, should be a life-long commitment. Therefore, it is important fully to appreciate the responsibilities you will be taking on, even before you choose a particular breed. To feed a dog correctly can be expensive and provision will have to be made for the payment of the occasional veterinary bill. Dogs can also be a tie and will interfere with some of your plans. However, if you are prepared to put up with such inconveniences, you will be richly rewarded by the addition of a loyal member to your family.

FINDING A BREEDER

After careful consideration you have decided that an Irish Setter is the dog for you, but how do you go about obtaining one? Maybe you know somebody who already owns an Irish Setter who could help and also answer some of your questions concerning the breed. Or you could contact your national Kennel Club for a list of breeders in your area. The Kennel Club will also be able to supply you with the names and addresses of the Secretaries of Breed Clubs for Irish Setters. They often keep a register of litters that are for sale which were bred by members. Another good idea is to buy one of the dog papers or magazines. Not only do they

carry advertisements from breeders with puppies for sale, but they also contain information about shows where Irish Setters are being exhibited. If there is a show not too far away from you, try and attend. You can watch the dogs being judged and decide which type you might prefer. Most reputable breeders will be delighted to talk about their stock and will let you know if they have a litter at present, or if one is planned in the future.

MEETING THE BREEDER

After finding a suitable litter and after making contact with the breeder, you will be anxious to see the puppies. Do not be too surprised if the breeder 'interviews' you to establish if you are a suitable owner for one of the precious pups! Expect to be asked if you go out to work and if so, what arrangements you have made for the puppy. Most breeders do not like the idea of a young puppy being left alone for any length of time. Be prepared to pay a decent price for a puppy. Quality puppies do not grow on trees and are expensive to rear properly. Breeders with a good reputation for breeding and selling winning stock can expect to be well paid for their puppies.

During your visit to the breeder, try and have a good look at the mother of the pups and any

other relations that might be owned by the breeder. Not only will this give you an idea of what to expect when your Irish Setter is fully grown, but it will also let you assess the temperament of your future puppy's relatives. Puppies do not only learn from their mother by example, they also inherit her genes. Irish Setters should have happy, extrovert temperaments and should greet you with great friendliness and some enthusiasm! However, try and be diplomatic with the mother of the pups. Some bitches can be quite wary of strangers when they come to look at their brood.

Most reputable breeders will sell their puppies from about eight weeks of age. I always ask prospective owners who come to see my puppies, to wear clothes in which they have not been near other dogs and make sure their shoes are sprayed with an anti-parvo preparation. If this happens to you, do not think it unreasonable, the breeder is only trying to do the best for the puppies. If you are lucky enough to be allowed to choose your own puppy, leave yourself plenty of time to make the selection. It is extremely interesting to watch puppies not only during play but also when they are being fed. All their individual characters are already developing and taking shape and can be observed from an early age. The extroverts in the litter will try and attract your attention and will want to be picked up, but a shy puppy will be much more reluctant to come forward to greet you. Such a puppy does not necessarily grow into a nervous or timid adult, but it might need much more careful treatment and handling to bring it out of its shell. Therefore, it is probably best not to choose such a puppy.

DOG OR BITCH?

The most important decision you will have to make next is what sex your puppy is going to be. Both male and female Irish Setters make excellent pets and companions, and it is really a personal choice. Irish Setter dogs tend to be larger and stronger than the bitches, but they are just as devoted to their owners. A bitch will

Puppies, aged eight weeks, ready to go to their new homes. Photo: Eve Gardner.

come into season, usually twice a year, from the time she is about ten or twelve months old and then for the rest of her life. At that time she must be kept secure and well away from all male dogs in the neighbourhood for about three weeks. This is a very minor inconvenience, but if you do not want the bother, choose a male. However, if you do settle for a male Irish Setter it is important that you do not let him roam to find a bitch in season! If you are starting off with the intention of wanting to breed a litter sometime in the future you must, of course, choose a bitch. Whatever the sex of the puppy, make sure that the one you select looks healthy and bright-eyed.

PET OR SHOW PUPPY?

If you are choosing a puppy to be your pet or companion do not worry too much about a minor physical defect that will only offend in the show ring, but choose the one that appeals to you in character. The most important consideration in a pet must be a perfect temperament. One fault that may class a puppy as 'pet quality' is a male puppy that is not entire. This means that either one or both testicles are not fully descended into the scrotum. This will not preclude him from being exhibited, but his chances in the show-ring will be extremely low. But beware, he will probably need an operation to remove the undescended testicle and this should be reflected in the price. Another puppy may have faulty dentition or

The puppies should be bright-eyed and inquisitive. Photo: Pat Jones.

the eyes are considered to be too light. There are many such cosmetic faults which will determine a puppy's future as a pet or as a show dog. However, they will make very little difference to your Irish Setter if you are looking for a faithful, loving companion.

If you have decided that you would like to take up showing as a hobby then your choice will be influenced by very different considerations. To select a puppy for show not only requires a combination of experience and knowledge of the breed, but also 'an eye for a dog'. Therefore, allow the breeder to help and advise. Most experienced and successful breeders will know their own stock and what to look for in a puppy. However, even the most experienced breeders have been known to make mistakes!

Puppies are usually placed on a mat on a table in a show stance to assess outline and balance. The puppy should have a nice long neck, set into well-laid shoulders. The front should be

Left: Decide if you want your Irish Setter for show or whether you are looking for a pet.

Right: An experienced breeder will help you to evaluate show potential.

Photos: Mike Gardner.

Most older Irish Setters adore young puppies. However, do not ignore the older dog with the excitement of the newcomer.

Photo: Meier.

straight and well-boned, leading to tight, well-shaped feet. The body should be well ribbed back and leading to a good strong loin and a well-made rear end with a good finish. Stifles should be well-bent, and the hocks short and strong. The tail in young Irish Setter puppies can often be out of proportion to the rest of the body. Do not worry too much, as they will usually "grow into it".

A bitch should be pretty and obviously feminine; a dog should be stronger and more masculine, but also appealing and with a soft expression. The foreface should be balanced in relation to the skull with a well-defined stop. Eyes dark and eyebrows well-raised. Eyes and eyebrows are so important in an Irish Setter, as they help to give that desired quizzical look with just a hint of devilment! This look is often described as being 'typically Irish'. When you open the puppy's mouth the teeth should have a scissor bite. Quite often an undershot mouth may correct itself when the second teeth come in, but it is best not to take a chance with this.

As far as coat and feathering is concerned, it is often quite difficult to predict what it will be like in an adult. Some puppies have quite rough or even woolly coats, but others tend to have a very sleek and silky textured coat. I prefer the slightly rougher texture in a puppy as this usually indicates a better adult coat. Puppies with the more attractive silky coats often do not grow a decent coat and feathering when they are adults. Colour can also be difficult to assess, but a dark puppy coat is much more likely to grow into a dark adult coat than a very pale one. However, coats, like most other things, are hereditary and the parents of the litter and a good look at the rest of the relations will give you an idea of what you can expect.

The choice of a promising puppy has now been made and, hopefully, a rosy future lies ahead. However, it is worth remembering that it is impossible for any breeder to guarantee that even the best puppy will become a Show Champion, or even end up making a show dog. The best puppy in the world will not fulfil its early promise unless correctly reared and brought up by you. This does not only involve feeding, but also the right amount of exercise and training to bring out the very best in the puppy. Dogs that enjoy being shown and have the right happy attitude to the game, have a great advantage over dogs who do not really like the show ring. In order to achieve this happy attitude, early socialisation with other dogs is essential to develop the pup's sense of enjoyment.

PAPERWORK

When the day arrives and you come to collect your puppy, the breeder should give you a pedigree, a Kennel Club Registration Certificate and a Transfer Form. This form has to be completed by you and sent back to the Kennel Club, together with the correct fee. A new certificate will be posted to you, confirming you as the registered owner. You should also be given a diet sheet and advice on rearing your puppy, including regular worming. You might also be handed a certificate to show that the puppy has already had one of the necessary vaccinations, and a reminder to consult your vet. And, finally, do not forget to telephone the breeders to let them know that the puppy has settled down in the new home and that all is well.

THE "UGLY" PHASE

There will come a time during your puppy's development when you wonder why you ever chose this particular one! Irish Setter puppies go through stages when no part of the body seems to match another. Suddenly the legs are far too long and totally out of proportion to the rest of the body. One day you discover that your puppy is about an inch or so taller at the back, and by the time this has returned to looking normal, the head will have lost its stop and will look very plain. This can happen when the puppy is teething and the gums are badly swollen. Owners are usually told not to worry and to forget about looking at the puppy. This may well be good advice, but it is easier said than done! However, if all was correct and promising at eight weeks, all the good points should return – eventually!

CHOOSING AN OLDER DOG

Some people may find it more convenient to have an older dog rather than a puppy. Breeders often run on two puppies from one litter and will part with one at a later date. Many successful kennels have been founded by such "rejects"! Occasionally, owners have to part with their pets due to domestic difficulties or due to having to live abroad. If you take on such a dog, try to find out as much as possible about the animal from the previous owner. All dogs have individual characters and have their likes and dislikes. Changing homes can be very stressful, but patience and understanding from the new owner will help an Irish Setter to settle into a new home much more quickly.

The breed is well served by several rescue organisations and their addresses and telephone numbers can be obtained from your national Kennel Club. If an Irish Setter has fallen on hard times, they will try and re-home the dog with a suitable owner. Expect a home-check before being considered. To take on a rescue dog can be very rewarding, but if dogs have been mistreated or neglected, they may feel insecure and worried and will need very special care and attention – and lots of it – from their new owners. Some adoptive owners have, over the years, given homes to several Irish Setters in need.

COMING HOME

At last the day has come when you can bring your Irish Setter puppy home. The shopping will have been done to provide your new puppy with the correct food, in accordance with the breeder's diet sheet. If a long car journey is involved in collecting the puppy, it is sensible to take somebody with you who can hold and comfort the pup on the way home. Very often this will be the first car ride the puppy takes, and the reaction to it can vary from puppy to puppy. Some do not take any notice of the moving car, but others get

A puppy has much to get used to in a new home. This puppy has an international pedigree. Mitch v.d. Westerhuy was born in Holland in April 1997, her mother came from the Czech Republic and her father is an English import.

distressed and restless. Some puppies will suffer from travel-sickness, so an old towel plus a kitchen-roll should be at hand to clean up. I usually give my puppies a tablet against travel-sickness for the first few journeys and they quickly learn to like the car. If the puppy has managed to travel well on the first few journeys and has accepted the car as part of life, try without the tablets. Once the puppy has been fully vaccinated, take frequent short trips in the car. Choose a destination where you can give the puppy a good run. In this way the pup will learn to associate travel with something enjoyable to look forward to.

When you arrive at home with your new member of the family, slowly let the puppy get used to the new surroundings, as everything will be very strange. If you have children, teach them right from the start that the puppy is not a toy and that, just like a baby, the puppy will

need a lot of sleep and rest. All dogs, and not just puppies, should have a place they can consider to be their own. You will have given some thought to where the new arrival will sleep during the first night, and this will probably provide the first test of your character! During the day the puppy will probably be quite happy to explore the new home, but the night, when all is quiet, can be quite a different story. The youngster will suddenly miss the litter brothers and sisters that have been left behind and feel very lonely and dejected. Some puppies will cry and test your resistance to the noise, but others will curl up and go to sleep, quite resigned to their fate. You will feel extremely cruel leaving the poor puppy all alone in the kitchen, or wherever the bed may be, but if you give in now and take the puppy to the bedroom, you may come to regret it, as it can become very difficult to break the habit.

A large cardboard box lined with a fleecy blanket such as a vetbed should provide plenty of warmth and comfort for your lonely puppy. If there is no response from you, the puppy will soon become exhausted and eventually fall asleep. Some owners have found it beneficial to leave the radio on for the puppy. It is worth a try if your puppy persists in being difficult when left alone. If you own another dog, maybe another Irish Setter, be diplomatic when you introduce the youngster. Most older Irish Setters adore young puppies, but you do not want to put their noses out of joint by making a great fuss over the newcomer and ignoring the older Irish. After a careful introduction, probably best done in the garden, the puppy will enjoy curling up with the older friend. My Irish Setter adults, including real oldies, have been known to make complete fools of themselves when playing with a puppy. However, if they are caught in the act, they will pretend that it did not really happen!

To begin with, your puppy may miss the competition of eating with the littermates.

HOUSE TRAINING

The next lesson for the puppy to learn is how to become clean in the house. As a rule, Irish Setters are naturally clean dogs and they hate to have 'accidents'. However, very young puppies do not have too much control over their bladders – but even at such a very young age they will try and be clean by getting well away from their bed, to avoid soiling it. Therefore, a newspaper placed near the door will help with the first steps towards house-training. Put the puppy out immediately after waking up and immediately after a meal. Most owners have a special command to encourage their puppy to perform. Afterwards, make a great fuss of the puppy and give a lot of praise when a penny has been spent.

There are certain warning signs to look out for if puppies want to be let out. They usually start to wander around in circles, looking for the right spot. This is the time for you to act by putting the puppy outside. If you are in time, praise the puppy – and the message will soon get through. To scold, or even punish, a puppy serves very little purpose as the pup does not understand the reason for this. If an accident has happened on a carpet, try and clean it up immediately as the puppy may return to the same spot again. There are many carpet cleaners on the market, but the best way to immediately neutralise the urine is to use soda water to soak the carpet, which can then be dried with paper towels and a cloth. Try not to make a drama out of the training, and you will be surprised how very quickly a young Irish Setter will become clean in the house.

FEEDING

The breeder of your puppy will have given you detailed feeding instructions. As a member of a litter the puppy had plenty of competition at feeding time but, now alone, there is no need to tuck in ravenously as there are no other siblings. Some puppies can develop a preference for just one type of food and will refuse to eat all others. This can present you with a dilemma, as Irish Setter puppies need substantial amounts of high-quality food to help in their rapid growth. Usually, this is just a phase the puppy will go through, especially around teething time.

At the age of eight weeks, puppies should still be on at least four meals a day. These should strike a balance between milk and meat meals. You can introduce your puppy to a variety of different types of protein by feeding some fish, chicken, eggs or even cheese to replace the more usual tripe or beef or tinned meat. The menu I suggest for my puppies will be given in a later chapter. The amount of food should be increased gradually as the puppy gets older and grows bigger. If the puppy eats up a meal quickly and still seems ravenous, give a little more with the next meal.

By the time the puppy is about three months old you can reduce the number of meals to three, but give an extra drink of milk. Vitamins and a calcium supplement should also be given to ensure strong bones and healthy growth. It is most important to get into a routine as soon as possible, and the puppy will learn to look forward to the meal-times. Once your Irish Setter is a fully grown adult, two meals a day should always be given. In the past, some Irish Setters had a reputation for being "skinny dogs" and "poor doers". This has changed considerably, and the great majority of pet Irish Setters one meets are well covered and look "prosperous". It is difficult to come to a conclusion about why this has happened, but some breeding lines used to be known as "bad doers", and it is possible that such lines no longer feature prominently in present-day pedigrees. Another reason could be the much greater variety and choice of different pet foods that are available now to accommodate a difficult feeder.

VACCINATION AND WORMING

All puppies will need to be vaccinated to protect them against the infectious diseases common to all canines. Your puppy might have had the first injection against Parvovirus before coming to you, but will also need to be protected against Distemper, Hepatitis, Leptospirosis and Para-influenza; a second booster injection against Parvovirus must also be given. I prefer to have my vet come to the house to give the first injection as I do not like to take an unprotected puppy into a surgery where other dogs are present. This is more expensive, but I like my puppy to be safe from infections that could be picked up in the surgery.

If your vet does not make house-calls and you have to visit the surgery, stay in the car with your puppy until it is your turn to be seen. It is probably best to make contact with the veterinary surgeon of your choice before the puppy arrives, to discuss the details and the timing. After the full course of vaccinations has been completed, the puppy should be kept safely away from other dogs for at least another week to allow the injections to become effective and to give their full protection to the puppy. The puppy should have been wormed thoroughly by the breeder; however, this will have to be repeated from time to time all through the dog's life, but only in accordance with your vet's advice.

TEETHING

Puppies usually start to change their baby, or milk teeth, between fourteen and sixteen weeks of age. Some puppies really suffer at this time and often lose their appetite. A quick look will usually confirm that the puppy is teething, because the gums will be swollen and red. Sometimes the face can also be swollen giving the puppy a very strange appearance. To ease the discomfort, the puppy will probably gnaw on anything that can be found. To avoid your furniture being damaged, provide the puppy with toys or a hard marrow-bone that can be chewed quite safely. If a new tooth is already coming in before the milk tooth has fallen out, try to gently move and loosen the old tooth. If the tooth proves to be particularly stubborn, the vet will be needed to remove the one that refuses to budge.

SOCIALISATION

Only when your puppy has been fully protected through vaccination can you start thinking about mixing with other dogs. Some canine societies run training classes for basic obedience where you can take your youngster. Very young puppies are really only taken along to get them used to being with other dogs without being frightened, or without getting over-excited. As the puppy gets older, the training sessions will become more serious. However, some Irish treat obedience classes as a huge joke and have a good time showing off – but some are very sensible and will try their very best to be good. If you intend to show your Irish Setter, ring-craft classes will be much more useful to you. If you are a budding exhibitor yourself, this type of training will be as instructive for you as it is for the dog, and you can learn together what is expected, once you get into the show ring.

LEAD TRAINING

Probably the most important lesson in early training is to get your puppy used to a collar and to walking on a lead. Some puppies do not take any notice of the strange thing around their neck and also learn to walk on the lead without any trouble. However, other puppies will make the most terrible fuss! When you put the collar on, they will throw themselves to the ground, rubbing their heads and necks in order to get rid of the collar. Others become quite rigid and hang their heads dejectedly. Try not to get angry when the puppy will not budge. Gentle coaxing with a treat will usually convince the puppy that this is not so bad after all.

Getting some puppies to walk on the lead can also be quite a trial! The worst case I have had was a puppy called Dougal. He became quite hysterical whenever I tried to put a collar and lead on him. In the end, I succeeded by first laying a trail of treats along the ground which Dougal greedily hoovered up while I was putting collar and lead around his neck. Next, I tempted him into following me on the lead by offering him more rewards. Eventually he learned to walk nicely on the lead and without too much pulling. However, some Irish Setters never seem to learn to walk quietly on the lead and will always try to pull their owners along! In such cases, I recommend the use of a Halti. This looks like a head-collar and fits over the dog's nose and around the head and is attached to the lead. There is no cruelty involved and even the most unruly Irish Setter will usually learn to walk quietly when a Halti is being used.

SIT AND STAY

Puppies should also be introduced to basic obedience such as sit and stay. Again, I use food as a teaching aid and make my youngsters sit and stay when a meal is put in front of them. Puppies learn very quickly to sit in anticipation

and I give lots of praise once they have learned to wait for their food. Just remember, patience is a virtue and will bring you great rewards when dealing with puppies.

YOUR PUPPY'S COAT

Puppies do not need a lot of grooming, as their baby coats are usually quite sleek and the feathering is still very short. However, it is a good idea to get the puppy used to being brushed and combed. By starting early, this will become part of the routine instead of something that has to be endured. Mine are real country dogs and during exercise usually manage to find all the disgusting things in a field. They love to have a good roll to make quite sure that it is rubbed in well before I can drag them away.

There is no need to bath a puppy; just leave the offending patches to dry and then brush them off. If the smell is really bad, such as fox, I might have to resort to washing it off with a bucket of warm water and a little shampoo.

EXERCISE

Very young puppies do not need to be taken out to be exercised, as long as they have access to a garden where they can play. Puppies tend to be extremely active one minute and are sound asleep the next. If puppies are allowed to run about too much without the chance to rest, they become overtired and fractious – in fact they are just like their human counterparts! Once the puppy is about four months old, more exercise can be introduced gradually, such as a walk on the lead followed by a short run in a field or the park, but this should not be overdone. Before you start to go out into a public place and to let the puppy off the lead, train your puppy to return to you. Start training in the garden, and give a reward every time the puppy returns to you when called, but do not repeat this too many times as a puppy's attention span is very limited.

5 *THE IRISH SETTER'S COAT*

The Irish Setter's coat, with its rich, chestnut colouring, is one of the most beautiful features of the breed. Like so many things, a good coat tends to be inherited and should be taken into consideration when planning a litter. However, even if an Irish Setter is born with a naturally good coat, correct diet and exercise are essential in order to maintain that glossy look which reflects a dog's good health. Regular grooming and careful trimming will then be needed to keep coat and feathering looking immaculate. This applies to all Irish Setters whether they are kept as pets or as show dogs – when coat care will have to be taken much more seriously.

ROUTINE CARE

It is most important to keep the coat free from tangles and knots. Regularly check all feathering and fringes and carefully remove anything that may have become entangled during exercise. If you do not do this the coat will soon become matted. Use your fingers to tease out, gently, any small twigs and burs, but take care not to pull too hard, for this will damage the coat. There are some excellent lotions available which can be sprayed directly onto the feathering to help to disentangle a Setter's fringes.

Once all debris has been removed, gently comb through the feathering with a wide-toothed comb. If you still meet with resistance, stop and check for further tangles. Once it is possible to comb through easily, a finer-toothed comb, or a coarse brush, can be used to complete the job. The same procedure should be used on the ears. From time to time, check behind your Setter's elbows and in the groin, to make sure that the rather finer, softer hair which grows there has not become knotted. If growth is particularly profuse, some of the hair can be carefully thinned out.

Always brush and comb the body coat in the direction in which it grows. First, comb through with a good, strong comb to remove any dried mud or dirt. Follow with a thorough brushing, for which I use a 'body brush' which is made for horses and can be bought in a riding shop. Made from pure bristle, it is oval in shape and quite large, which makes the job of brushing very easy. Vigorous brushing will remove any finer dirt and dust and stimulate coat growth. When brushing the body coat, I spray a coat conditioner containing mink oil on to the brush, but never directly on the coat. There are many different sprays available which will make the coat easier to manage and which will nourish and condition it. Do experiment to find the one that suits your dog's coat best, but be careful about using it at shows – in the UK, for example, the Kennel Club only allows water to be used for the final preparation at shows.

TRIMMING

The first, and most important, lesson any novice will have to learn is that trimming should only be undertaken to enhance a dog's natural appearance and that no attempt should be made to alter it in any way. Fortunately, trimming fashions, such as the excessive use of a razor or even electric clippers, have come and gone. They do nothing for an Irish Setter's looks, but rather tend to make a dog look hard and untypical. Most of us pick up the art of trimming from fellow exhibitors and our skills improve through practising on our dogs.

There really is no need to spend a small fortune on trimming equipment, even though this would be extremely easy, if the number of products for sale at shows is anything to go by! However, there are a few basic items that are essential and will help to make a good job of trimming. Look upon them as an investment and as the tools of the trade. Always buy the best quality scissors that you can afford. With proper care, they should last you for a very long time and, despite their initial high price, they will be cheaper in the long run than a less expensive pair that may not last for very long.

TRIMMING TOOLS

Thinning Scissors: There are two types available. One has double thinning blades and is best used for coarser coat, the other has just one thinning blade and a straight blade, best for more delicate work. Buy a pair for each job. Thinning scissors are used to remove excess hair from the ears, from behind the ears and from the neck. They are also used on the hocks and feet and to thin out any feathering that has become too profuse.

Straight Scissors: They are mainly used to trim feet and tail feathering, but are also used on ears.

Stripping Knife: This is mainly used to remove dead coat from the top of the head, the ears and from the neck.

Nail Clippers: I prefer to use the pliers type on my dogs, but many prefer to use the guillotine type, which has an opening into which the nail is inserted; the nail is then cut by a blade coming down onto it.

Combs: You will need a wide-toothed comb for the first comb through the coat; this is then repeated with a finer-toothed comb. I prefer combs with handles as I find them easier to hold.

Rubber Finger Stools: They are probably more familiar on a cashier's fingers in the bank! However, they are very useful for removing the last bits of dead coat from a dog's head.

Brushes: I really prefer to use natural bristle brushes on the body. However, the brush I use on the feathering after combing is made from synthetic fibres. A body brush is a good investment and can be bought in a riding shop. It is oval in shape and has a hand strap for better control. To give a dog the finishing touch to the coat, I use a cushioned, pure bristle brush. Such a brush is very expensive but is worth every penny and will last a long time.

TRIMMING STEP BY STEP

EARS

Before starting, make sure that the hair on the ears is clean and well combed. This is particularly important if dogs have not been trimmed for some time, as the longer hair may have come into contact with their food and drink. Hold up the ear and, with thinning scissors, thin out the hair on the back of the ear, as well as on the neck under the ear, by using the thinning scissors in an upward direction. The best way to judge how well you are doing is to cut once and then to comb out the hair that has been cut. Repeat this several times until sufficient hair has been removed, so that the ear now hangs closely to the head. Then, turn the ear over and also trim the inside of the ear, taking great care not to cut the delicate skin.

Once you have finished tidying up behind and inside the ear, hold the tip of the ear down and, carefully, start to reduce the feathering on the front of the ear. Push the thinning scissors upwards under the coat and only thin out the lower layer of hair. Again, after each cut, stop and comb the hair away. Trimming from

THE EARS

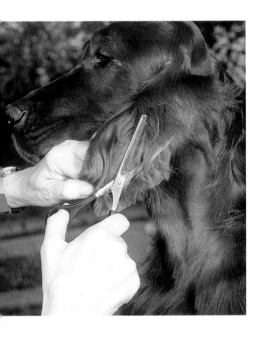

LEFT: Hold the tip of the ear down to start thinning out the feathering on the ear.

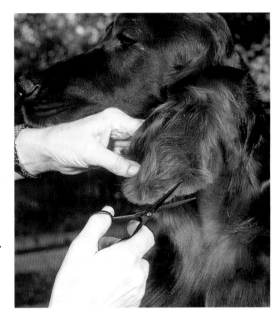

RIGHT: Use straight scissors to give a neat line along the length of the ear.

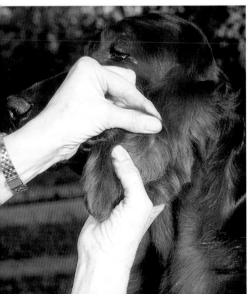

LEFT: To achieve a really good finish, use the finger and thumb method.

RIGHT: Well trimmed to enhance the natural appearance.

underneath will prevent you from leaving scissor marks on the ear's more silky top coat – and you should remember never to use the thinning scissors to cut across the growth of the hair. When the feathering has been thinned out sufficiently, use your straight scissors to give a good, clean line along the length of the ear to its tip, but do not trim the hair from the fold downwards with straight scissors. A little attention with thinning scissors is all that is needed here, as feathering should be left longer to help achieve the desired soft expression.

When both ears have been trimmed, carefully check that they are even in length and texture, and adjust where necessary. To achieve a really good finish, now use finger and thumb to remove any dead hair from the top of the ear's feathering. This is my favourite way of dealing with an Irish Setter's ears as it allows them to retain the desired, natural look. If you regularly pluck out any re-growth, ears will always look tidy and trimming will never have to become a major job again. However, if you prefer it, you could use the stripping knife instead of using the finger-and-thumb method. When trimming ears, remember to remove any dead coat from the dog's skull. Many Irish Setters are prone to growing yellow fluff on their heads which should *never* be touched with scissors, but should be carefully plucked out with finger and thumb.

NECK

To trim the neck, get your dog to sit down and comb the coat thoroughly. Hold the thinning scissors in one hand and, with your free hand, support the dog's head. Start to thin out the coat from a point just above the breastbone by trimming in an upward direction towards the dog's chin, following the growth of the coat. Cut once, and comb as you go along. This is usually a very satisfying activity as plenty of coat tends to come off, but you should stand back from time to time to look at your work.

Start to thin out the coat from just above the breastbone by trimming in an upward direction.

A tidy neck and front.

Lift the dog's ear and trim to the line where the growth of the coat changes direction and where it is joined by the longer, more silky coat which has grown forward from the back of the neck and from over the shoulder. This is topcoat and it has a different texture from the hair you have just removed. Use the finer thinning scissors and thin out enough undercoat to allow the topcoat to blend into the already trimmed-out neck. If there are any wayward tufts of coat

45

sticking up over the shoulder they should be thinned out and shaped to lie down flat. Again, stand back from time to time to view your work, not only from the front but also from the side, in order to judge the effect.

FEET AND NAILS

Even if you have no intention of ever showing your Irish Setter, you should always trim your dog's feet. This is for your dog's benefit and for the sake of your home! If left unattended, the hair on a Setter's feet can easily become matted and will tend to stay wet or damp. This is not only uncomfortable for the dog, but it can also lead to infections and other foot problems. Neatly trimmed feet will prevent this, and will stop extra dirt from being brought into the house – especially after a good gallop across a muddy field. Before trimming, make sure that the dog's feet are really dry and clean or you may damage your expensive scissors. If matts have been allowed to develop, tease them out

between your fingers before starting to work. Hold the foot firmly in one hand and trim off the excess hair from the bottom of the pads with straight scissors. Next, carefully trim around the toes, with straight scissors, to define the correct shape of the foot. Do not remove the feathering that grows between the toes completely, but only thin it out, as it helps to protect the tender tissues between the toes. To complete the neat appearance, taper the leg feathering towards the foot, by starting to reduce it slightly at the pasterns. This will also stop the feathering from trailing on the ground.

Toe-nails need to be cut regularly. This is best done when the nails are wet and therefore softer. It is also easier to see the quick when the nails are wet and held up against the light. Cut close, but do avoid the quick as, if this is cut, it can be very painful to the dog and can also lead to bleeding. Nails that are cut back regularly to their correct length will ensure that the dog walks correctly on the pads of the feet.

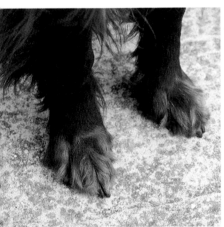

Untidy feet with long nails.

Trim around the toes to define the correct shape of the foot.

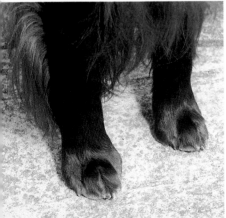

Correctly trimmed feet and toe-nails.

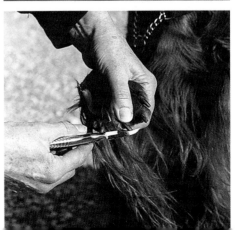
Toe-nails need regular clipping.

Angle the thinning scissors towards the heel of the dog's foot and thin out the coat.

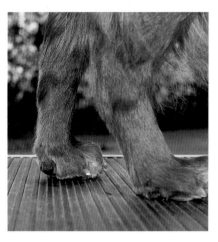

The finish should be as smooth as possible.

own devices, the feathering will usually grow with a curl at the end of the tail and the fringe tends to become uneven and untidy-looking. Therefore, some careful trimming is needed to achieve the desired effect. Brush the tail feathering with the cushioned bristle brush and hold your dog's tail straight out, away from the body. Gently wrap the feathering around the tail and towards its tip. Cut off the excess hair across the tip of the tail by using a pair of straight scissors. This will give an even, gentle taper to the tail feathering.

After wrapping the feathering around the tail, cut off the excess hair across the tip of the tail, using straight scissors.

HOCKS

The feathering which grows from the hocks down to the heels should also be trimmed. First, comb out thoroughly, then brush the coat upwards and against the direction in which it grows. Angle your thinning scissors towards the heel of the dog's foot and start thinning out. Stop occasionally, and comb through, to check how much more coat has to come off. The final result for which you should be aiming is as smooth a finish as possible, one without any "steps" having been cut into the coat and without any ragged edges being left.

TAIL

A well-fringed tail is extremely desirable in an Irish Setter and, according to the Standard of the Breed, "the tail should have a fringe of moderately long hair decreasing in length as it approaches point." Unfortunately, if left to its

A well trimmed fringe of moderately long hair, decreasing in length as it approaches the point.

BATH-TIME

Buy a top-quality shampoo which suits your dog's coat. There is a very large selection available and it is really by trial and error that you find the most suitable one. Buy a low-foaming shampoo which will make rinsing-out much easier. I bath my dogs in my own bath-tub which is by far the easiest way. My dogs really enjoy their bath and will get in by themselves. However, I strongly recommend the use of a non-slip mat to prevent dogs from slipping. Always bath your dog several days before a show to allow time for the natural oils to be restored.

Start by wetting the dog's coat thoroughly. You can buy a special shower attachment for the taps which makes this easier, but I am still using two plastic jugs! This works quite well but takes much longer. The shampoo I use is very thick and concentrated. Therefore I pour some into a jug and dilute it with warm water in accordance with the manufacturer's instructions. This produces a shampoo which is very easy to use. Start at the head, taking great care that the shampoo does not get into your

dog's eyes. Apply it all over the body and work well into the coat, including the legs and feathering and under the chest and tummy. Rinse, and then shampoo a second time. Rinse again thoroughly and check that all traces of soap have been removed, leaving the coat really clean. Squeeze out the excess moisture and, if necessary, use a special rinse which will help to make the coat more manageable. While the dog is still standing in the bath, brush lightly with the cushioned bristle brush.

Wrap the dog in towels and gently lift out of the bath. To speed up the drying process, a blow-drier can be used, but continue with brushing to ensure that the coat settles correctly. Try and avoid using a blow-drier too often as the heat will damage the coat. Once dried, use a special coat, or pin a towel around the dog, to make sure that the body coat remains as flat as possible. There is some debate about whether to bath a dog before trimming or whether to trim before bathing. I prefer to do most of the trimming before a bath and make adjustments, where needed, after the coat has settled after bathing.

6 *THE BREED STANDARDS*

The original Standard of the Breed for Irish Setters was drawn up and approved by the Committee of the Irish Red Setter Club, Dublin, and published in 1886. The Club had been founded in 1882 to promote the Irish Red Setter rather than the Red and White Irish Setter. From the outset the Standard did not contain any reference to size nor any other measurements. This lack of all dimensions has often been criticised by breeders and exhibitors, as well as by aspiring judges of the breed. However, it can be said that their absence has served the breed rather well by making the overall balance of the Irish Setter much more important than just a series of measurements or weights. The Standards of several breeds which include references to size have, over the years, had to be altered and adjusted, usually in an upward direction, to accommodate fashionable trends from within a breed. Irish Setters of merit have gained their titles despite their size – or lack of it, because they were well-balanced and in proportion.

However, this does not mean that there has been no debate concerning size and other measurements over the years. In answer to some criticism that her Ch. Winifred was too small, Mrs Ingle Bepler published a reply in *Our Dogs* which compared the measurements of Palmerston and Winifred. She had obtained Palmerston's measurements from Dalziel's book *British Dogs* (all shown in inches)

	Palmerston	Winifred
Height at shoulder:	23.5	24.5
Length from nose to set-on of tail:	44	44.5
Length of tail:	15	13
Girth of chest:	30	29
Girth of loin:	24	22
Girth of head:	16	15.5
Girth of muzzle:	10	10

When the Standard was revised in Dublin in 1930, the inclusion of size was discussed but was, once again, firmly rejected. However, an important addition to the revised version was the introduction of 'Style' which read: "Must be racy, full of quality, and kindly in expression", which placed a greater emphasis on the essential raciness of the breed; and by changing the description of the body from "should be long" to "should be proportionate", the importance of overall balance was reinforced. Later on, when the English Kennel Club decided to adopt the Dublin Standard as the official description of the breed, the Scale of Points it had contained was dropped.

REVISIONS

The Standard of the Breed for the Irish Setter, in common with all others, was laid down to serve as a 'blue-print' for the breed, enabling breeders to produce stock of the correct type and to provide a standard for judges by which to assess the breed. In fact, the Standard should serve as the 'Bible' for both breeders and judges alike.

During the 1980s the KC undertook a revision of all the Breed Standards in consultation and with the co-operation of the breed clubs. On the whole, this did not make any changes to the important points of the Irish Setter Standard, but only clarified some of the details. It also gave a common format to all Standards, which were then published in 1986.

The current American Standard of the Breed was approved by the American Kennel Club in August 1991 and replaced the June 1960 version. It is much more detailed in its descriptions than the British Standard, and the most obvious difference between the two is the inclusion of a guide to height and weight.

THE BRITISH BREED STANDARD (1986)

GENERAL APPEARANCE Must be racy, balanced and full of quality. In conformation, proportionate.

CHARACTERISTICS Most handsome and refined in looks, tremendously active with untiring readiness to range and hunt under any conditions.

TEMPERAMENT Demonstratively affectionate.

HEAD & SKULL Head long and lean, not narrow or snipy, not coarse at the ears. Skull oval (from ear to ear) having plenty of brain room and well-defined occipital protuberance. From occiput to stop and from stop to tip of nose to be parallel and of equal length, brows raised showing stop. Muzzle moderately deep, fairly square at end. Jaws of nearly equal length, flews not pendulous, nostrils wide. Colour of nose dark mahogany, dark walnut or black.

EYES Dark hazel to dark brown, not too large, preferably like an unshelled almond in shape, set level (not obliquely), under brows showing kind, intelligent expression.

EARS Of moderate size, fine in texture, set on low, well back and hanging in a neat fold close to head.

MOUTH Jaws strong, with a perfect, regular and complete scissor bite, i.e. the upper teeth closely overlapping the lower teeth and set square to the jaws.

NECK Moderately long, very muscular but not too thick, slightly arched and free from all tendency to throatiness, setting cleanly without a break of topline into shoulders.

FOREQUARTERS Shoulders fine at points, deep and sloping well back. Forelegs straight and sinewy having plenty of bone, with elbows free, well let down and not inclined either in or out.

BODY Chest as deep as possible, rather narrow in front. Ribs well-sprung leaving plenty of lung room and carried well back to muscular loin, slightly arched. Firm straight topline gently sloping downwards from the withers.

HINDQUARTERS Wide and powerful. Hindlegs from hip to hock long and muscular, from hock to heel short and strong. Stifle and hock joints well bent and not inclined either in or out.

FEET Small, very firm; toes strong, close together and arched.

GAIT/MOVEMENT Free flowing, driving movement with true action when viewed from front or rear, and in profile showing perfect co-ordination.

TAIL Of moderate length proportionate to size of body, set on just below the level of the back, strong at root tapering to a fine point and carried as nearly as possible on a level with or below the back.

COAT On head, front of legs and tips of ears, short and fine, on all other parts of body and legs of moderate length, flat and as free as possible from curl or wave. Feathers on upper portion of ears long and silky; on back of fore- and hindlegs long and fine. Fair amount of hair on belly, forming a nice fringe which may extend on chest and throat. Feet well-feathered between toes. Tail to have fringe of moderately long hair decreasing in length as it approaches point. All feathering to be as straight and flat as possible.

COLOUR Rich chestnut with no trace of black. White on chest, throat, chin or toes, or small star on forehead or narrow streak or blaze on nose or face not to disqualify.

FAULTS Any departure from the foregoing points should be considered a fault and the seriousness with which the fault should be regarded should be in exact proportion to its degree.

NOTE Male animals should have two apparently normal testicles fully descended into the scrotum.
Reproduced by kind permission of the Kennel Club.

THE AMERICAN BREED STANDARD (1991)

GENERAL APPEARANCE The Irish Setter is an active, aristocratic bird dog, rich red in color, substantial yet elegant in build. Standing over two feet tall at the shoulder, the dog has a straight, fine, glossy coat, longer on ears, chest, tail and back of legs. Afield, the Irish Setter is a swift-moving hunter; at home a sweet-natured, trainable companion.

At their best, the lines of the Irish Setter so satisfy in overall balance that artists have termed it the most beautiful of all dogs. The correct specimen always exhibits balance, whether standing or in motion. Each part of the dog flows and fits smoothly into its neighboring parts without calling attention to itself.

SIZE, PROPORTION, SUBSTANCE
Size There is no disqualification as to size. The make and fit of all parts and their overall balance in the animal are rated more important. Twenty-seven inches at the withers and a show weight of about 70 pounds are considered ideal for the dog; the bitch 25 inches, 60 pounds. Variance beyond an inch up or down is to be discouraged.
Proportion Measuring from the breastbone to the rear of thigh and from the top of the withers to the ground, the Irish Setter is slightly longer than it is tall.
Substance All legs sturdy with plenty of bone. Substance in the male reflects masculinity without coarseness. Bitches appear feminine without being slight of bone.

HEAD Long and lean, its length at least double the width between the ears. Beauty of head is emphasized by delicate chiselling along the muzzle, around and below the eyes and along the cheeks.

Eyes Expression soft, yet alert. Eyes somewhat almond-shaped, of medium size, placed rather well apart, neither deep set nor bulging. Color dark to medium brown.

Ears Ears set well back and low, not above level of eye. Leather thin, hanging in a neat fold close to the head, and nearly long enough to reach the nose.

Skull The skull is oval when viewed from above or front; very slightly domed when viewed in profile. The brow is raised, showing a distinct stop midway between the tip of the nose and the well-defined occiput (rear of skull). Thus the nearly level line from occiput to brow is set a little above, and parallel to, the straight and equal line from eye to nose.

Muzzle Muzzle moderately deep, jaws of nearly equal length, the underline of the jaws being almost parallel with the top line of the muzzle.

Nose Nose black or chocolate; nostrils wide. Upper lips fairly square but not pendulous.

Teeth The teeth meet in a scissor bite in which the upper incisors fit closely over the lower, or they may meet evenly.

NECK, TOPLINE AND BODY

Neck Neck moderately long, strong but not thick, slightly arched; free from throatiness and fitting smoothly into the shoulders.

Topline Topline of body from withers to tail should be firm and incline slightly downward without sharp drop at the croup. The tail is set on nearly level with the croup as a natural extension of the topline, strong at root tapering to a fine point, nearly long enough to reach the hock. Carriage straight or curving slightly upward nearly level with

the back.

Body Body sufficiently long to permit a straight and free stride.

CHEST AND FOREQUARTERS

Chest Deep, reaching approximately to the elbows with moderate forechest, extending beyond the point where the shoulder joins the upper arm. Chest is of moderate width so that it does not interfere with forward motion and extends rearwards to well-sprung ribs.

Loins Loins firm, muscular and of moderate length.

Forequarters Shoulder blades long, wide, sloping well back, fairly close together at the withers. Upper arm and shoulder blades are approximately the same length, and are joined at sufficient angle to bring the elbows rearward along the brisket in line with the top of the withers. The elbows moving freely incline neither in nor out.

Forelegs Forelegs straight and sinewy.

Feet Strong, nearly straight pasterns. Feet rather small, very firm, toes arched and close.

HINDQUARTERS

Hindquarters should be wide and powerful with broad, well developed thighs. Hind legs long and muscular from hip to hock; short and perpendicular from hock to ground; well angulated at stifle and hock joints, which, like the elbows, incline neither in nor out. Feet as in front. Angulation of the forequarters and hindquarters should be balanced.

COAT AND COLOR

Coat Short and fine on head and forelegs. On all other parts of moderate length and flat. Feathering long and silky on ears; on back of forelegs and thighs long and fine, with a pleasing fringe of hair on belly and brisket extending onto the chest. Fringe on tail moderately long and tapered. All coat and feathering as straight and free as possible from curl or wave. The Irish Setter is trimmed for the show ring to emphasize the lean head and clean neck. The top third of the ears and the throat nearly to the breastbone are trimmed. Excess feathering is removed to show the outline of the foot. All trimming is done to preserve the natural appearance of the dog.

Color Mahogany or rich chestnut red with no trace of black. A small amount of white on chest, throat or toes, or a narrow centred streak on skull is not to be penalized.

GAIT

At the trot the gait is big, very lively, graceful and efficient. At an extended trot the head reaches slightly forward, keeping the dog in balance. The forelegs reach well ahead as if to pull in the ground without giving the appearance of a hackney gait. The hindquarters drive smoothly and with great power. Seen from the front or rear, the forelegs, as well as the hind legs below the hock joint, move perpendicularly to the ground, with some tendency towards a single track as speed increases. Structural characteristics which interfere with a straight, true stride are to be penalized.

TEMPERAMENT

The Irish Setter has a rollicking personality. Shyness, hostility or timidity are uncharacteristic of the breed. An outgoing, stable temperament is the essence of the Irish Setter.

Reproduced by kind permission of the American Kennel Club.

INTERPRETATION OF THE STANDARDS

GENERAL APPEARANCE

The most important characteristic of the Irish Setter is described in the very first sentence of the British Standard of the Breed: *Must be racy, balanced and full of quality*. This choice of words is deliberate and unequivocal: *Must* be racy, balanced and full of quality. Therefore, the conformation of the Irish Setter must be in harmony and without exaggeration to any part of the body, and the description should immediately conjure up the picture of a true Irish Setter: A fit, balanced, sporting dog with every part of the body flowing smoothly into the next without any ugly breaks or lumps and bumps; and the first impression an Irish Setter *must* give is that of a racy, elegant thoroughbred.

The American Standard refers to the Irish Setter as an aristocratic bird dog of such balance and beauty that artists have termed Irish Setters the most beautiful of all dogs, and very few of the fans of the breed in the UK would argue with such an apt description! Just as in the British Standard, the American Standard calls for the Irish Setter to be balanced and with each part of the body fitting smoothly into the next "without calling attention to itself", and describes the Irish Setter's build as "substantial yet elegant", but does not use the word racy. However, the description of "active, aristocratic bird dog of substantial yet elegant build" really equals the mental picture of "racy".

An initial reference to size is made under General Appearance by describing the animal as "standing over two feet tall at the shoulder". In the UK many worthy Irish Setters, and bitches in particular, have gained their titles over the years without "standing over two feet tall at the shoulder". This was also true of the great Elcho, who was imported into the USA from

Points of anatomy

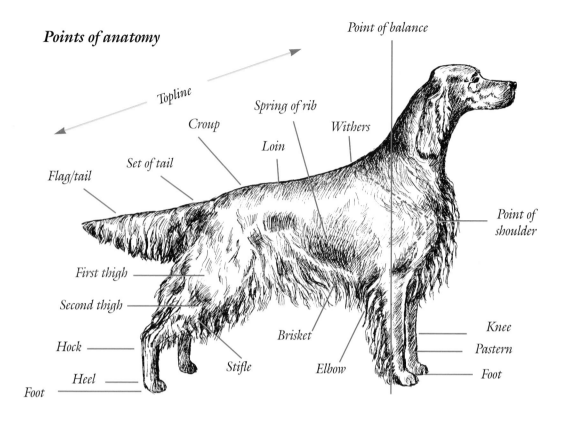

Point of balance

Topline

Spring of rib

Croup

Withers

Loin

Set of tail

Flag/tail

Point of shoulder

First thigh

Second thigh

Knee

Pastern

Hock

Brisket

Foot

Heel

Stifle

Elbow

Foot

Skeletal system

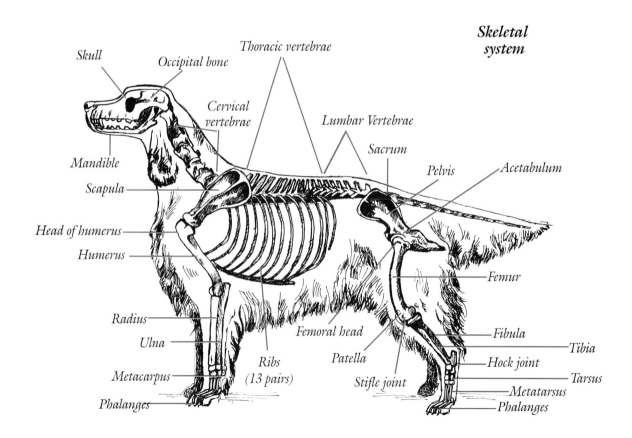

Skull

Occipital bone

Thoracic vertebrae

Cervical vertebrae

Lumbar Vertebrae

Sacrum

Mandible

Pelvis

Acetabulum

Scapula

Head of humerus

Humerus

Femur

Radius

Femoral head

Fibula

Ulna

Patella

Tibia

Metacarpus

Ribs (13 pairs)

Stifle joint

Hock joint

Tarsus

Phalanges

Metatarsus

Phalanges

Ireland in the 1870s and became the first bench Champion there. He was said to have been just 24 inches at the shoulder. There has clearly been a preference for a taller type since those days which has been accommodated in the American Standard in the section called SIZE, PROPORTION, SUBSTANCE. The ideal height for a male Irish Setter is considered to be 27 inches at the shoulders with a show weight of 70 pounds. The ideal height for a bitch is considered to be 25 inches at the shoulders and weighing 60 pounds. An additional measurement is given by stating that the length from the breastbone to the rear of the thigh should be longer than the measurement from the top of the withers to the ground, thereby requiring the Irish Setter to be slightly longer than it is tall. There is no disqualification as to size, but a variance beyond an inch up or down is discouraged.

CHARACTERISTICS AND TEMPERAMENT

The handsome physical appearance must be matched by the correct temperament. Irish Setters should be extremely active and untiring during their work and at exercise, and their happy-go-lucky attitude to life should be reflected in their ever-wagging tails. Most Irish Setters love to greet their friends, both human and canine, with some enthusiasm, but often have to be restrained from being just a little too 'demonstratively affectionate', which is the term used in the British Standard, as they can be quite boisterous, especially when young.

The American Standard describes the Irish Setter's personality as "rollicking" which, according to my dictionary, can mean "wild, unruly, exuberant, boisterous and frolicsome". The American Standard also lists some of the undesirable traits in the Irish Setter's temperament such as shyness, hostility or timidity. The correct temperament is of the utmost importance in the Breed and the call for

"an outgoing, stable temperament" as the essence of the ideal character, is excellent.

HEAD AND SKULL

Both Standards call for the head to be long and lean, but the American Standard includes an additional, dimensional reference by stating that "the length (of the head) should be at least double the width between the ears". By insisting on a minimum length for the head, length alone becomes an important issue. As balance is of the utmost importance, the head should be proportionate and in harmony with the rest of the body. The American Standard goes on to describe the chiselling and moulding of the head. Strangely enough, the British Standard does not contain any reference to this, but a finely chiselled and moulded head is usually described as possessing "plenty of work".

The British Standard calls for the skull to be oval and with plenty of brain room. The American Standard seems to agree, but specifies that the skull should be oval when viewed from above or from in front, but when viewed in profile it should be slightly domed. Both call for a well-defined occipital protuberance (the rear of the skull) which lends the Irish Setter the desired air of refinement. The back of the skull should be level and not fall away, but show a good finish with a nice nape to the neck.

When viewed in profile the Irish Setter's head has often been compared to two bricks on top of each other with the top brick pulled halfway back over the lower brick. With this picture in mind, both Standards agree that skull and foreface should be well-balanced and on parallel lines. Therefore, downfaced or "Roman noses" are undesirable, as are "dished" faces. The distances from occiput to stop and from stop to tip of the nose should be of equal length, creating a balanced picture. The line from occiput to stop is set a little above and parallel

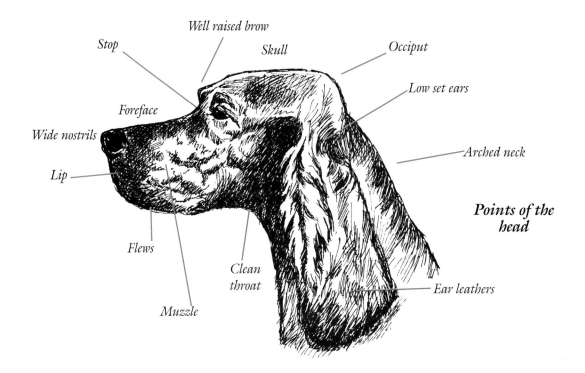

Stop

Well raised brow

Skull

Occiput

Low set ears

Foreface

Wide nostrils

Lip

Arched neck

Points of the head

Flews

Clean throat

Ear leathers

Muzzle

to the line from stop to tip of the nose. The forehead should be raised at the brows, showing a well-defined stop, which is the depression between the eyes at the junction of skull and foreface. A lack of stop and a lack of the characteristically raised brows spoils the true expression of an Irish Setter and both are untypical for the Breed. The head should never be coarse and heavy, but also never be narrow and pointed.

The muzzle should be moderately deep – which does not mean as deep as that of an English or Gordon Setter – with jaws that are of nearly equal length. The desired finish to the muzzle is fairly square at the end and not pointed or snipy; and, when viewed from the front, the chin will be visible.

As the Irish Setter relies on a well-developed sense of smell to find game, the nose must be of good size and the nostrils, according to both Standards, must be wide. There is nothing more pleasing than an Irish Setter's head with a good square finish to the foreface and a nose that ends in wide, moist nostrils. The British Standard describes the colour of the nose as dark mahogany, dark walnut or black, with the American Standard calling for the nose to be black or chocolate. Most Irish Setters have excellent pigmentation, not only to their noses, but also around their eyes, and any loss is often associated with the time of the year – as in a "winter nose". In bitches a loss of pigment can often coincide with the time of their seasons, but it usually returns very quickly afterwards.

EYES
The description of the shape of the eyes was reviewed and improved during the revision of the British Standard of the Breed in 1986. Following the advice of veterinary eye experts, the phrase "preferably like an unshelled almond in shape" was added to the Standard, which replaced "ought not be too large". Many breeders had aimed at the smaller, undoubtedly attractive, almost almond-shaped eye in their breeding programmes, but it was felt that the description of 'unshelled almond' was not only more accurate, but also much safer. Veterinary eye specialists advised that breeding for an eye that "ought not be too large", was not definite

enough and might eventually lead to an eye that would not completely fill the eye-socket. This, in turn, could give rise to such problems as entropion. If any reader has difficulty in visualising this reasoning, it is very easy to compare the shape of a shelled and an unshelled almond! An Irish Setter's eye should never be slanted, as this gives a hard or alien expression, as does a light eye. In a working gundog a loose eye is potentially dangerous, as grass-seeds can more easily get into the eye. An eye that is too prominent is equally undesirable as it increases the chances of damage during work.

The British Standard calls for the expression to be kind and intelligent. The American Standard describes, similarly, a soft, yet alert expression, and with eyes to be "somewhat" almond-shaped, of medium size and placed well apart, neither deep set nor bulging. The correct expression is one of the characteristics of the breed, but to put it accurately into words is quite a challenge! An Irish Setter's expression should be able to change from being soft and kind to being bright and alert, to quizzical and mischievous. All in the flicker of an eye! Without this ability, something of the true Irish character is lost.

According to the American Standard the colour should be dark to medium brown. The British Standard describes a similar range of colour from dark hazel to dark brown.

EARS

The British Standard calls for ears to be of moderate size – which does not mean the length of a Cocker Spaniel's ears, nor should they be as broad – and with a fine and soft texture. The set-on should be quite low. Short ears which are set on too high are unattractive and tend to spoil the classy appearance of the Irish Setter.

The American Standard is more explicit by calling for the ears to be set well back and low. They should not be set on above the level of the eye. Both Standards agree that the ears should hang in a neat fold close to the head, but the American Standard calls for the leathers to be nearly long enough to reach the nose. In the UK exhibitors tend to be rather surprised when judges measure an Irish Setter's ears in this fashion!

MOUTH

The description in the British Standard is very clear. The correct scissor bite means that the upper incisors fit closely over the lower. Two faults in the show-ring are 'undershot' mouths, where the bottom teeth protrude in front of the top teeth, and 'overshot' mouths where the top teeth project too far over the bottom teeth and therefore leave a gap. As a rule, neither fault interferes with a dog's ability to eat properly, nor do they affect an Irish Setter's ability to perform the work for which the breed was intended. However, both faults tend to exclude the dog from winning at shows.

An important difference between the two Standards concerns the bite. The American Standard permits a level bite, but the British Standard only allows for a perfect, regular and complete scissor bite. A level bite is not acceptable in the UK as it is felt that it could eventually lead to more undershot mouths appearing in the breed. The majority of Irish Setters have a correct bite with good strong teeth, but this can change very quickly. Faulty dentition is, like many faults, a genetic problem and should be guarded against in any breeding programme.

Normal dentition for Irish Setters is forty-two teeth, but judges in the UK do not usually count an exhibit's teeth. In some countries, Germany for example, missing teeth are penalised, and judges are required to record their absence in their show-reports. This is also taken into consideration when permission is sought for an Irish Setter to be bred from.

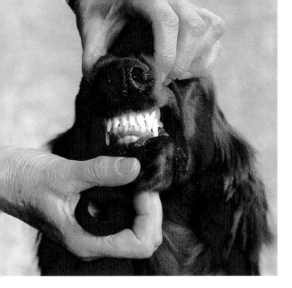

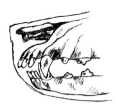

Incorrect: Overshot.

Incorrect: Undershot.

Incorrect: level bite.

THE BITE
Correct scissor bite.

NECK

Both Standards are agreed on a moderately long and well-arched neck, which lends a look of elegance to the Irish Setter. It should be well muscled, but if the neck is too short and thick, the desired outline of the Irish Setter will be spoilt. However, the opposite, a very long and rather thin neck, is just as undesirable. A clean throat without excessive folds of skin under the throat is correct, and the clean neck should be set into the shoulders smoothly and without a break in the flowing lines. Because the Irish Setter is a galloping breed which relies on air-scents to find game, a correct neck and a correct head carriage are essential.

FOREQUARTERS

Both Standards agree that shoulders should be well laid back. The British Standard calls for shoulders to be fine at points and deep; the

FRONT VIEWS

Correct:
Straight front.

Incorrect: Elbows out,
feet turning in.

Incorrect: Elbows tied
in, feet turning out.

Correct.

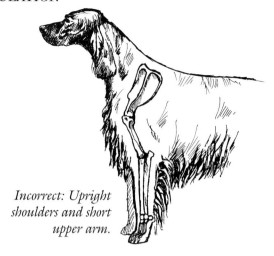

*Incorrect: Upright
shoulders and short
upper arm.*

American Standard requires them to be fairly close together at the top with wide shoulder blades. It is absolutely essential for shoulders to be correctly angulated to enable an Irish Setter to move forward with a long and reaching stride. An animal with straight or upright shoulders and straight upper arms cannot move with such a stride, but will move with short, mincing steps. The correct angle formed by the junction of the upper arm and the shoulder blades should be about 90 degrees. The American Standard much more eloquently explains that "upper arm and shoulder blades are approximately the same length, and are joined at sufficient angle to bring the elbows rearward along the brisket in line with the top of the withers". When viewed in profile, the Irish Setter should have a good forechest which can only be achieved through the correct layback of the shoulders. Both Standards ask for elbows to be free and not inclined either in or out and agree that front legs should not only be well-boned, but that they should also be sinewy. Thick and heavy front legs detract from the elegant and racy appearance of the Irish Setter, but a lack of bone is just as undesirable as it tends to make the dog look weedy.

BODY
According to the British Standard the chest should be well-developed and as deep as possible, but the American Standard specifies that the chest should reach approximately to the elbows. Therefore, when assessing a heavily-coated Irish Setter it is necessary to use the hands to feel just how far the chest reaches, and judges are often surprised to discover just how shallow some dogs are under their coats!

When viewed from the front, the chest should appear to be rather narrow but this does not mean that the front legs should look as if they came out of one hole, but a "rather" narrow front allows the front legs to extend and to reach well forward. The ribs should be well-sprung and carried well back, giving plenty of lung room which is essential in an untiring, active gundog. However, "well-sprung" should not be confused with barrel-ribbed. Nor should an Irish Setter be slab-sided, which is flat and without spring. The ribs should reach well back to the loin, which according to the British Standard should be muscular and slightly arched. The American Standard calls for the loin to be firm, muscular and of "moderate length". The call for "moderate length" is excellent as it seems to reinforce the quest for overall balance. It is essential for the loin to be strong, as it provides the coupling that connects the front and the rear of the animal. The two Standards are in agreement that the loin should be muscular.

The gently sloping topline distinguishes the Irish Setter from the other Setter varieties. It should be firm and flow gently from the withers, without a break nor with a sharp drop at the croup. Therefore an exaggerated 'ski slope' is not correct, nor is a flat, 'coffee-table' topline. Here, the two Standards are substantially in agreement. However, in addition, the American Standard calls for the body to be sufficiently long to permit a straight and free stride. A "sufficiently long" dog is also a much more scopy dog, and an Irish Setter with a very short back not only looks wrong and lacks elegance but, much more importantly, is unable to get into a long, ground-covering stride; crabbing will result as the dog has to move sideways to prevent the back feet from touching the front feet.

HINDQUARTERS
The hindquarters represent the "powerhouse" of the Irish Setter and, in a galloping breed, they must be wide, muscular and well-developed. The hindlegs should be long from hip to hock, well-angulated and with plenty of muscular substance through both the first and second thighs. Straight stifles with a lack of angulation are incorrect, leading to movement without drive. Over-angulated hindlegs lead to unsteady or wobbly movement, with the dog having difficulty getting the hindlegs under the body. The hindleg from hock to heel must be short and strong, enabling Irish Setters to propel themselves forward with great drive. In addition, the American Standard calls for the forequarters to be balanced by the hindquarters. This is essential in a balanced mover to cover the ground efficiently and accurately.

FEET
Both Standards call for small, very firm feet, with strong, arched toes which are close together. Poor feet are a handicap in a working dog that has to gallop over heather and rough terrain during a long working day. Therefore, hare feet, which are thin and splayed are incorrect, as are flat feet. The ideal foot is extremely neat in appearance and should be well-padded, turning neither in nor out. The American Standard calls for "nearly straight" pasterns. This does *not* mean completely straight. The pasterns act as shock absorbers and a slight angle will give much better protection to the leg of a hard running dog.

REAR VIEWS

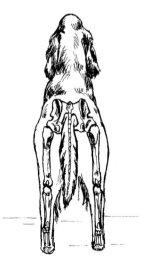

Correct.

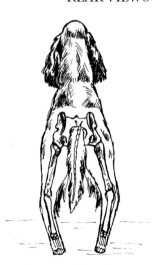

Incorrect: Bowed.

Incorrect: Cow-hocked.

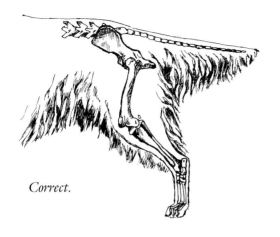

Correct.

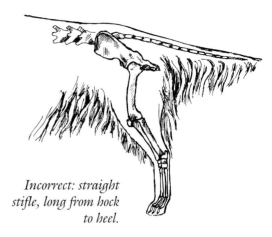

Incorrect: straight stifle, long from hock to heel.

GAIT/MOVEMENT

The British Standard requires a free flowing, driving movement with a true action from all angles. It should never be forgotten that the Irish Setter was originally bred as a free-ranging, tireless worker, which requires an animal that can cover the maximum of ground with the least amount of effort. Therefore, the action must be efficient and smooth, but if a Setter is incorrectly constructed, this true action cannot be achieved. A hackneyed gait where the forelegs are raised excessively is inefficient and incorrect, as is a lack of reach and drive. A "daisy-cutting" action is desirable. On the move, the correctly constructed Irish Setter remains balanced at all times, keeping a firm topline, and when viewed in profile, movement should be perfectly co-ordinated.

The American Standard is rather more detailed in the description of the gait, but basically calls for the same as the British Standard. Accordingly, at the trot the gait is described as big, very lively, graceful and efficient. At the extended trot the head reaches slightly forward, keeping the dog in balance. Perfect co-ordination is not mentioned, but the description that "when seen from front and rear, the forelegs, as well as the hindlegs below the hock joint, move perpendicularly to the ground, with some tendency towards a single track as speed increases", seems to mean just that. The American Standard adds that any structural characteristic which interferes with true movement should be penalised.

BELOW: Sh. Ch. Danaway Debonair demonstrating free, flowing movement with a firm topline, on his way to winning Best in Show at Crufts 1993. Photo: Dalton.

Correct movement viewed from the side.

Incorrect: Hackney action.

Incorrect: Over-reaching.

Incorrect: pacing.

TAIL

The British Standard calls for the tail to be of moderate length, but the American Standard includes, as a guide to length, that it should be nearly long enough to reach the hock. Both agree that it should be set on just below the level of the back. A lower set is often associated with a "goose rump" or a too steep finish over the croup. A tail that comes straight off the back is also incorrect. The tail should be strong at the root and taper to a fine point. When it comes to tail carriage, the British Standard calls for the tail to be "carried as nearly as possible on a level with or below the back". The American Standard allows for carriage to be straight or curving slightly upward nearly level with the back. However, this would be interpreted as a first step towards accepting a higher tail carriage as correct in the UK, where the spread of persistently gay tails, often flown over the back, is (and hopefully) remains extremely undesirable. On the move Irish Setters tend to make good use of the tail, thereby not only demonstrating their happy disposition, but also aiding their balance when moving. This is particularly important when working in the field and turning sharply, at speed.

COAT

The two Standards are agreed on their descriptions of the coat and its texture on head and body; also that it should be as free as possible from curl and wave. However, this does not mean that the coat should be as short and fine as a Pointer's coat. The Irish Setter should have a good undercoat as protection from the elements, which is then covered by a moderately long top-coat. Agreement concerning the feathering on the belly and chest also exists. However, the American Standard goes on to concern itself with trimming and presentation for the show ring. It states that all trimming is supposed to be done to preserve the natural appearance of the dog. There was no reference to trimming in the earlier American Standard but it was added to the revised 1991 version. It must be questioned whether a Breed Standard is the correct place for a guide to trimming, which is purely cosmetic and does not have any bearing on the animal under the coat. The British Standard does not contain, nor has it ever contained, any reference to trimming because it only concerns itself with the correct construction and conformation of the Irish Setter.

COLOUR

The Irish Setter's coat and its glorious colour are the crowning glory of the Breed. Both Standards call for a rich chestnut-red coat without any trace of black. Small amounts of white on the chest, throat or toes, or a narrow centred streak on the skull are not to be penalised. In addition, the British Standard allows for white on the chin and a small star on the forehead or a blaze on the nose or face, and the frequency with which white markings appear in litters of Irish Setters serves as a reminder of the Breed's beginnings and history.

FAULTS

The British Standard points out that any departure from the Breed Standard should be considered as a fault. To a greater or lesser degree, all dogs have faults, and the seriousness with which a fault is regarded should be in exact proportion to its degree and how it affects an Irish Setter's ability to perform the tasks for which it was bred. Neither the British nor the American Standard contain any disqualifying faults.

CONCLUSION

There are, quite obviously, differences in the text of the two Standards. However, they alone cannot account for the gap that now seems to separate American Irish Setters from their

PRESENTATION
Am. Can. Ch. Sametsuz Ard-Righ: Born in the UK, crowned in North America.
Breeder: Magi Henderson, Scotland. Owner: Jean Ryan, USA.
Same dog – different styles of presentation.

Trimmed and presented in the American style.

Ashbey Photography.

Trimmed and presented in the British style.

Photo: Ryan.

British cousins. Therefore it must be a question of interpretation and the amount of emphasis that is placed on certain points of the breed. On the whole, the various changes and additions that were made to the American Standard seem to reflect the search for a much more spectacular animal for the show ring. The British Standard has remained, in essence, very close to the original and any adjustments have only been minor. It remains to be seen if the differences have now become so great that the American Irish Setter will develop into a completely separate breed, in much the same way that the American Cocker Spaniel did in the past

7 *SHOWING AND JUDGING*

There seems to be a definite pattern to the way in which happy pet owners end up getting involved with dog showing, and how this changes their lives. They usually acquire an Irish Setter purely as a pet – until the day that someone suggests that their excellent specimen should be shown. This is what happened to me and, after reading how others got started, it is a classic route! My first bitch Molly came from a famous kennel and had a splendid pedigree containing many Champions and Show Champions. However, after I had attended my first few shows, I soon realised that my beautiful pet was not really good enough to go very far in the show ring.

After looking at different Irish Setters I decided that I liked Molly's type and contacted her breeder to order a show puppy. A second Irish joined our family and the rest, as they say, is history. Gradually, my new hobby became more and more important, and life has never been quite the same since. From time to time my husband tells me that he would still like to catch up with the man who suggested that I should show Molly but, on the whole, showing Irish Setters has been a great hobby with some exciting highs, but also with some desperate lows!

Many Irish Setter exhibitors tend to be like

their dogs in character and enjoy nothing more than meeting their friends at shows to have a good time – win or lose! In fact, a friend of mine, who shows a different breed, insists that Irish Setter exhibitors are inclined to have far too much fun. But showing your dog should be just that. However, if you have had a really bad day at a show, it helps to remind yourself that you are going home with the same dog that you came out with in the morning when you were still full of hope.

Some people show for a while but, unless they have immediate success in the ring, they drop out of the game; other exhibitors become disillusioned very quickly when they see dogs from certain kennels winning all the time. If your Irish Setter does not win as much as you think it should, do not immediately blame the judges for being dishonest or incompetent, but have a good hard look at your dog to discover the reasons why. Maybe you could improve your dog's chances through better schooling, or through better presentation in the ring. Maybe your handling could be improved, or maybe your dog is quite simply not good enough to go to the top in hot competition. I have found that if I show a good Irish, I tend to win, but if I show one less good, I do not win as much! Watch and learn from exhibitors with consistently winning stock, and never be afraid of seeking their advice. You will be pleasantly surprised to discover just how helpful most successful Irish Setter people are.

SHOWS IN THE UK

The British Kennel Club is responsible for all aspects concerning the exhibition of dogs at shows of all levels. They are held under Kennel Club rules and regulations and Kennel Club licences have to be obtained by the organisers before they can stage such events. The different types of shows where you can exhibit your Irish Setter are described below.

EXEMPTION SHOWS: These shows are really fun events and are usually run in aid of a charity or other good causes. Quite often they take place in conjunction with the village fete or similar local events. The time and place where exemption shows are held are usually published in the local press, and there is no need to enter in advance as entries are taken at the venue, on the day, and dogs do not have to be registered at the Kennel Club to compete at Exemption Shows. There can be up to five classes for Pedigree dogs, and an unlimited number of novelty classes for all, including mongrels. They can be great fun and can provide excellent experience for novice exhibitors and their dogs. Very often Exemption Shows attract huge entries and some of the prizes on offer to the winners are

extremely generous; however, no cash prize shall exceed £1.00! Champions, CC, Reserve CC and Junior Warrant winners are not eligible to compete at Exemption Shows.

MATCHES: Matches are usually organised by local canine societies and are held on a regular basis. Match meetings are ideal for young dogs and novice owners to learn about showing. However, even the most experienced exhibitors will quite often bring out their promising youngsters at matches to gain experience before launching them on their serious show careers. Dogs are judged in pairs and on a knock-out basis.

There is usually a match for puppies and a match for adult dogs. Owners have to be members of the canine society which is holding the match and entries are taken at the event. Dogs must be registered at the Kennel Club, and Champions and CC winners are not eligible to compete.

In recent years so-called Super Matches have become regular events where the top winning dogs from their breeds compete, usually by invitation. Some Matches are organised on a regional basis to find a Top Dog and others are run by breed clubs to find their Dog of the Year from the CC winners. Such Matches can seem a long way removed from the more humble, local events, but they are still organised on a knock-out basis. They often become great social

The British show scene: Three Counties Championship Show 1993.
Sh. Ch. and Ir. Sh. Ch. Autumnglow Masquerade, judge Liz Rose, and Sh. Ch. Tatterslee Toute Seule.

Photo: Dalton.

events and can raise large sums of money for various canine charities. The Kennel Club grants special permission for such events.

SANCTION SHOWS: It is regrettable that this type of show has almost disappeared from the canine show calendar, as Sanction Shows used to provide excellent practice for novice exhibitors and young dogs. Sanction Shows are restricted to members of the canine society and entries are made in advance. The classification is only for variety classes up to Post Graduate, which eliminates top winners from competition.

LIMITED SHOWS: Unfortunately, Limited Shows seem to be heading for the same fate as Sanction Shows and are becoming much rarer. Entry is made in advance and is open to members only. CC winners are not allowed to compete.

OPEN SHOWS: As the name implies, Open Shows are open to all. Irish Setters are a popular breed and can expect separate classes at most Open Shows. The classification usually includes a Puppy class, Junior, Novice or Graduate and Open classes. In addition, there are variety classes in which to compete against other breeds. Some Open Shows are staged by Gundog Societies and usually provide a much better classification for Irish Setters, with separate classes for dogs and bitches. Again, Any Variety classes are scheduled, but competition will be against other gundogs only.

Breed Clubs run Single Breed Open Shows with an even more comprehensive classification. Most of the Irish Setter Breed Clubs run their own Open Shows which take place in a relaxed atmosphere and, if staged during the summer months, tend to have a garden-party air about them.

Open Shows are of great importance as a training ground for up-and-coming judges who

need the required experience before they can be considered eligible to award Challenge Certificates at Championship Shows. Show Champions and CC winners may enter Open Shows and should be encouraged to do so, especially at the breed club events. This will give aspiring judges a chance to go over some good dogs and to learn from their experience. Open Shows are advertised in the canine press and entries are made in advance.

CHAMPIONSHIP SHOWS: In the UK, Kennel Club Challenge Certificates are only awarded at Championship Shows and entry is open to all. With some exceptions, Championship Shows are the only shows where a dog can qualify for Crufts or for entry into the Kennel Club Stud Book. General Championship Shows in the UK tend to be huge events, with judging on the Group System. They are often spread over several days to cope with the large numbers of dogs. Irish Setters usually provide one of the top entries in the Gundog Group, if not for the whole of the show, and competition in all their classes tends to be fierce. The Kennel Club has put a restriction on the number of dogs a judge can assess in one day, and the organisers often have to appoint two judges for Irish Setters to cope with the large entries. Dogs and Bitches are shown in separate classes, and if there are two judges, they will judge one sex each. At the end of judging, both judges decide on the Best of Breed winner and the Best Puppy. If they cannot agree, the referee is called to make the decision. The Group Judge also acts as referee. Breed Clubs usually stage their own Championship Shows and can attract in the region of 500 Irish Setters. Some Clubs send out voting lists to their members, allowing them to cast their votes for the judges of their choice.

Championship Show judges can either be 'Specialists' or 'All Rounders', but both must have had sufficient judging experience at Open Shows before being approved by the Kennel Club to award CCs. Championship Shows are well advertised in the canine press and entries usually close a long time in advance of the show-date and tend to be rather expensive. Therefore, it is far more sensible to test your youngster first at cheaper Open Shows before you try your luck at a Championship Show.

SHOWS IN THE USA

The American Kennel Club governs all aspects of dog showing in the USA. There are many more shows in the USA than in the UK, but entries in individual classes tend to be lower. However, Specialty Shows, organised by breed clubs, are the exception and tend to attract very large entries.

MATCHES: Matches are organised by Specialty breed clubs as well as by all-breed clubs and, as in the UK, they provide a good training ground for puppies and youngsters. Championship points are not awarded and Champions are not eligible to take part.

ALL BREED CHAMPIONSHIP SHOWS: Winners Dog and Winners Bitch gain points that count towards their Champion title. Breed Clubs can back "Supported Entries" with special prizes.

SPECIALTY SHOWS: These are held annually and are run by a breed club and usually attract very large entries. The maximum number of points awarded to the Winners Dog or Winners Bitch is five, regardless of the size of the entry. To win a Specialty is often the highlight of an Irish Setter's show career, and to win all the necessary points at Specialty Shows is considered to be a major achievement. Judges are usually specialists or respected all-rounders. Once an Irish Setters has gained enough points to qualify for the title of American Champion, he or she can only be entered in the Best of Breed Class.

FCI SHOWS

Shows run under the Rules of the Fédération Cynologique Internationale (FCI) are either National or International. At National Shows the CAC is on offer to the winners of the Open and Champion classes, as well as to the winning dog and bitch from the Working Gundog classes. The winners of the Junior Classes, as well as the winners of the Veteran Classes, can only compete for Best of Breed. At International Shows the CACIB, or International Certificate, is on offer to the winners of the Open, Champion and Working Gundog Classes. The best dog and best bitch must have been graded Excellent before they can challenge for the CACIB, and they must be

The American show scene: Am. Ch. Meadowlark's Expectation.

at least 15 months old before they can be awarded a CACIB. At International Shows, the National CAC is also on offer. In addition, Breed Clubs also award CACs.

MAKING UP A CHAMPION

UK RULES: It is generally accepted that to make up a Show Champion under Kennel Club Rules is extremely difficult. Dogs must win three Challenge Certificates from three different judges. If a dog wins three CCs before his first birthday, another CC must be won after that date before the title can be awarded. As Irish Setters are a slow-maturing breed, this does not happen very often, if at all. A CC is awarded to each best of sex winner at Championship Shows where CCs are on offer.

Judges should never take awarding a CC lightly. The Kennel Club issues a Special Direction to Judges at Championship Shows requesting them "to refrain from awarding CCs, unless the winning exhibit in each sex is of such outstanding merit as to be worthy of the title of Champion". Only if judges can satisfy themselves that this is the case should they sign the famous big green card. I cannot recall the CC being withheld in Irish Setters, but it does happen, from time to time, in other breeds.

A Reserve CC is awarded to the second best Irish Setter dog and bitch. They do not count towards the title, but if the CC winner is disqualified, the Reserve CC winner is awarded the CC. Therefore, Reserve CCs should not be handed out without due consideration. There is no limit on the number of CCs a dog can win and Show Champions can continue to compete for CCs. The current record holder in the breed has won 40 CCs, all under different judges.

Irish Setters are awarded the title of Champion by gaining a qualifier in the field in addition to the three CCs which are required for Show Champions and a number of Irish

Setters have gained their Show Gundog Working Certificate after being tested in the field. Others have run in Field Trials and have been awarded a Certificate of Merit, or better still, have won a prize.

The title Show Champion for Gundogs is a relatively recent innovation as it did not gain recognition until 1958. Up to that time the only title, apart from Field Trial Champion, which an Irish Setter could gain was that of Champion, which meant three CCs plus a field trial qualification. In 1958 the Kennel Club decided to award the title of Show Champion to gundogs which had won three CCs but were without a qualification in the field. The new title Show Champion was awarded retrospectively.

FIELD TRIAL CHAMPIONS: The winner of the Setter and Pointer Champion Stake is entitled to be called a Field Trial Champion, as is a dog that wins two first prizes under different judges at two different Field Trials in an Open Stake for Setters and Pointers. There must be a minimum of 16 runners.

USA RULES: Irish Setters gain their American Champion titles on a points system and need a total of fifteen points to qualify. Of these, two have to be 'Majors' which have to be awarded by different judges. A 'Major' is a show where three or more points are awarded to the Winners dog and to the Winners bitch. The maximum number of points that can be awarded for each sex, at any show, is five, regardless of the size of the entry. The USA is divided into different areas and each year the points system is assessed for shows, depending on the previous year's entries. Dogs and bitches, in the same breed and at the same show, can win different points, and the number of dogs an Irish Setter has to beat to gain the Champion title, can vary considerably.

Once Irish Setters have become American

Carnbargus Continuity pictured at six weeks.

Looking leggy at four and a half months.

At 16 months, the winner of a Reserve CC and Junior Warrant.   Photo: Claire Prangle.

Sh. Ch. Carnbargus Continuity, aged two years and three months.   Photo: Mike Gardner.

Champions they no longer compete for points. They can only be entered in the Best of Breed class. After the Winners Dog and Winners Bitch have been awarded their points, they go into the Best of Breed class with the Champions to decide the Best of Breed.

FCI COUNTRIES: CACs are awarded to the best dog and the best bitch. To become a Champion an Irish Setter needs to win 4 CACs under three different judges. Between the first and last CAC award, a time of one year and one day must have elapsed. Some national titles also require a field trial qualification specific for Pointers and Setters.

To become an International Champion, an Irish Setter needs two CACIBs from two different judges in two different countries.

Furthermore, a field trial qualification, specific for Setters and Pointers, is required to gain the International title. A timespan of one year and one day must elapse between the two qualifying CACIBs. In addition, dogs can win special titles which require them only to be Best of Breed on the day. A title such as 'World Champion' is won at the annual 'World Show' and is awarded in addition to the CACIB.

THE REPUBLIC OF IRELAND: In order to become an Irish Show Champion, a dog must win 40 Green Star points, including four Majors of at least five points each. The number of points available at a show depends on the number of dogs or bitches actually present at the show, but some shows carry a guaranteed Major, irrespective of the number of dogs exhibited. Dog and bitch awards do not always carry the same number of points, but the BOB winner will receive the same number as the opposite sex winner if the latter has won a higher number. To become a Champion, a "qualifier" is required.

YOUR FIRST SHOW
Once you have decided to take the plunge and to have a go at showing, you will need to find out where the shows are due to be held and how to make your entry. Probably the best way of obtaining details of forthcoming shows is through the canine press. Once you are hooked on showing, these papers and magazines will become essential reading! Not only do they contain all the information concerning shows, but also the critiques which are written by the judges and are eagerly awaited by exhibitors.

Once you have entered for a show, you will usually go on the society's mailing list and a schedule for the next show will be sent to you. Apart from Exemption Shows, entries for most shows close well in advance, in particular those for General Championship Shows. The secretary of the show society will send you a schedule on request, and it is customary to enclose a stamped addressed envelope when asking for one. Schedules contain all the information concerning the show, including the classification for the different breeds as well as for variety classes, together with the names of the judges and a copy of the show rules. It will also give you important details concerning the parking arrangements, the time when the show opens and when judging is due to commence.

Together with the schedule you will receive a printed form on which to make your entries for the show. Complete this carefully and check all the details before writing out your cheque for the correct amount. Before sealing the envelope, make sure that you have signed both the entry form and your cheque. Entries which are received without payment are usually not accepted. Correct entries will help a busy show secretary who often has to check hundreds or even thousands of forms, many of them containing careless mistakes that have to be referred back to the exhibitor. If you want to know that your entry has been received, enclose a stamped addressed card on which the secretary can acknowledge your entry. Entries have to be posted before or on the closing date, and I like to use a Certificate of Posting, which is date-stamped. Not only do I have proof that my entry was actually posted, but also that it was sent in good time. In the UK this service is free at all Post Offices.

WHICH CLASS?
If you are showing a puppy for the first time at an Open Show, enter in the breed's puppy class, if one is available, and perhaps in Any Variety Minor Puppy or Puppy class, depending on the youngster's age. This should give you and the puppy plenty of experience without tiring the puppy too much. It is surprising how much the excitement of going to shows can take out of a youngster. Therefore, it is much better not to do too much at first and to let the puppy enjoy

the day at a show. Promising puppies have been spoilt by being taken to far too many shows and having to compete in far too many classes. I used to think that it was travelling long distances that tired my dogs, but over the years I have discovered that it is the actual show and all the excitement that has tired them most.

If you are starting off by showing an adult Irish Setter, enter for the lowest available class to test your dog in competition. If you have a good day first time out, there will be plenty of incentive for you to keep going. Once you have become a seasoned exhibitor at Championship Shows, let your Irish Setter win through the classes, instead of entering higher, and probably more competitive classes. Not only is it much more fun, but if your dog is good enough, success will come from whatever class you have entered.

The entries for many shows close so far in advance that it is often difficult to decide if a dog will still be in good coat by the time the show actually comes around. This can be particularly difficult if you are showing a bitch, as she may have come into season by the time of the show, or she could well have lost her coat by then. Make a note when your bitch was in season last and calculate the expected time of her next, before entering an expensive show. The majority of bitches tend to be quite regular with their seasons. If you are showing a male, you will not have to worry and it should be an important consideration when deciding whether to have a male or female Irish Setter just for show.

PREPARING YOUR DOG

Dog shows are beauty competitions and since the opposition in the Irish Setter ring is extremely hot, no time or effort should be spared to prepare and present your dog in the peak of condition. This does not only mean the condition of the coat, but also includes physical fitness, with the correct muscle-tone and just the right amount of bodyweight. None of this can be achieved overnight, but must be worked for over a period of time. A correct diet plays an important role in conditioning, and once you have discovered what suits your dog best, stick to it, instead of trying the latest product that has just been launched. Keep an eye on your dog's waistline and, if you own several Irish Setters, decide at feeding time who may have a little extra, and who should have a little less!

Regular exercise is most important to help to produce the racy, active Irish Setter the Standard calls for. It is much better to give a dog regular, daily exercise than a long run maybe only once or twice a week. Roadwork will help to build up and tone the right muscles and will also discipline an Irish Setter to walking on a lead.

Correct trimming is important, but should never be done the day before a show. Toe nails should always be kept nice and short. This makes the feet look neat and tidy and will also enable a dog to move much better. Bathing before every show is not absolutely necessary. However, if the dog needs it, it should be done a few days in advance of the show to enable the coat's natural oils to be replaced. Good, regular grooming is usually sufficient. Most Irish Setters in the show ring are presented in clean condition and judges often remark, that after having judged a very large entry of the breed, their hands are still clean. This is quite a compliment for Irish Setter exhibitors! A detailed guide to bathing and trimming is given in a later chapter.

THE SHOW LEAD

A clean, well-presented Irish Setter also needs a special show lead. Ideally, the show lead should be quite narrow and should complement the dog's colour. Dark brown or black is ideal for the breed. Some exhibitors like to use a fine leather slip lead, but others tend to use nylon leads. Both types are fine, but they must be long enough to lay loose over a dog's shoulders to show off the flowing lines over the neck and shoulders. In my opinion, this cannot be achieved with a broad, brightly-coloured show lead which can give the impression that the dog is rather short and stuffy in the neck. I have seen Irish Setters being exhibited with bright red, bright blue and even bright yellow leads. This will do nothing for the dog and may well attract a judge's attention – but for the wrong reason! Many seasoned exhibitors have a favourite lead which they have used for years to campaign their winning dogs to the top. If they are made of leather, they tend to be lovingly saddle-soaped or oiled to maintain them in good condition. Nylon leads will have been washed regularly to keep them looking clean. Some owners are quite superstitious about leads and make sure that they only use their 'winning' one!

THE SHOW BAG

When I first started going to dog shows, my show bag tended to be rather large and heavy but, over the years, this has changed, and now I only take the absolute minimum. At most of the General Championship Shows the walk from the car park to the entrance of the show can be quite a trek and having to carry a heavy show bag, when also trying to control a Setter or two, is not much fun. However, there are certain essential items that have to be taken and must be accommodated in the show bag.

For a benched show a good strong collar and a benching chain are required with which to secure a dog on the bench. As dogs are required to spend quite a long time sitting on their benches, they should be able to do so in some comfort, and a soft blanket or a benching rug is essential. At outdoor shows we are very much at the mercy of the weather and a good-sized towel is essential to dry off a dog after a shower of rain. You will also need your grooming kit.

All dogs have a number in the catalogue and handlers wear the number in the ring when competing in a class. Therefore, make sure that you take a safety pin or buy a special ring-number clip.

A dish and a small bottle of drinking water from home, or a small carton of milk for your Irish Setter should also be packed. Some exhibitors give their dogs regular meals at shows, but my dogs just have some of their favourite biscuits. They also like to scrounge special treats, such as cooked liver, from my friends! Take along some 'pooper scoopers' to clean up after your dog. Exhibitors are constantly being reminded to do so, but there is still a selfish element that does not bother, and many show venues have been lost over the years due to such people's irresponsible behaviour. Do not forget to take your schedule, the pass for admission, which will also be needed when leaving the show, as well as the pre-paid car park label before setting off in the morning.

THE EXHIBITOR

Having decided what to take for your dog, it is time to consider your requirements for a day at the show. Give some thought to your outfit and select colours that will not clash with your dog but will help to show off an Irish Setter to advantage. Make sure that your clothes are comfortable for a long day, but try to look neat and tidy. Exhibitors are usually asked to move their dogs first in a triangle and then straight up and down. Therefore, sensible shoes are essential to enable you to move as well as your dog does. High-heeled shoes are quite unsuitable, even at an indoor show, and should be avoided. Be prepared to cope with rain and mud and have some waterproof clothing handy. I usually carry a pair of Wellington boots and a raincoat in my car – just in case! The schedule will contain information about catering at shows; however, you may prefer to take your

Showing And Judging

own food, tea or coffee etc. There is usually a bar at most of the bigger shows, but make sure that any celebrations stay within the drink-driving laws!

Arrive at the show in good time. All dogs need time to settle down after a journey and hate to be rushed. It is so much better to give your Irish Setter the chance to get used to the venue and to meet the other dogs. At some benched shows the ring-numbers will have been placed above your bench, at others, you will be given your number in the ring by the steward. Find out before you go into your class. Despite the added expense, I usually buy a show catalogue to study the entry, not only at the show, but also at home after the event. Catalogues make fascinating reading for a long time to come and provide me with a record of all the shows I have attended.

SHOW RING PROCEDURE.

It is up to the exhibitor to arrive in the ring in time for the class for which the Irish Setter is entered. If you miss your class, you only have yourself to blame. Once you are in the ring with your dog, concentrate on making the most of your dog as there is only a very short time in which to impress the judge. I have already mentioned that the competition in Irish Setters tends to be very hot, and that a very busy judge will only have a limited amount of time to spend on each exhibit. Before the class is called, have a look at the ring and decide where to stand your dog. Try and avoid facing downhill as you may not be able to show off your Irish Setter's gently sloping topline. On a windy day, place your dog so that the wind does not blow the coat the wrong way. Give yourself enough room to show off your dog to the best advantage, and if you find yourself being crowded out by neighbouring dogs, move away or ask for extra space.

Some exhibitors like to be seen first, others prefer to be seen last. I do not think it makes

IN THE RING
It is customary to set up Irish Setters in front of the judge in show stance. Here are two ways of making the most of your dog – and your chances!

Jeremy Bott handling Sh. Ch. Thendara Kennedy to win the Group at Bath in 1996. He prefers to kneel. Photo: Carol Ann Johnson.

Rachel Shaw and Sh. Ch. Starchelle Chicago Bear winning the Gundog Group on their way to Best in Show at Crufts 1995. She uses a different technique.

Photo: Marc Henrie.

any difference. During the time when the judge examines the other competitors, try and relax with your dog. A large class can take a long time to be completed, giving you the opportunity to observe the judge before your turn arrives. Some judges can be quite specific about what they want you to do – so be ready. On a very hot day you can protect your Irish Setter from the sun by using a cool, damp towel for the head while awaiting your turn to be seen.

Once all the dogs have been examined, the judge will usually make a short-list of dogs for further consideration. The chosen few will be called into the centre of the ring, usually in no particular order. The rest of the class will then be dismissed and the remaining dogs will move back to be stood again. Judges tend to have another close look at the exhibits and will probably move them again. Once a decision has been made, the judge will place his winners in descending order from left to right in the centre of the ring. If you are lucky enough to have been placed, remain until the judge has written down the dogs' numbers in the judging book. The prize card will then be handed to you by the ring steward.

At Championship Shows, the judge will write a critique on the dogs that were placed first and second, for publication in the dog papers. At Open Shows, a critique is usually only required for the first prize winner in each class. If you are disappointed with the result, do not show your feelings, but congratulate those placed above you. Remember this is only one judge's opinion and the placings could well be reversed at the next show. At the end of the judging, the unbeaten class winners meet in the challenge and the judge will select the Best of Sex Winners before deciding on a Best of Breed Winner from those two. The best puppy will be chosen from the best dog puppy and best bitch puppy. Best of Breed winners are expected to stay on to represent the Breed in the Group. If

there is a Puppy Group competition, the Best Puppy is also expected to stay. Many famous Irish Setters have not only won Groups, but have gone on to win Best in Show at Championship Shows.

JUDGING IRISH SETTERS

After you have been actively involved with the breed for some time, through owning and campaigning your Irish Setters, you may, one day, receive an invitation to judge your first show. In the UK there are no hard and fast rules on how long an apprenticeship you should have served before being asked to judge at an open show, but in some countries rigorous training of judges is undertaken. This training often culminates in quite difficult, written examinations. Learner judges also have to gain practical experience by accompanying experienced judges into the ring where they write reports on the exhibits and, after the show, the learner judge's critique is submitted to the senior judge for appraisal. In the UK, the Kennel Club does not have to approve the choice of judges for open shows. However, judges who award Challenge Certificates at Championship Shows have to be approved by the Kennel Club, and to a very large extent, approval depends on the number of breed classes a candidate has judged at open shows.

In the USA aspiring judges are expected to have had ten years experience in the breed, to have bred at least five litters and to have made up two Champions, as well has having acted as ring stewards, before being considered as judges. They will start off by judging Sweepstakes, for dogs aged up to 18 months, before being able to apply for a judge's licence.

YOUR FIRST INVITATION

Receiving an invitation to judge for the first time can be very exciting, but most novice judges will approach their first appointment with some fear and trepidation. If you have studied and understood the Standard of the Breed, and have a good knowledge of canine anatomy and construction, you should have little to worry about. Approach the appointment with an open mind and try not to think, in advance, of the show or what dogs could be entered under you. Carefully avoid pre-judging from the ring-side at other events. It is much better to allow yourself to be pleasantly surprised, or otherwise, at how good some dogs are when you get the chance to go over them in the ring. Put everything out of your mind and just concentrate on the dogs in front of you. Even if you think a dog does not stand a chance of being placed, remember that the owner has paid the same entry fee as all the others and deserves the same courtesy and consideration from you. Try and do your best and be honest. That is all anyone can ask of you.

Novice judges have a tendency to 'fault judge' when fulfilling their first few appointments. This can be an easy way of dealing with an entry as, to a greater or lesser degree, all dogs have their faults. They are usually obvious to all! However, after gaining more experience, most judges will learn to look far more for a dog's virtues rather than only for the shortcomings.

ACCEPTING THE INVITATION
An invitation to judge will usually be sent to you by the secretary of the canine society which is holding the show and will arrive quite some time in advance of the actual date of the show. You will probably be asked to agree not to judge the same breed within a certain time before that show, as well as within a certain radius of the show venue.

You are usually expected to judge in an honorary capacity, which means that you will not be paid for your efforts. However, some societies are prepared to pay something towards your travelling expenses if you live a long way from the show venue. If you are expecting financial rewards for your activities as a judge, forget it! Only very few judges, usually the well-known all-rounders, are paid for their judging. The experience you gain through judging at open shows is absolutely essential if you want to go on to greater things as a Championship show judge and, therefore, you should regard it as part of your training.

Keep an accurate record of your judging experience, ready for the day when you are invited to award Challenge Certificates. The Kennel Club will then expect you to provide full details of your experience, on the questionnaire, and it is best to keep all the catalogues, as well as all your judging books. Attempts to falsify judging records have been heavily penalised by the Kennel Club. It is important to remember that once you have agreed to judge at a show and written confirmation of the invitation has been received, you have actually entered into a contract. Unless there are very special circumstances which will prevent you from keeping the appointment, this contract should not be broken, or you could find yourself in serious trouble with your national Kennel Club or governing body.

WHAT TO WEAR
Judging a large entry of Irish Setters can be extremely hard work and it is essential for a judge to wear an outfit that is not only suitable for the occasion but is also very comfortable. The same applies to your shoes. Most of our breed judges tend to be exhibitors and are usually seen in the ring showing their dogs. Exhibitors in the UK are often criticised for the clothes they wear which can often leave a lot to be desired! I am particularly guilty of wearing less than smart clothes when I show my dogs and well-worn, rather scruffy jeans are usually the order of the day. I have photographic evidence going back over many years, and it

comes as a shock to realise that there has been no improvement in my clothes during all that time!

However, when I am invited to judge, I like to push the boat out and wear something rather smart. Before coming to a decision what to wear, give some thought to the type of venue where the show is being held and, above all, if you are judging in the UK, remember the British weather when judging at an outdoor event. Always take your wet-weather gear, a change of shoes and some spare dry clothing – just in case you have to stay out in the rain and get soaked. As usual, male judges have it so much easier. They look good in a neat suit or in a jacket and trousers. Ladies probably find it more difficult to decide what to wear but, whatever it is, they should check in front of a mirror, that when bending over, they will not reveal more to the ringside than they would really like!

THE DAY OF THE SHOW

Over the years I have learned, from bitter experience, that it is much better to leave home really early before a judging appointment. There is no point in spoiling your day by worrying about the time or by getting flustered when stuck in a traffic jam. Therefore, allow plenty of time so as to arrive in a calm and relaxed mood. Traffic jams have become a part of modern life and due allowance must be made for them. This is particularly true if you are judging at one of the agricultural shows where the entrance to the show ground is often heavily congested, not only by dog exhibitors, but also by all the other show traffic.

Let the secretary know that you have arrived, and pick up your judging book. As a rule, you will be offered a cup of tea or coffee which will give you the chance to have a look at the number of entries in the different classes. Once you have seen how many entries there are for each class, you can pace yourself accordingly.

Go to your ring early and introduce yourself to your steward or stewards. An experienced steward will help to make your ring run smoothly and efficiently. Decide where you want the unseen dogs to stand, and where you would like to have the "old dogs" waiting during subsequent classes. Check the light and select the spot where you want to examine the exhibits.

Once the steward has called the first class into the ring and the absentees have been marked in the judging book, I take a good look at all the competitors together in the ring. In my opinion, there is very little point in moving all the dogs together around the ring, as it tends to get everybody rather excited and unsettled. After my initial glance around the ring, individual dogs come forward to be examined. It is customary to set up Irish Setters in front of the judge in show-stance. I like to see the dogs first in profile, making a mental note of the first impression. Then I walk to the front to see the dog's expression and to study the front assembly. Only after that do I look at the head in more detail, including a check of the dentition.

Neck and shoulders come next, as well as elbows. I run my hand along the ribs to check that they are well carried back and also feel how far down they reach. The loin and hindquarters follow, making sure that the tail is set on correctly and that a male Irish Setter has two testicles fully descended into the scrotum. It soon becomes obvious if a dog is in good, hard, muscular condition, and since dog shows are a beauty competition, I take a good look at the dog's coat and general presentation. After a thorough examination and probably after spoiling a dog's stance, I like to give a handler sufficient time to set up the dog again for me to have another good look.

After this, I will ask to see the dog being moved; first in a triangle and then straight up and down. By moving a dog in a triangle, I will have the opportunity to see the dog moving in profile which is essential. Sometimes, when the ring is too small or is the wrong shape, it becomes impossible to see very much of the movement in profile. In such an event, I step to the side of the ring to get a better view when the dog is moving up and down. After carefully examining the entry, I select the dogs I want to see again. Once the others have left the ring, I move the short-listed animals again, and maybe check on some details. This is the time when I, just occasionally, ask to see the finalists running around the ring together. I then place my winners from left to right and mark my judging book with the numbers of the placed dogs. Give a thought to the ringside and place the dogs in such a way that they can mark their catalogues as well.

SHOW REPORTS

In the UK it is customary for judges to write a report for the dog papers, and the two leading weekly papers will provide you with a stamped addressed envelope in which to post your report to them. At open shows you are expected to write about the winner of every class, and at Championship shows you should write a critique on the dogs that are placed first and second.

After you have finished marking your judging book, and when the dogs are still standing in front of you, take some notes which will help to remind you at home of what they were like. There is no need to write too much and, over the years, you will probably develop your own kind of "shorthand" to express quite accurately what you particularly liked or disliked about a dog and why you made a certain decision. Critiques should, above all, be constructive and should achieve a balance of the good with the bad. After having had a good day at a show, we all eagerly await the write-up by the judge, and it can be very disappointing when it does not appear in print. Therefore, once you are back at home, sit down straightaway to write your piece while the dogs are still fresh in your mind, and consider it as part of your judging appointment.

In FCI countries judges have to write a critique for each dog, which can be a lengthy procedure and therefore it restricts the number of dogs a judge is able to assess in any one day. In the USA the maximum number of dogs a breed judge is allowed to judge in one day is limited to 175.

8 THE WORKING IRISH SETTER

By Peter Heard (Dunroon)

The Irish Setter is one of the five specialist gundog breeds that locate game birds, point or "set", and then finally flush them into the air. They locate their birds by methodically hunting the ground with style and pace, making use of the prevailing wind to obtain air scents. They indicate to the handler the presence of birds by stopping or pointing or setting. An Irish Setter should remain motionless until the handler comes up and, on command, the dog should advance on the birds until they fly, when he is required to drop. Up to the mid 19th century, sportsmen enjoyed shooting over pointing dogs, with their main quarry being grouse in the summer and partridge and pheasant in the autumn and winter. The advent of the driven shoot almost made the breed redundant and shooting over Setters has now become a sport which is largely restricted to the grouse moors, where driven shoots are not economical.

I am describing in this chapter the basics of training a young puppy for the shooting field. The late John Nash, owner of the great Moanruad kennel, always said that the best soup was the one which was allowed to cook the longest. By this he meant that young Irish Setters need time to learn – therefore, allow them to have it! It is worth remembering that the main reason why young dogs fail to reach their full potential is that they are being pushed too early.

Peter Heard with four of his Field Trial winners.

TRAINING AN IRISH SETTER

Many years ago I asked George Abbott, the great professional handler employed by the late Mrs Florence Nagle "how does one train an Irish Setter?" His answer was "kindness, patience and firmness". His advice holds as true to-day as it did when it was first given to me.

Irish Setters have long been regarded as being the most difficult to train of all the pointing breeds. However, a fully fit, properly trained Irish Setter is as good as any of the other pointing breeds and, on inclement days, the breed can be without equal in the field. They are, by nature, highly intelligent, exuberant and, at times, obdurate. It has been suggested that Irish Setters do not settle down mentally before the age of three, but their mental development can vary tremendously. I have seen very young Irish Setters that were virtually trained at nine months of age, but it is my belief that training should only start when the dog is capable of understanding what is required.

There are no hard and fast rules concerning age and at any age it can appear that Irish Setters have forgotten everything that they have ever learnt! In my experience, some of them almost have to be retrained at the start of a new season; but they can also be sensitive, almost to the point of neurosis, and it is possible to ruin a potentially good young Irish Setter in a moment of thoughtlessness. Here I write from experience and yet, if one approaches the training of a young dog with care and with a system in mind, training is not only rewarding but also intensely satisfying.

These days, when a new book on canine psychology seems to appear every week, it is easy for a novice trainer to become confused and side-tracked. For me, the essentials are that the dog accepts me as his master and that mutual trust is built up to a point of perfect understanding between dog and trainer. The old adage that we only get out what we put in has never been more true than when starting to train an Irish Setter. In practical terms there are three basic commands and lessons that *must* be taught and learned:

The Drop
The Recall
Ground Treatment/Quartering

THE DROP

All dogs must be taught to drop, in any situation and at any time, and Irish Setters are expected automatically to "drop to wing" when birds fly. This is the one command that could, possibly, save your dog's life. For the purpose of describing the simplest way of teaching a dog to drop, I would suggest starting off by using the voice as the primary command tool. This should later be replaced by the whistle. An upright arm signal should be used as a secondary command in conjunction with the voice, or later with the whistle.

Assuming that the dog is receptive enough to be trained, traditionally most gundog trainers will use the word Hup, but Down, Drop or Deck, or any other word, will suffice, so long as you use it consistently. Find a quiet secluded spot with as few distractions as possible, put your Setter on a lead and, after getting his attention, give the dog the command word and gently, but firmly, push the dog down by the shoulders. At first a youngster may struggle or even roll over on his back. If this is the case, walk away with the dog and start again. Once your dog has learned what is required, and has completed a down to your satisfaction, give plenty of praise.

Never over-do the exercise; young Irish Setters can get bored very quickly. There is an old maxim that one should never give a command that cannot be enforced. Every time the dog is allowed to ignore a command it will become more difficult to enforce it the next time. Some young Setters will learn immediately what is required, others will be slower to grasp the lesson. Patience is the only way forward.

Once the youngster is entirely proficient in dropping on a short lead, exchange this for a short trailing-cord, possibly eight to ten feet long, and repeat the lesson. If the dog refuses to drop, go to him and put him down on the exact spot where he was when you gave the original command. Some trainers use the tidbit method of reward once the dog has dropped successfully. The moment of truth will come when the trailing-cord is taken off and the youngster is allowed to run freely.

I have a small, enclosed paddock and use an arm-signal, together with either a verbal or a whistled command for the dog to drop. By this point in their training the dog should know what the command means, and failure to obey will be pure disobedience, but, hopefully, your dog will have dropped. Walk over to him, praise him and then call it a day. It is best to finish the day on a high – if not, the dog will remember.

If your youngster did not drop, take him back to the exact spot where the command was given. If the dog is obdurate it can become a battle of wills, but there can only be one winner – the trainer. However, in some cases this can take all the patience one has. Irish Setters are capable of tapping into our moods long before we know them ourselves and, if the dog becomes insecure, the trust that has been built up so carefully can be broken. If a dog will not stay, put the light cord back on, complete one

drop on it and make new plans for the next day. I am firmly convinced that some dogs enjoy ignoring a command. My old Ch. Adriano chased lark for six months, totally ignoring my drop whistle. One day I blew the whistle, he dropped – and never looked at another lark!

Some young Irish are capable of accepting a mild form of punishment without losing their confidence in you. If you, as the trainer, are satisfied that the dog is wilfully disobedient, take him by the scruff of the neck and give him a good shake before taking him back to the spot where the crime took place. Irish Setters have great dignity, so *do not forget* to make it up with him after the lesson is over.

At some stage, whistled commands take over from the voice as the primary command, and it is essential to establish, right from the outset, which sequence of "peeps" one is going to use. Most trainers use *one* peep for the drop, *two* peeps for the turn and *three* peeps for the recall.

THE RECALL

Teaching the recall is a much simpler affair. The young Irish Setter will now know what training is about, but may also have learned what he can or cannot get away with. Just as before, find a quiet and secluded place and attach a short trailing-cord to the dog's collar, allowing him to play at the end of it. Command him to come back by using his name, followed by the firm command Come. If he does not come back to you, pull him towards you, repeating the name and the command. On completion, praise the

Casting off.
Photo: Peter Heard.

Working out a point.

Photo: Peter Heard.

dog and put him away. Repeat the lesson, using a longer line, until you are satisfied that he knows what is required.

When you think that the line work is good enough, remove the line and allow the dog free running. Wait until you have the dog's attention and either call or whistle him in, using a different arm signal. I drop on one knee and extend my arms to encourage the dog. If he does not come in, turn and slowly walk away from the dog. When he does come, praise him. If a dog persists in not coming in to your command, when you catch up with him put him back on the line and remind him of the lessons. Never run at a dog, it only scares him. The golden rule for the drop and recall is always to walk to the dog that you have dropped, and always to wait for the dog to come in, once he has been recalled.

QUARTERING

As it is a Setter's function to locate birds, it is necessary to teach a youngster how to cover his ground in the most methodical and efficient manner. Setters use air scents and one should always work a young dog directly into the wind. It is preferable to put a youngster on a light running-cord, maybe 40 to 50 yards long. Some dogs may have a problem carrying it, but most get used to it. Again, the trainer must decide from the outset which whistle commands are to be used.

Take the young dog out and, once facing the wind, cast him off. If he attempts to pull forward, pull him across you and walk for a few steps in the direction in which you want him to go. Then turn and retrace your steps, pulling him across you at the same time. He will very quickly get the idea. Always make sure that he lines up into the wind and does not "back cast", and return down-wind. If he does line up wrongly, walk forward more quickly and, when he looks for you, he should turn up-wind. Most Irish Setters will quarter naturally and quickly learn to associate quartering with the finding of game. It is important that the handler walks in a straight line once the dog has the idea of a pattern; and always make sure that the youngster works to the handler.

On a shooting day it is extremely rare to get a head-wind all day and a young dog will soon learn to run at right angles to the wind direction. If one is forced to run a dog on a "back" wind, the technique is to stand still, the dog runs out in a straight line and then proceeds to quarter back to the handler into the wind.

Once you have decided that your youngster understands what is required, take him to a game-free, enclosed field, and set him off into the wind. At the end of the first cast, blow the turn signal and work him across with a hand signal to indicate the direction. The late Dr J.B. Maurice always said that he could turn his dogs by simply moving his shoulders! Once a young Irish has become proficient in both the drop and the recall, the rest of the lesson consists of practice. Should he ever go off the rails, do not hesitate to put him back on the running-cord. Always keep in mind that the Irish Setter should run with a high head-carriage and, if he starts to drop his head to scent on the ground, tell him to get on and move on. In my opinion, it is better to flush a brood of birds than to allow a Setter to get into the odious habit of running head down.

GUN TRAINING

Most modern dogs are used to man-made noise. In the past, war horses were trained to accept noise by having their bowls banged together at feeding time, allowing them to become accustomed to the noise. The theory behind the training of young dogs, to some extent, is the same. If Irish Setters are out, galloping around a paddock or on a point, the sound of a cap-gun, or of a fire-arm, some 100 yards away will not scare them. They will quickly learn to associate the sound of a shot with the great pleasure of hunting and pointing game. Dogs usually become gun-shy when a fire-arm is discharged too closely to them.

TRAINING FOR THE SHOOTING FIELD

Only when a young Irish Setter has learned the drop, the recall and ground treatment, is it time to take him to game. Some youngsters will point at an early age, but I have owned two Irish Setters that were incapable of pointing until they were about three years old. In the wild, pointing is recognised as the prelude to dogs springing in when capturing game. Therefore, it is essential to train Setters to remain motionless. When a youngster is taken out on a moor for the first time, his senses are assailed by hundreds of new scents and time must be given for the dog to adjust to them. A young Irish will point lark, but miss a pheasant completely because he cannot work out as yet, through his nose, what is going on. However, once he has pointed grouse, partridge or pheasant, all else will be ignored.

When a young dog is working on game for the first time, it is advisable to attach a short running trailer. Set the dog off and allow him to do his work. Once he comes on point for the first time, quietly walk up to him from behind and allow him to enjoy the scent. Old handlers used to say that young dogs should be allowed to stay on point for at least two minutes. When you are ready, gently encourage the dog to road in, holding the cord at all times. When the birds rise, drop the dog and praise him. After the initial point, take him forward to clear his ground. If he points again, repeat the lesson. Do not allow him to go back to where he originally pointed.

Once you are satisfied that the young dog has done well enough, put his lead on and take him home to allow him to dream about his day out. All dogs will make mistakes if they are over-run, especially when they start to get tired.

BUILT RIGHT, RUN RIGHT

I would like to end where I began, with Mrs Nagle and her Sulhamstead Kennel. I spent a great deal of time with her during the last years of her life, and it is my belief that she was so successful because she gave an immense amount of thought to her breeding, training and field trial programme. Shortly before she died I ran one of my dogs for her. She complimented me by saying that it could have been one of her own. She went on to say that one should be able to balance a full glass of water on the back of an Irish Setter at full gallop and not spill a drop; and that if they are bred and built right, they run right! I took this to mean that if the modern Irish Setter conforms to the Breed Standard as laid down by shooting men, then the future of the breed, on the bench and in the field, must be assured.

9 BREEDING IRISH SETTERS

It is probably correct to say that many Irish Setter owners embark on their careers as breeders by just wanting to have a litter from their bitch. However, owners who have been showing their bitch probably want to go on to greater things with a puppy that carries their own prefix. Whichever, no owner of an Irish Setter bitch should ever embark lightly on breeding a litter from her without first considering all the implications and responsibilities that such a litter will create.

TO BREED OR NOT TO BREED

Prospective breeders should start off by asking themselves whether a litter is really necessary and whether they would be able to cope. It is often said that bitches should, for health reasons, have at least one litter in their lives as this will prevent them from suffering false pregnancies after their seasons. Do not allow yourself to be misled as, even after a litter, some bitches will continue to have false pregnancies. As far as pyometra is concerned, a bitch that has had a litter is just as likely to develop it as a maiden bitch. I have owned bitches that, for one reason or another, have never been bred from, and they have been quite as healthy as the bitches with litters.

MONEY MATTERS

Another myth is that breeding a litter will make you a lot of money. I have tried and failed! I consider I am doing well if I can cover my costs and end up with having the pick of the litter. The expense of breeding and rearing a litter correctly is considerable. If you are prepared to cut corners and to stint on all the good things that Irish Setter puppies need and must have, you may well be able to make it pay. I would never consider breeding a litter unless I had sufficient funds in the bank to give my pups a really good start in life without having to worry about the cost. Remember that you will have to pay a stud fee to the owner of the dog you use, pay for your travelling expenses to get to him, often more than once, and that you will have to find the money for the Kennel Club Registrations for the litter. No doubt, you will also want to register your own prefix to use on your puppies, which is not cheap.

You should also hold enough money in reserve in case something goes wrong and the brood bitch or the puppies need expensive veterinary attention. This is only the start, as you will also have to pay for the vast quantities of food a decent-sized litter can consume. And all this before you have the chance of selling a puppy! It is also worth remembering that you

Five generations of Cairncross Irish Setters. Front (left to right): Am. Ch. Rossan's Xanadu; her son, Am. Ch. Cairncross Second Wind; his daughter, Am. Ch. Cairncross Deja Voodoo; her daughter, Am. Ch. Cairncross Sierra Class; and the puppy is her daughter, Cairncross Hurricane Wind.

may be left with one or two unsold puppies for several weeks, or even months, before you can find suitable homes for them. No wonder I have often thought that it probably would have been cheaper, and certainly easier, if I had gone out and had bought in a puppy.

TIME AND SPACE

The next consideration must be your time. Puppies will be born nine weeks after mating and will not be ready to leave for their new homes until they are about eight weeks old, at the very earliest. Not only will they take up a great deal of your time, but rearing a litter is

also hard and demanding work, especially during the last three weeks before the puppies are ready for their new homes. At that time it can seem that a day consists of nothing more than preparing meals for the ever-hungry litter, which is followed by the necessary cleaning up, followed by yet another meal! Most owners who have to go out to work tend to take their holidays to coincide with their litters, but I am still full of admiration for how they manage to combine the two, as I find rearing a litter to be a full-time job!

You will also have to give some thought to the accommodation for your puppies. Is there a suitable place where your bitch can have her litter in peace and quiet? Bitches do not like whelping in busy places where other dogs are present. Therefore, a sufficiently private area must be made available to her. Where will you rear the puppies? Anyone who has not reared a litter of Irish Setter puppies before cannot quite appreciate what they are letting themselves in for. Once the puppies start having several meals a day, your kitchen will not be the ideal place for them, as cleaning-up will become a major task. I shall never forget a friend's reaction to the state of her kitchen after she had come downstairs one morning. During the night her puppies had turned the kitchen into a battlefield; not only with ripped-up newspapers but far worse! She quickly arranged for some new outdoor accommodation for her puppies but, so far, she has not bred another litter.

RESPONSIBILITIES

One final word of warning before you make your decision about whether to breed or not: if you do go ahead, do not think that your responsibility will end the minute you have sold a puppy and the cheque has been cleared by the bank. For one reason or another, things can go wrong, and even the most carefully chosen owners may not be able to keep the puppy and so the Irish Setter you helped to bring into the world will need your help.

THE BROOD BITCH

If my words of warning have not put you off breeding, it is time to take a good look at your potential brood bitch. Above all, she should be healthy and free from major faults. It is also helpful if your bitch comes from lines that have, over the years, consistently produced sound Irish Setters of a definite type. Such a foundation bitch will make it very much easier for you to start your own line of typical stock. Fortunately, it is not always the top winning bitch that produces the Champions, but it is

often the well-bred bitch with many virtues, but without being spectacular, that has the ability to pass them on to her offspring.

If you have shown your bitch, you will have had the chance to compare her honestly to some of the winning bitches and will have discovered her strong points, and her weak points too. This does not just mean physical imperfections, but also concerns her character and temperament. A nervous bitch should not be bred from, as she is quite likely to pass on this trait to her puppies. Fear can very quickly turn to aggression, which makes any dog a danger to the owners, especially so to their children. To the best of your knowledge, your brood bitch should be free from hereditary diseases and defects and should not be a carrier of such conditions. Try and find out as much as you can about problems in the breed that can be passed on, and make use of any available tests to discover the status of your bitch before going ahead with the proposed mating. Make sure all the required vaccinations are up-to-date and that your bitch has been thoroughly wormed.

I like to mate my bitches for the first time when they are about three years old. At this age they are sufficiently mature in mind and body to enjoy their puppies and they tend to be confident and relaxed about the whole affair. Other breeders prefer to mate their bitches before that age, but no Irish Setter bitch should be bred from before she is at least two years old. Irish Setters are late in maturing and need more time to develop properly than some other breeds.

Some years ago the Kennel Club decided to restrict the number of litters a bitch can have in her life to six. I think that this is still a large number of litters, especially when one considers that Irish Setters tend to be quite prolific and that litters of 12 or 14 puppies are quite common. The Kennel Club will not normally register puppies born to a bitch after she has

Sh. Ch. Sorrel of Andana of Reddins with some of her children. Pictured (from left to right): Sh. Ch. Reddins Jonah, Sh. Ch. Reddins Ferdinand, Sh. Ch. Reddins Justin of Stylersetts, Reddins Jessica, Sh. Ch. Sorrel of Andana of Reddins, Reddins Marianne, Reddins Morgan, and Ch. Ir. Ch. Reddins Fintan of Riqitta.

reached the age of eight but, under certain, very special circumstances, this rule can be lifted to allow a bitch to have another litter. In some countries, Germany for example, dogs and bitches have to be X-rayed for hip dysplasia before permission is given for them to be bred from. Special permission will also have to be obtained to breed from a bitch on two consecutive seasons.

THE STUD DOG

Now that you have decided to go ahead with breeding a litter, you will have to give some thought to finding a suitable mate for your bitch. The correct choice of a good stud dog will not be easy, but is of great importance. All good breeders should aim to improve their stock with each subsequent generation, and the ideal stud dog will not only help to improve the weaker points in a bitch, but will also complement her good points.

Do not be tempted to use the dog from down the road. He may well be handy and save you the expense and bother of travel, but if that is all he has to offer, forget it! Years ago, when we lived in Cornwall, I wanted to mate my Sh. Ch. Mattie to a lovely dog. The fact that he lived in Scotland and the mating involved a round trip of about 1000 miles failed to deter me because I felt he was the right dog for her.

Many novice breeders tend to use the current top winners, regardless of whether they have anything in common with their bitch or not. This is fine if a dog happens to be a prepotent sire with the ability to produce good-quality stock to a variety of bitches of different bloodlines. Unfortunately, such dogs are few and far between. You may well be lucky enough to have a bitch with the same ability, and breed a 'flyer' from a complete outcross mating to an

Sh. Ch. Twoacres Troilus and Sh. Ch. Cornevon Primrose, pictured in their tenth year. These influential dogs had winners in many countries.

Sh. Ch. Wendover Vagabond: An important stud dog. Photo: Sally Anne Thompson.

Am. Ch. Meadowlark's Vindicator ROM: A prolific sire who has had a major influence on the breed in North America.

unrelated dog, but this could be a one-off, and there is no guarantee that there will be more such winners in the next generation.

A safer bet is to contact the breeder of your bitch to discuss your plans and to ask for advice. Most successful breeders tend to line-breed, and the breeder of your bitch will know all about her background and ancestry. Line-breeding is the mating of related animals such as cousins, or those more distantly related but with lines to a common ancestor or ancestors. This should not be confused with inbreeding, which can mean a father and daughter mating or brother to sister and should never be undertaken by a novice. An experienced breeder should be in an excellent position not only to recommend some suitable candidates, but also to warn about the dogs to avoid.

Try and go to some Championship shows to study some of the suggested dogs, together with some of their offspring that are being shown. Looking at a dog's progeny can often be the deciding factor when choosing a stud dog. Make sure that the eventual dog of your choice has a good temperament and does not display any signs of aggression, whether in or out of the ring.

Sh. Ch. Jason of Andana: The sire of 10 Show Champions. Bred by Joan Anderson, owned by Pat and Jim Rutherford.

Once you have decided which stud dog you would like to use on your bitch, you should contact his owner. Some stud dog owners like to see a bitch before they agree to a mating; others just want to see the bitch's pedigree. A responsible stud dog owner will want to make sure that the dog will not be used on an inferior bitch which, in turn, could produce an inferior litter. Also be prepared to answer some questions concerning the rearing of the planned litter and the general welfare of the puppies. If everything is agreeable, do not forget to ask what the dog's stud fee is, and arrange to contact his owner as soon as your bitch decides to come into season.

THE BITCH IN SEASON

By the time your bitch is due to be mated, she should have been in season before, and you will have been able to observe her pattern. It is probably best to mark a calendar with her dates. Most bitches tend to come into season regularly every six months, and it should be relatively easy to forecast when you can expect her to be in season again. Some bitches have different cycles and go for eight or nine months between seasons; others only come into season once a year. This is quite normal and should give you no cause for concern. I only worry when their seasons come closer and closer together and the bitch ends up being on heat every three or four months. This is a sign that all is not well and should be investigated by your veterinary surgeon.

Around the time when you have calculated that your bitch is due in season, check her regularly to see if her vulva has started to become swollen and if there is a blood-stained discharge. A good guide is when males start paying your bitch a lot more attention than usual. Even two or three weeks before a bitch comes on heat they will find her scent extremely interesting, giving you a pretty good idea that things are about to happen! With

some bitches it can be rather difficult to be accurate about day one, as Irish Setters can be fastidiously clean. However, their persistent cleaning is a good indicator, reminding you to check your bitch. When you have established that she is in season, let the stud dog owner know, but leave the final date for the mating fairly flexible.

THE CORRECT DAY

During the first ten days or so the bitch's vulva will become much enlarged and will gradually change from being hard to the touch, to being soft and flabby. After the first few days the drops of blood-stained discharge will become much more profuse and darker in colour. When the flow reduces again, the colour will change from dark red, via paler pink, to straw-coloured when the bitch should be ready to meet her mate. At this stage, if you gently rub her back, she will move her tail to one side, signalling that she is starting to stand. Maybe you own another bitch, and you can observe how she behaves with her companion. If she turns her tail to one side and pushes herself into her friend, hoping to be mounted, then this is the time to contact the owner of the stud dog again to finalise the date for the mating. As usual, there are exceptions, and some bitches not only continue to show colour right through their seasons, but some sexy bitches will also turn their tails throughout, making it difficult to judge accurately when they are ready to go to the dog.

The usual day for a bitch to be mated is between the tenth and fourteenth day of her season. Again, there are exceptions, and no two bitches are alike. Furthermore, they may also vary from season to season. I have had a bitch who produced a decent-sized litter after getting herself mated, by accident, on the fifth day. Another bitch had an equally good-sized litter after having been mated on the 21st day of her season. This bitch had been to visit the same dog on consecutive seasons, on what seemed to be the correct day, but each time she refused to be mated. In fact, when we went the second time, she seemed to know where we were going and refused to get out of the car! On both occasions, she had given off all the right signals at home, and the dog was very keen. Unfortunately, every time he approached her, she turned into a bit of a monster. She was given another chance with a different dog who came to visit us at home and, finally she had a litter from a successful mating on the 21st day.

When I planned a second litter from her, she was quite happy to be mated on the thirteenth day. It was only by chance that several days later she was observed playing some very sexy games with her mother. I dropped everything and decided to take her back to the dog. This was just as well, as the resulting litter was conceived to the second mating. Fortunately, her daughter, grand-daughter and great grand-daughter have all reverted to a much more orthodox pattern!

All this happened some years ago before Pre-Mate, which originated in the USA, was widely available. This product has been proven to be accurate in predicting the correct time for mating a bitch. But it does involve several visits to the vet for blood-tests from the time the bitch starts her season, and the test is not cheap. You will also have to be in a position to act very quickly to visit the dog at the predicted time. However, it is worth all the effort and expense if you manage to get a difficult bitch in whelp.

THE MATING

The correct day has arrived and you are setting off with your bitch to keep the appointment with her chosen mate. If you have to travel a long way, allow yourself plenty of time for the trip. There is nothing worse than getting caught up in heavy traffic and to start worrying about being on time. It is important to be

punctual for the mating, as some stud dog owners have to take time off from work to fit in your visit. If the dog lives at a busy kennel, the daily routine of walking and feeding the dogs has to be changed to accommodate the mating. If you feel that you would like to have an experienced friend come along to lend a helping hand, check with the dog's owner first if this acceptable. An extra pair of hands to assist at matings can often be quite useful, but do not take the whole family!

I like matings to be as natural as possible and everything should be done to make the bitch feel relaxed and in the right frame of mind. After your arrival, take your bitch for a short walk and let her relieve herself. She will, no doubt, appreciate a drink of milk or water after her journey, but neither the stud dog nor the bitch should be fed before a mating. If there is a secure field or paddock available, allow your bitch to have a run to get used to the strange place and all the different smells.

Dog and bitch are usually introduced to each other on collars and leads. This will prevent a keen and excited stud dog from frightening the bitch. Once they have been introduced in this way, let them off their leads to have a game in the garden, but leave their collars on in case you have to get hold of the pair in a hurry. If you are lucky and the weather is fine, a secure garden is an ideal place for a mating. However, if it rains or the weather is too cold for the owners, a garage is probably the next best thing.

Some stud dogs really love to court their bitches and tend to make absolute fools of themselves in their attempt to appeal to them. There is usually plenty of ear-washing and excited rushing around by the dog going on. It is surprising how quickly some bitches learn to enjoy the dog's attentions and they will soon flirt with the him. Quite often, at this stage, a mating will take place quite naturally and without any human assistance. However, if after a while, the courtship does not seem to lead anywhere, it is best not to let it go on for too long as the dog can exhaust himself with his antics. You will soon discover if your bitch is receptive to the dog's advances by the way she responds to him. If she is ready, she will turn her tail to one side, inviting the dog to mate her. However, despite giving off all the right signals to the dog, a bitch may growl when he actually attempts to mount her. This is the time to get hold of her firmly by her collar in case you have to prevent her snapping at the dog. If all is well, the bitch will brace herself to take the dog's weight and a mating can be achieved very quickly.

Not all stud dogs indulge in foreplay and they want to get on with mating the bitch straightaway. Even on the right day this can be quite alarming to a maiden bitch, and she may need your reassurance. However, some bitches behave in a rather confused way in the presence of their owner: they snap and snarl at the dog from the front, but turn their tail for him at the rear! Bitches often identify too much with their human owners, rather than with their own kind, and protest against the eager stud dog who seems to want to assault them. Usually, as soon as the devoted owner has been sent away to have a cup of tea or coffee, the bitch will stop her protesting and the mating can proceed.

I hate forced matings, but some bitches are extremely reluctant to be mated and will struggle and do their level best to get away from the dog. They can be so opposed to the whole idea that it becomes impossible for the dog to get near enough to even attempt a mating. Bitches can be physically restrained with the assistance of several helpers, or even be muzzled to get them quiet enough to be mated. Many forced matings result in the bitch not producing a litter and it is much better to try and find out why she is behaving in such a reluctant way. If she has gone past her peak and is no longer receptive to the dog, there is always her next season. Fortunately, the most common reason why bitches can be very difficult is their owners! Most are far too anxious about missing the right day for their bitch and come to the dog far too early. If this is the case, a return trip a day or two later will usually lead to a happy ending.

10 *WHELPING AND REARING*

et us assume that all has gone well with the mating and that you have returned home with your bitch. It is very important to remember that she will continue to be in season for some time and that she will have to kept away from all other male dogs until you can be quite sure that she has completely finished her season. It would be a great shame if she was to get out now and meet with another dog after all your careful planning.

AFTER THE MATING

The normal term of pregnancy is 63 days – nine weeks. Calculate the day on which your bitch is due and mark your calendar. Specialist diaries are available which not only publish canine events, but also give easy-to-follow charts for calculating the date when a bitch is due to whelp. However, it is not unusual for bitches to whelp a day or two earlier, or a day or two later, than expected. Whelping early or late can run in certain families but, so long as the bitch is fit and well, it should give you no cause for concern.

About three weeks after being mated, the brood bitch should be thoroughly wormed for roundworms. It is quite safe to worm an in-whelp bitch, but you should consult your vet,

who will recommend a safe but efficient product. The release of hormones during pregnancy activates the roundworm larvae which have been lying dormant in the tissues of the bitch. Some will migrate to the bitch's uterus and, from about the forty-second day onwards, into the developing puppies. All dogs suffer from worms, and the larvae that are already present in the puppy at birth will have developed into adult worms by the time the puppy is about two weeks old. To help prevent this initial infestation, or at least reduce it quite considerably, a small dose of a recommended liquid wormer in a 10 per cent suspension can be added daily to the bitch's food from about day forty of her pregnancy onwards. Again, this should be discussed with your vet.

Following the mating the bitch should be allowed to return to her normal routine for feeding and exercise. There is no reason why an in-whelp Irish Setter bitch should not be allowed to continue with her normal free-running exercise right until the time she is due to whelp. In fact, it is most important to keep a bitch as fit as possible – not only for her own well-being during whelping, but also for the health of her litter. Some bitches will slow down naturally, due to the extra weight they are carrying, but most tend to forget the family they have on board once they are out and running in the fields! One of my bitches took no notice of being in whelp and continued to hunt for mice in our wood-pile. By the time her puppies were due, she had become quite heavy, but this did not deter her from her hunting activities, and it was quite a sight to see the rather rotund body disappear into the timber store. My bitches tend to give their puppies many a bumpy ride, but because they are fit and well-exercised, they tend to whelp easily and without much trouble.

IS SHE IN WHELP?

It is only natural for an owner to want to know, as early as possible, whether their bitch is going to have puppies or not. Because I spend a great deal of time with my Irish Setters, I get to know their individual characters really well and can usually detect even the slightest change in a bitch's behaviour which indicates that she probably is in whelp. Such changes become noticeable well before there are any physical signs. Some bitches become more affectionate and tend to cling to their owners. They will want to be stroked and touched all the time and seem to need even more love and attention than usual.

Often the first physical sign to look out for is morning sickness. Just like some human mums-to-be, Irish Setter bitches can suffer from morning sickness. They will usually refuse to eat their breakfast for a few days and, occasionally, will be sick. This does not last for very long, and their normal appetite will return very quickly.

Another good early sign to look out for is an enlarging and reddening of the teats. This can usually be observed when the bitch is between three and four weeks in whelp. Around the same time it becomes possible to detect the presence of puppies by gently placing your hands around the bitch's tummy. At this stage in their development the puppies are about the size of a pea and each puppy is surrounded by only a small amount of amniotic fluid. To find the small balls tends to be much easier at this stage as, later on, the increasing amounts of amniotic fluid will make detection much more difficult.

By the time five weeks have passed since your bitch was mated there should be no doubts left in your mind. Especially after eating a meal, the signs of pregnancy should be there for all to see! If she is in whelp, your bitch should look well filled out by now and, if you put your hands under her stomach, it will feel rather heavy. Looking down on your bitch, you will see that the normally trim waistline has disappeared. However, beware, some bitches can go through all the signs of being pregnant without actually being in whelp. Bitches suffering from a false or phantom pregnancy can fool their owners quite convincingly that a litter is on the way by filling out and even by producing milk for their non-existent litter!

If that list of helpful signs has failed to convince you that your bitch is in whelp and you want to be absolutely certain, you can have her scanned with an ultrasound scanner. This is one of the more modern ways of establishing pregnancy in bitches and was originally developed for use in sheep. Many veterinary surgeons offer this service – and can even forecast the number of puppies the bitch is carrying. If your local vet does not have the necessary equipment, you will be able to find skilled operators through their advertisements in the canine press. To use their services can be rather convenient, as some will come to your home to scan the bitch, provided, of course, that you pay the travelling expenses. The most sophisticated of the scanners will also allow you to listen to the puppies' heartbeats and will print polaroid-type pictures of the litter in the bitch's uterus. An even more up-to-date method of confirming pregnancy is through blood-testing. This can be done between four and five weeks after mating and is reported to be extremely accurate.

I have to confess that I have never used any of the modern pregnancy tests on my bitches as I do not like to interfere with nature nor to put my bitches under any kind of stress at such a delicate time. If my bitch is in whelp I will know soon enough!

FEEDING

There is no need to increase or change a bitch's food for the first four weeks after mating provided that she is normally fed on a well-balanced diet containing meat, cereals, vitamins and calcium. Once you are certain that your bitch is in whelp her food intake should be changed to containing more protein, but less bulk. As my dogs are normally fed twice a day, it is easy just to add extra milk and eggs to an expectant mum's breakfast, and to add more meat instead of cereals to the main meal in the evening. By the time a bitch is about six weeks in whelp and getting heavier, I reduce the evening meal, but give a third meal at lunch-time. In addition, I use a multi-vitamin powder which supplies the bitch and her growing puppies with all the necessary trace-elements and calcium. If you are normally feeding your bitch on one of the many complete diets which are now widely available, make sure that it is the very best, and closely follow the manufacturer's feeding instructions. A complete diet, as the name implies, does not need any extra additives, but the in-whelp bitch should be fed on a product which contains higher protein and vitamin levels. The best manufacturers offer feeds that are carefully balanced to meet the specific needs and demands of the pregnant bitch. Whatever you feed your bitch during pregnancy, it should be of the highest quality to help ensure that her puppies will have the very best start in life. However, do not allow her to get fat – a healthy brood bitch should be fit, but never fat.

THE WHELPING QUARTERS

It is an excellent idea to get your bitch accustomed to the place where she is going to have her litter well before she is due to whelp. I am very fortunate in having a downstairs cloak-room which I use as a nursery and it is ideal for the purpose. The room is just about the right size to accommodate the whelping box: it has a small hand-basin with hot and cold water, and enough room for a small table to take all the bits and pieces that are needed during whelping and for the puppies. A reasonably comfortable

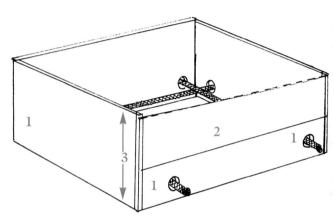

1. Removable guard-rail.
2. Slot-in front to prevent escape.
3. Height 18 inches (45cm).

View from above

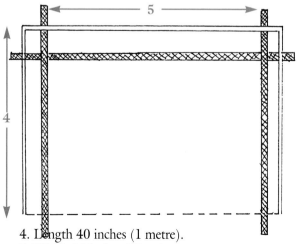

4. Length 40 inches (1 metre).
5. Width 36 inches (90cm).

folding chair can also be fitted in for me when I have to spend the night with my bitch.

This cloak-room is not only nice and quiet for the bitch, but it is also ideally placed for any human attendants keeping a watchful eye on the proceedings. I find it very easy to keep the room at the correct temperature for the puppies by using the central heating radiator or an infra-red lamp which is suspended over the whelping box. These lamps emit heat only and come in different sizes to give maximum coverage to a whelping box. Therefore make sure that you buy the right one for the size of whelping box you are using. Some years ago, during re-decorating, my husband fixed some permanent hooks into the ceiling, which make it very simple to hang the lamp in just the right spot. In order to prevent any accidents, there are two separate anchor-points in the ceiling from which the lamp is suspended by a chain. Not only does this ensure safety, but also makes it very easy to raise or lower the level of the infra-red lamp over the whelping box.

About two weeks before a bitch is due to whelp, I like to introduce her to her new quarters. After moving the whelping box into the cloak-room, I just put her normal blanket into the box and let her spend some time in there every day. This will let her get used to her new bed and to the new surroundings. As I only ever keep a small number of dogs, they all live together as a family group and some bitches really resent being taken away from their usual environment and from their friends. If a bitch seems at all unhappy about being left alone, I will also feed her in her new quarters. This usually does the trick and avoids putting the expectant mum under any kind of stress. When my bitch Cashmere was due to have her second litter, she knew exactly what was going on as soon as she saw the whelping box coming out of storage! After it had been carefully cleaned and disinfected, it was brought into the house and Cashmere made herself at home

immediately and did not seem to want to return to the rest of her family in the kitchen.

THE WHELPING LIST
Apart from getting the room fitted out as a maternity ward, I also prepare a box with all the necessary bits and pieces for the happy event. It is so much easier to have everything ready in advance, and well before the bitch goes into labour, rather than having to search for the following, necessary items.

A strong, clean cardboard-box.
Two pieces of vet-bed or some other fleecy bedding material to line the box with.
A larger vet-bed or two for the whelping box.
One or two hot-water bottles.
Some clean towels (I save our old and frayed ones for this purpose).
Kitchen roll.
Sterilised scissors.
A dropper feeder and a tin of bitch's milk substitute. This is necessary just in case the bitch does not have any milk.
Scales for weighing the puppies.
Pen and paper for recording the time of the births and the puppies' weights.
A large supply of newspapers.
Large plastic sack and plastic gloves.
A torch.
A good supply of milk and glucose for the bitch and tea or coffee for myself.

The reason why you should have all these items prepared and ready will become clear in the rest of the chapter.

THE FIRST STAGE OF LABOUR
The onset of the first stage of labour is often marked by the bitch refusing to eat her meal. Most text-books on the subject suggest that this is the case, but some of my girls have proved to be most unreliable on this point! When the first litter I bred was imminent, the bitch ate her

meal quite normally, thereby lulling me into the false sense of security that nothing could possibly happen just yet. After all, I had read that a bitch is supposed to go off her food before going into labour. However, within a short space of time, and after she had quite obviously enjoyed her meal, she started to display some of the well-known symptoms of the first stage of labour.

She became extremely restless and began to pant and shiver. I tried to reassure her, but she seemed very anxious as she frantically tried to scrape up the carpet to make a bed for her puppies. In order to satisfy her urge for nesting, I managed to find enough newspapers to keep her busy for a while. This gave me a chance to hastily assemble all the other necessary things and to get ready for the whelping. This bitch was not unique, as several others of mine have since managed to eat a hearty meal just prior to going into labour. Fortunately, I have learned my lesson and, nowadays, I am well prepared to deal with the unexpected.

Another sign that the bitch is going into labour is a drop in her temperature. Her normal temperature is 38.5. degrees Celsius (101.5 Fahrenheit), but a few hours before whelping, this will drop to 37 degrees Celsius (98 Fahrenheit). In order to be able to identify this drop, you will have to take the bitch's temperature several times. As most bitches are not used to having their temperature taken regularly, they may find it quite stressful now. Once again, some bitches like to be different, and their temperature can go up again and return to normal just before whelping.

Many bitches like to prepare their own bed for whelping, but it may not necessarily be the one you had in mind! Over the years, some of my pregnant bitches have chosen some very strange places where *they* would have liked to have had their puppies! Some have excavated holes in the garden, usually in places that were

quite inaccessible for me, and others were really determined to have their puppies under a hedge. I usually indulge them in their activities for a while, but when I think that the time for whelping is getting closer, I insist on a return to the nursery and that the whelping-box must be used.

The duration of the first stage of labour can vary considerably; it may be quite fast and last for only about two hours, or it may take as long as 24 to 36 hours. Let your bitch have a good supply of newspapers which she can tear up to make a bed for her puppies. This frantic nesting can go on for hours before the start of the second stage of labour and can be quite exhausting for the bitch, as well as for her anxious owner who has to watch. I do not interfere, but stay on hand in case the bitch needs my help and reassurance. Apart from panting frantically, she may also pace about restlessly or even whine or cry a little.

Some bitches insist on wanting to go out into the garden to relieve themselves. Do not let her go out on her own, as she is quite likely to return to the special place she had prepared earlier on. Many bitches seem to whelp at night, so if you have to take her out, make sure she is on a lead and that you take the torch in case she might surprise you by producing a puppy in the garden.

Fortunately, most bitches will take a break and sleep for a while before resuming their activities, giving their owner the chance to have a quick cup of tea or coffee, before returning to watch over her. Make sure that she has access to fresh drinking water or, better still, tempt her with some milk and glucose which will help to preserve her strength for the actual whelping. Now is the best time to inform your vet that a whelping is under way in case help is needed later on. Most Irish Setter bitches whelp easily and without veterinary assistance, but it is always best to have a contingency plan to cope with any emergency.

THE WHELPING

The second stage of labour starts with the first contraction or straining movement to expel a puppy. To be on the safe side, you should write down the exact time of the first contraction, as it can be quite easy to lose track of time during a long whelping. If the first puppy has not been born after an hour, contact your vet immediately to ask for advice.

A contraction can easily be observed as it moves along the bitch's body. Gradually, the contractions become more frequent and, when the bitch is not straining, she will pant or try and lick her vulva, which is quite a task for a pregnant bitch. She will also arch her back and tail in a quite unmistakable way. Normally a dark-coloured sac of fluid will appear at the vulva ahead of the first puppy and, after further contractions, the puppy will make its appearance, normally head first and enveloped in its own membrane. It will probably take several more contractions for the entire puppy to be expelled, but once the head is through, the rest will follow very quickly. A further strain will then produce the placenta or afterbirth. Most Irish Setter bitches are wonderful mothers and usually know what to do with their newly born puppy by instinct. A bitch will quickly clear the membrane from the puppy's face, allowing the pup to take its first breath, and then sever the umbilical cord by biting through it with her teeth.

Sometimes, a first-time mum can be rather confused about what is going on and will ignore her puppy. If this happens, use your fingers to gently break open the membrane; first clear it away from around the puppy's head and then from the rest of the body. Wipe away all excess fluid from around the puppy's mouth and nostrils with a small piece of towel to enable it to breathe properly. You will also have to sever the cord yourself by pinching it hard between your finger and thumb, about half-way between the puppy and the placenta, and then cut the cord in that place with the pair of sterilised scissors. There is no need to tie up the cord; it will dry and shrivel up and then fall off, quite naturally, a few days later. Dry the puppy thoroughly by rubbing it very gently with one of the towels. This should start the puppy crying and make the bitch take notice. Offer her the puppy to lick while you to talk to her gently. After a while the puppy will migrate to look for a teat and will start to suckle. The bitch may find all of this a little strange, but your reassurance and the puppy's suckling should soon bring out all her maternal instincts and, by the time the second puppy is being born, she will probably have discovered what motherhood is all about.

It is quite natural for a bitch to want to eat the afterbirth and I let her eat a few. Not only is a placenta full of nutrients which the bitch needs at this time, but eating it will also help her milk production. However, be warned – if the bitch eats too many she is quite likely to end up suffering from a bout of diarrhoea after whelping, and it is probably best to restrict the number she should be allowed to eat. Once the bitch has eaten a few, wrap up the remaining placentas in some newspaper and dispose of them in the plastic bag. It is important to make quite sure that a placenta arrives with each puppy, as a retained afterbirth can lead to problems later on, but keeping a check on all the placentas can occasionally prove to be quite difficult, especially, when the bitch is producing several puppies in very quick succession.

As the whelping box can get quite crowded with all the new arrivals, I remove some of the puppies that were born earlier into the cardboard box which has been lined with a good layer of newspapers and a vetbed. Place a securely wrapped hot-water bottle between the paper and the fleecy bedding. This will keep the puppies safe and warm until the mother has finished producing her litter. The whelping box should be kept as dry as possible and the newspapers will have to be changed from time to time. First remove the soiled paper carefully and put it into the plastic sack, then replace it with dry newspaper – but try to do this without upsetting the bitch too much.

I like to keep a record of the litters being born and write down the time of each birth, the sex of each puppy and the weight. I also record whether I saw the placenta or not. Such records can make fascinating reading in later years, and I have often tried to recall how I felt when I had a litter of eleven dog puppies. After I had given up all hope for a bitch puppy, the mother managed to squeeze in one when I was exhausted and having a quick nap in my chair. The bitch puppy was perfectly healthy and had not suffered from her delayed entry into the world. Unfortunately, and much to my disappointment, she was not of show quality, but she went on to live a long and happy life as a much-loved pet.

PROBLEMS DURING WHELPING
Fortunately, Irish Setter bitches tend to have few problems when they have their litters and the large majority of whelpings pass without incident or veterinary intervention. However, and I have already suggested this, you should always inform your veterinary practice that a litter is on its way. Just in case!

At any time during a whelping, even if a bitch has good contractions, she may be unable to expel a puppy. There could be a very large puppy stuck in the birth canal, or two puppies could be presented at the same time. If this happens, keep an eye on your watch and consult the time-chart you started with the first contraction. Do not hesitate to call your vet if an hour has gone by without the arrival of a puppy. Prompt action now will increase the chances of survival for the puppy or puppies. You do not want to weaken the bitch by leaving her to strain for too long without success, as she will need all her strength to produce the rest of her litter, whether naturally, or by surgical intervention.

Some vets will come to the house to assess the situation, but others will ask you to come to the surgery. This makes good sense as all the necessary equipment will be there, ready and available, in case a caesarean section is needed. If the bitch has already had some puppies, keep them warm and safe at home in their cardboard box with the hot-water bottle. However, you should take some more towels and another box with you, in case more puppies are born on the journey or at the surgery. It is surprising just how many bitches have managed finally to whelp the puppy that was stuck for so long on the way to the surgery! On arrival, check the car and make quite sure that the bitch did not have a puppy during the journey, and that a newborn puppy has not slipped behind the seats.

Some bitches can suffer from uterine inertia, which is an inability to expel the puppies due to very weak contractions. Inertia can occur right at the beginning of a whelping or after the arrival of several puppies. One of my bitches suffered uterine inertia with her first litter only recently. She gave birth very easily to two healthy bitch puppies and then decided that this was quite enough! It was obvious from her size that she still had a number of puppies on board, but she just went to sleep. Help was clearly needed, and I telephoned my vet, who came out very quickly. After an injection of pituitrin, things got going again and Lottie whelped the rest of her litter without any further delays. It is said that uterine inertia can run in some families, but as I have not experienced it before, I will have to wait until this bitch has another litter, or until her daughter is going to have a family.

POST-WHELPING CARE
When I think that a bitch has finished whelping her litter, I try to persuade her to come out into

A contented bitch with her puppies a few hours after birth.

Pictured just two days later, the puppies are filling out well.   *Photo: Mike Gardner*

the garden to relieve herself. It usually takes a great deal of gentle persuasion to get a bitch to move and to leave her puppies, but once you have managed to get her to stand up, you will also be able to check and feel if she has another puppy tucked away. Because it is so very difficult to get a new mum away from her puppies, help is needed, and I usually ask my husband to take her out. This gives me the chance to clean up the whelping box but it has to be done quickly, as no bitch wants to be kept away from her new litter for too long.

I remove all the soiled paper and place it into the plastic sack, wipe the whelping box with disinfectant and line it again with a thick layer of newspaper. Then I place all the puppies on a clean vetbed in the whelping box before the bitch returns from outside. Veterinary fleeces are a wonderful invention. They allow any moisture to soak through to the layer of newspapers underneath, which keeps the surface dry. Puppies love the warmth and texture of the artificial fur and seem to be much more contented on their vetbed than any other bedding. Because they are machine-washable and dry very quickly, they can be used again very soon after washing. I usually have several

on the go for a litter and often wonder whatever did we do before vetbeds were invented?

Before the bitch comes back to her brood I like to check the temperature in the room and in the whelping box. If necessary, I adjust the height of the infra-red lamp above the box. Puppies need to be warm, but not hot. The temperature should also be comfortable for the bitch and the ideal temperature, at this stage, is an even 21 degrees C (70 degrees F). Do not overheat the room where the pups are kept, and remember that the vetbed and the mother's body will also provide additional warmth. Observe the puppies – they will soon let you know if they are feeling comfortable. If they are too hot, they will crawl away from each other, crying. If they are too cold, they will pile on top of each other and cry when seeking warmth and comfort from their siblings. A concerned mother will usually try and curl herself around her cold puppies in order to keep them warm.

After a lengthy whelping, the bitch will probably be exhausted and hungry. I first offer her some more milk with a beaten egg and glucose. This should help to restore some of her lost energy, and after a sleep, she will probably be ready for a meal of cooked chicken or rabbit, or some other light, but nutritious, food. Some bitches take a while before their normal, healthy appetite returns after whelping and they may have to be coaxed into eating. Fortunately, mine have always demanded their dinners soon after they have finished having their families and I have never had to worry about a lack of appetite.

You can tell very quickly if all is well with a mother and her puppies, as the only sound you will hear is a contented humming from the puppies as they suckle or sleep while the bitch rests quietly, trying to recover from her great effort. This quiet humming, which is only interrupted by an occasional squeak from a puppy, is a lovely sound and the sight of a contented bitch with her beautiful puppies soon makes you forget all the sleep you may have lost during their births. If the puppies whine and fret, and the bitch refuses to settle, then there is usually a problem such as a retained puppy or an afterbirth which should be investigated immediately.

I always ask my vet to come out and check the bitch after whelping to make quite sure that all is well. If the litter was born in the middle of the night and without any problems, it can wait quite safely until the morning for the call-out. Vets will usually give the bitch an injection of pituitrin (Oxytocin), often together with a long-acting injection of antibiotic. This will deal with anything that may have been left behind and will prevent complications.

Should you have any worries concerning the puppies, this is the time to ask your vet to check them over. If a bitch has had a very large litter, and Irish Setters can be extremely prolific, you should consider culling back to more manageable numbers. A bitch can manage eight puppies very well, and most Irish Setter bitches can cope with ten puppies, provided you give lots of help. However, I would rather have eight bonny puppies that the bitch is

rearing well, than twelve or fourteen that are not thriving properly. Quite apart from the expense of rearing all the puppies really well, I do not believe that you can manage to find such a large number of suitable homes for *all* the puppies at any one time. Leave it for a few days, in case you lose a weakling puppy, before calling in your vet to put any puppies to sleep. In any case, you will have to make arrangements for the vet to return to remove the puppies' dewclaws. This is usually done when the puppies are about three or four days old. It is essential to have the dewclaws removed at this age, as later on a full anaesthetic will be required to do the same.

I usually spend at least the first night with the new mother and her puppies to make quite sure that all is going well, and that she is coping with her family. Once I am confident that the bitch is sensible, I return to sleep in my bed, but leave the bedroom door open so that I can hear any strange sounds or disturbances that may come from the nursery. Fortunately, over the years, there have been very few disturbed nights caused by a bitch or her puppies.

THE EARLY DAYS

After your bitch has presented you with the carefully planned litter, it will be up to you to rear the puppies correctly to bring out their full potential. The foundation for strong, healthy puppies should already have been laid with the extra food and vitamins the mother had during her pregnancy. This now needs to be carefully built on.

For the first two to three weeks of their lives the puppies will be dependent on their mother for their nourishment, and she will need all the care and attention that you can lavish on her. Lactation makes great demands on a bitch, and it takes a considerable amount of high-quality food to produce all the milk the puppies need. Research has shown that, at the height of lactation, a bitch needs up to four times her

normal intake. This represents a very large amount of food, which should be divided into four smaller meals. I like to give my bitches two meals of meat and biscuit, and two meals of milk and cereal to which I add an egg and a vitamin and calcium supplement.

For a change, one of the milk meals can consist of tinned rice pudding which can be bought in the local supermarket or, better still, can be cooked at home when the oven is on. Naturally, the exact amount of food a bitch will need very much depends on the number of puppies she is rearing and whether you are helping her by supplementing the pups with a bitch's milk substitute. In addition, nursing bitches really appreciate special treats such as cooked chicken or steamed white fish. Both of these are not only extremely palatable and nutritious, but also make a welcome change from the more usual tripe, or beef, or tinned meat. My dogs have milk as part of their daily diet and it does agree with them. However, after whelping, some bitches can suffer from diarrhoea, especially after having eaten too many placentas, and their digestive system cannot cope with milk. If this is the case, do not worry, but cut out the milk for a while and give her extra meat meals.

A bitch does not have to drink milk to produce milk, but she does need good food and plenty of liquid which she converts into milk for her puppies. Therefore, it is extremely important that a bitch should have easy access to an unlimited supply of fresh drinking water.

For the first few days after whelping, a bitch will probably be extremely reluctant to leave her puppies, even to eat her meals. If this is the case, feed her in her box with her puppies. Irish Setter bitches tend to be excellent mothers who take great care of their puppies by not only licking and washing them very thoroughly, but also by cleaning up after them. Bitches can often appear to be quite rough when licking their pups, but their tongues do not only clean their brood, but also stimulate their tiny systems and their bodily functions.

REMOVING THE DEWCLAWS
When the puppies are three or four days old, I ask my vet to come to the house to remove their dewclaws. It is sensible to have them removed as, later on, they can easily be torn off, especially if they grow outwards and at an odd angle. If they have to be removed at a later date, a general anaesthetic will be required. This calls for great diplomacy to prevent the mother from getting too distressed. As soon as I hear the vet's car on the drive, I try to coax the mother out of the bed and ask my husband to take her into the garden. I always hope that this will prevent the bitch from hearing her puppies crying when the deed is being done. However, most bitches are very suspicious when they are being removed from their puppies, and my poor husband usually has a battle on his hands trying to restrain the very anxious mum. A skilled vet can remove dewclaws very quickly, without much blood

being shed and without too much crying. Check the puppies for dewclaws on their hindlegs and have them removed as well.

I usually hold the puppies for my vet, but I have to confess that I hate it and that I cannot bear to look when the pups are being dealt with. Once the dewclaws have been removed, I place the puppies back in their bed, but on a clean vetbed to cut down the risk of infection. By this time the poor bitch will probably have realised that something terrible has been happening to her puppies and will want to get back to them as fast as possible. Once she has been allowed back with her puppies to comfort and feed them, they will soon forget their nasty experience. As a rule, my vet stays on for a while to make quite sure that there is no bleeding and that all is going well.

EARLY DEVELOPMENTS

Puppies are born with their eyes and ears closed and do not start to open their eyes until they are about ten to fourteen days old. The first sign is usually a little glint in the corner of one of the puppies' eyes and, gradually, little slits will appear in all their eyes which will widen over the next few days until the eyes are fully open. However, not all the puppies open their eyes at the same time and some will take a little longer than others. At first the puppies appear to have blue eyes and are unable to focus properly. This will change and, once their sight improves, together with their hearing, they will become animated and start to play with their litter mates. I waste a great deal of time by just sitting with my puppies to watch their first, rather feeble attempts to get hold of each other's tails, falling over in the process.

Once puppies become more mobile, they will start to rush around their box, trying to bark. In no time at all, the puppies will also learn to recognise you and will greet you with wagging tails. Their nails will need regular attention from a very early age. It is best to cut them when the puppies are about one week old and to keep them trimmed regularly. At first, when they are still very soft, this can be done with an ordinary pair of nail-scissors; later use a pair of special nail-clippers. If left, the nails will soon grow into very sharp talons which must be agony for the nursing bitch during feeding time when the puppies pummel her to encourage the flow of milk.

WEANING

I usually start to wean my puppies when they are about three weeks old. The exact time really depends on the size of the litter and how the bitch is coping with feeding her pups. Larger litters have to be weaned earlier than smaller ones, not only for the sake of the puppies, but also for the good of the mother. Nursing bitches can put so much into their puppies that they rapidly lose condition and become extremely thin. However, if the bitch is coping well and the pups are thriving, I prefer to delay weaning for a little longer because slightly older puppies get the hang of taking solid food so much more quickly than pups that are just a few days younger.

The first solid food I give to my puppies is raw scraped beef, but only the very best will do. Try and keep the bitch away for a while before introducing them to the new food. It will be easier when they are hungry. I take one puppy at a time, put it on my lap and push a tiny amount of meat into the puppy's mouth. Hopefully, the puppy will like the new taste and accept the offer. At this stage, puppies do not really chew, but they suck the meat down in much the same way as they take their mother's milk. Some puppies do not like what is being offered and will reject the meat. Therefore, it is best to wear a plastic apron which can be wiped down easily, or to spread a towel across your lap to prevent your clothes from being soiled. I keep a cardboard box with a clean vetbed by the side of the bed and, once a puppy has been fed, I put the puppy into the box. This will prevent one of them from being fed twice.

Gradually increase the quantity of meat you give as well as the frequency of the tiny meals. After a few days of individual tuition, puppies will usually become quite expert at taking the meat from your finger. This is the time to try and get them to feed from a saucer, which I place in their bed. It is best to roll up the vetbed first and to put the saucer on newspaper because, during their first attempts, a fair amount of the meat will be wasted and spread around. Some will continue to need a bit of help to get their share and, even at this early age, it is possible to pick out the slower eaters from the more greedy ones.

Once the puppies have got the hang of eating scraped beef, it is time to introduce them to lapping milk. There are a number of excellent products available which are specially formulated to closely resemble a bitch's milk, but it is most important to prepare the milk in strict accordance with the manufacturer's instructions. Again, I introduce each puppy individually to the warm milk on a saucer by gently dipping their noses into the liquid. Some puppies will learn to lap very quickly, but others will recoil from the saucer in a state of shock. In fact, some make such a fuss that they scream and shake with disapproval. In such cases, it can be quite helpful first to put a little bit of the milk around the puppy's nose and mouth and, hopefully, the puppy will start to lick and gradually learn to lap the milk.

After persevering for a few days, most puppies will have got used to taking milk from a saucer and a larger dish can be introduced. I like to use a circular feeder which is specially designed for weaning puppies and can usually accommodate all the puppies at the same time. It is practically impossible to tip up and you can easily observe how each puppy is coping. Getting the hang of lapping can be quite a messy business, and I love to watch my puppies after they have finished their milk. By this time they are usually covered in the white, sticky stuff and will spend some time licking each other clean, before falling fast asleep again on a dry, warm vetbed.

FEEDING THE GROWING PUPPIES
Puppies have very special feeding requirements because their stomachs are very small, but they need large amounts of food in relation to their body-weight. Therefore, their daily rations must be divided into four or five small meals that are spread as far apart as possible during the day. After my puppies have mastered the art of eating meat from a dish and having milky drinks from their feeder, it is time to introduce them to cereals and other types of meat. At this stage I also like to put my puppies on to goat's milk which is excellent and is much more convenient to use than the powdered milk.

Therefore, when the puppies are about four weeks old, their daily menus will be as follows: breakfast and tea – warm goat's milk with a human baby cereal stirred into it. Lunch and dinner – minced beef. There is now no need to scrape the meat as the pups can cope with

A circular feeder can accommodate a number of puppies, and it is almost impossible to tip it up!

Photo: Mary Gurney.

minced beef. Supper – warm milk mixed with some rusks that have been crushed and turned into a porridge.

By the time another week has gone by, the puppies will be ready to have some well-soaked puppy meal mixed in with their meat. One of the milk meals can be replaced by tinned or home-made rice pudding, which mine usually find delicious. I also add a vitamin and calcium supplement vitamin powder to one of their meals. During this time the puppies will still help themselves to their mother's milk but, as their meals increase, the bitch should be kept away from her puppies more and more frequently.

Cut down gradually on the amount of food the bitch is getting, as well as on the amount of liquid she has been drinking during the time of maximum demand. This will help to reduce the amount of milk she produces and will allow it to dry up gradually. By the time my puppies are about six weeks old, they will also have been introduced to tinned puppy meat and to finely minced tripe. The quantities of food will gradually be increased for the four meals, but I cut out the rusks from their supper last thing at night. I like to give my puppies as much to eat as they want, and if they finish their meal quickly and still look for more, it is time to give them more. Irish Setters grow rapidly and need all this food for their healthy growth and development.

By the time my puppies are six-and-a-half to seven weeks old, they will have become completely independent from their mother, but some bitches insist on continuing to go in with their pups. The weaning process should be as natural as possible, and I allow my bitches to have access to their puppies, if they insist. Most puppies will leave their breeder when they are at least eight weeks old and by that time their food intake should have been increased to the following quantities.

BREAKFAST: Half a pint of goat's milk with baby cereal or porridge.
LUNCH: 8 ozs of meat, either beef, tripe or tinned, together with soaked puppy meal and a vitamin and calcium supplement.
TEA: Same as breakfast. Or rice pudding as a change. Babies' rusks and milk also make a welcome change.
DINNER: Same as lunch. Feed cooked chicken or some white fish as a change; also an occasional egg. Drink of milk. There is no need to give the vitamin and calcium supplement again.

Gradually increase the quantities as the puppy grows. By the time the puppy is about three to four months old, cut out tea, but add the milk to the remaining meals. Continue with three meals for as long as the puppy will eat them. By the time a youngster reaches twelve months, only breakfast and dinner should be fed, and my adult Irish Setters continue to have two meals throughout their lives.

WORMING
All puppies need to be wormed, and the earlier the better. I usually discuss worming with my vet, as there always seems to be an even better preparation available than I used with the previous litter, probably some years ago. My most recent litter was wormed for the first time when the puppies were only two weeks of age. Following the manufacturer's instructions, each puppy was weighed and then given one quarter of a tablet of the preparation. I had the distinct impression that after the initial worming the litter made rapid progress, but before leaving for their new homes the puppies had to be wormed twice again, each time with an increased dose and according to their weight. It is important to remember also to worm the bitch at the same time. Thorough worming is essential to ensure the puppies' health and growth rate, which can be affected by a severe worm burden.

HOUSING

Once I have made quite sure that all the puppies can eat and drink without my help, I like to move them out into their puppy kennel. By this time I usually find that the puppies are getting just a bit too smelly for the house! Moving is done in easy stages. At first the puppies and their mother will spend just a few hours during the day in their new quarters. Then the time is gradually increased until, eventually, the family will spend their first night outside. The kennel is divided into two sections which are separated by boards that can be raised as the puppies get older. The bitch has her bed on one side of the partition which allows her to escape from her demanding brood when she wants to.

My puppy shed is warm and draught-free, having been lined with ply-wood, and the infra-red lamp is used to top-up the temperature when needed, especially at night. If you have a winter litter and the weather turns very cold, do *not* be tempted to use paraffin heaters. If there is insufficient ventilation their fumes can be lethal to the puppies and, if they knock a heater over, a fire can start very quickly. Extra heat can be provided by adding another infra-red lamp, or through a wall-mounted electric convector heater which must be kept safely away from the pups.

Once the litter has been moved to the puppy kennel, I start to use a different type of bedding which is made from off-cuts of tea-bag casing. It is soft and white and very absorbent and the puppies love it! It comes compressed in large plastic sacks and the puppies have a wonderful time when I replace their bedding, as it has to be fluffed up before use. It is very convenient to use outdoors and it does not need washing. However, I would never recommend it for use in the house as it gets strewn all over the place.

I also provide the puppies with an area which is covered with thick layers of newspapers where they can relieve themselves well away from their bed, as Irish Setter puppies like to be clean from a very early age. First thing in the morning, or whenever the bedding and newspapers are soiled, I roll up the lot and burn it. When the puppies are about four weeks old, I wait for a fine day and then bring them out of their kennel to introduce them to the great outdoors in their puppy run. This is attached to the puppy kennel and has been a wonderful investment. It consists of three panels, each is six feet long and about three feet high. Two are plain wire meshed and the third has a small gate, allowing easy access. One side of the puppy run is formed by the wooden fence that separates the yard from the garden and, once the panels are fixed together, they make up the rest. They are heavy duty and galvanised and can be left out in all weathers.

The first introduction to the big wide world is not always a great success. Some puppies are so shocked that they huddle together in a corner, or try to get straight back into the security of the puppy kennel. For this purpose my husband has provided them with a ramp which gives easy access in and out of the puppy kennel and prevents the puppies from having to cope with a rather steep step. It does not take very long for the puppies to get used to their new run where they can enjoy playing in safety and security.

SOCIALISATION

In order for Irish Setter puppies to grow up confidently and well adjusted, they will have to learn, from an early age, how to cope with all the complexities of modern life. My puppy kennel is situated very close to the backdoor of the kitchen and the pups soon have to get used to living with the noise of the washing machine, dishwasher and vacuum cleaner. We live in a part of the country where Royal Air Force pilots are given low-flying practice, but after the initial shock of hearing the tremendous noise puppies, just like the adults, do not take any notice. The same applies to the noise from the lawnmower and the hedge trimmer. I like to sit with the puppies, letting them climb all over me, and if there is a slightly more retiring puppy in the litter, this is the time to concentrate on that youngster.

Visitors are encouraged to talk to the puppies who soon learn to appreciate all the fuss that is being made of them. I also like to introduce the puppies to the family cat to teach them to accept other pets. This particular cat is a wise animal and has seen it all before! She can always easily get away from the puppies, but loves and seeks their company. If the puppies take too many liberties with her, she will hiss at them to teach them a lesson, or she will just leave. Once the rest of the litter have gone to their new homes, my chosen puppy copies the adult Setters and quite happily curls up with the cat. My puppies do not have shop-bought toys, but usually have great fun with a cardboard box or the cardboard from the inside of kitchen rolls. Both are safe and can be ripped up without causing any worry.

A BREEDER'S RESPONSIBILITIES

Breeders should be extremely careful about whom they sell their puppies to, and I like to meet my potential owners well before the puppies are old enough to leave for their new homes. Irish Setters can be a handful, especially if they are not correctly treated, and it is best to point out the pitfalls to new and unsuspecting owners. I never paint a rosy picture in order to sell a puppy, but make it quite clear that owning an Irish Setter is a commitment that will have its ups and downs. I also remind new owners to check the fencing in their garden before the new puppy arrives – Irish Setters always seem to find the only gap in your hedge or fence!

When the puppies are old enough to leave for their new home, you should make sure that all

'Katrein' pictured with her unusual foster child. Photo: Kind permisssion of KYNOS-Verlag, Germany. Taken from 'Rasse Portrait Setter', by Hilde Schwoyer.

the paperwork is ready to leave with the puppy. You should give the new owners a pedigree, the Kennel Club Registration and a diet sheet, together with worming instructions and advice on vaccinations. But, as many vets seem to have different ideas about the timing of vaccinations, it is probably best if new owners check with their vet before they collect their new puppy. Finally, I always remind the new owners that I would like to hear how the puppy is getting on in the new home and also stress that the puppy, or later the adult Irish Setter, should be returned to me if things go wrong and the owners can no longer keep the animal.

11 *HEALTH CARE*

Irish Setters are, on the whole, a healthy breed. However, there are certain conditions which tend to occur and I have drawn special attention to them. After the success of DNA testing for PRA it is hoped that more tests will become available to eradicate other hereditary conditions from the breed.

THE VETERINARY SURGEON

One of the most important people in the life of an Irish Setter owner is a good veterinary surgeon. Not only is it essential to have complete trust and confidence in a vet during an emergency, but a vet should also be approachable enough to discuss any worries owners may have concerning their animals. I have made it a golden rule not to delay consulting my vet and not to moan too much about the cost, as experience has shown that it is better to be safe than sorry.

One of the first considerations when looking for a suitable veterinary practice must be its location. This is particularly critical for those of us who live in the country and, invariably, some distance away from the centre of a town where most vets seem to be located. In an emergency every minute counts! Once you have found a vet with whom you feel you can get on, stay and develop a good relationship, not only with the vet, but also with the auxiliary staff such as the nurses.

If you have to consult your vet, find out if they operate an appointments system or whether their surgeries are run between certain hours. It is also advisable to find out if your vet will make house-calls. In cases of emergency, all vets have to provide a 24-hour service for sick animals. If you need the emergency service, try and stay calm and give the vet as clear a description of the problem as possible.

INSURANCE

All dog owners should have a third-party insurance cover for each one of their dogs. If a dog is the cause of an accident, or if it bites someone, the owner is responsible and could be liable to potentially enormous claims of damages and costs. Check your household policy, as some include such cover. If it does not, do not delay, and take it out as soon as possible. It is easy to arrange and does not cost a great deal of money. Over recent years, health insurance for dogs has become increasingly more popular. There are several companies that offer a variety of plans, therefore choose the one that suits you best. In view of the ever-rising costs, and the ever more sophisticated veterinary treatment that is now available, insurance cover could well be an option you may want to consider.

FIRST AID

It is sensible to keep a first aid kit handy to deal with any minor ailments or to give speedy assistance in an emergency before the dog can be seen by a vet. It should contain lint and bandages, a roll of elastoplast, and a pair of scissors. Disinfectant such as Dettol or Savlon is also essential, as well as an antiseptic cream such as Dermisol. I always keep a bottle of Arnica around the house – not just for the dogs, but also for the human family. It is excellent in cases of sprains and bruises and helps to reduce any swellings. In fact, we have been known to make use of the Dermisol as well! My kit also includes one of my husband's old ties that has, in the past, been successfully used as a tourniquet. A first aid kit would not be complete without a thermometer and I have recently invested in an electronic thermometer. Temperatures are much easier to read with that. Thermometers in Fahrenheit or Centigrade are available.

Some years ago one of my bitches had to be spayed and she simply would not leave the wound alone and seemed quite determined to take out her own stitches! Unfortunately, my vet did not have an 'Elizabethan' collar available which would have prevented her from paying too much attention to her wound. The Elizabethan collar closely resembles a lampshade that can be looped through the dog's collar which holds it in place. I telephoned around and eventually found a friend who had a 'lampshade', but who lived rather a long way away. I left the bitch in my husband's care and drove off to collect the object. Unfortunately, I was caught on a speed camera on my mission of mercy but at least the patient was prevented from taking out her stitches! I spent some anxious days waiting to

hear about a fine and endorsement of my licence but, fortunately, nothing ever came of it. However, ever since that time a plastic lampshade has become an essential part of my first aid kit.

HEALTH PROBLEMS OF PARTICULAR IMPORTANCE TO IRISH SETTERS

BLOAT: (Gastric Dilation Volvulus) *This life-threatening condition is an emergency!* The condition occurs when the stomach fills up rapidly with gas (thought to be air) and then twists about its axis. This is extremely serious and must be treated immediately! Pressure on the major abdominal blood vessels can induce irreversible shock which can quickly become fatal. Gastric Dilation can occur without any twisting; this is far less serious, but often precedes an episode of GDV. The condition is most common in very deep-chested breeds such as the Irish Setter, Great Danes, Bloodhounds and Borzois.

Symptoms: A sudden and noticeable swelling of the abdomen, quite often after eating a meal. The stomach rapidly becomes grossly swollen and hard. The dog is restless and in distress and often has difficulty in breathing. The animal may try to vomit or pass faeces but is unable to do so because, once the twisting has taken place, nothing can pass.

Action: This is a true veterinary emergency and you must *contact your vet immediately* whether by day or by night

Treatment: Counteracting shock. Relieving the pressure in the stomach and returning the stomach to the normal position through surgery.

Prevention: A nationwide case-control study in the USA has identified several factors which seem to increase the risk of bloat, and a survey undertaken in the UK appears to confirm some of those findings. It must be accepted that the make and shape of the Irish Setter has a considerable role to play in the cause of bloat, but the following precautions can help to reduce the risk factor:

Feed your Irish Setter twice daily.

Do not exercise immediately before or immediately after a meal.

Ensure that your Irish Setter is calm and not excited before being fed.

Do not feed a single food only. Add some tinned meat or similar to a mainly dry diet.

Irish Setters with an "easy-going" temperament seem to be less prone to bloat. I have owned Irish Setters for over thirty years and during that time two of my bitches have suffered from bloat. Both bitches survived their illness, but probably because I was at home with them and managed to get them to my vet immediately. However, this is where the similarities end, and a short account of the differences in their emergencies may be of help to an Irish Setter in the future:

Case 1: Carnbargus Red Silk. (born 13.3.1974). Silky showed no signs of bloat or distress during her early morning exercise but within half an hour after returning home she developed the classic symptoms of bloat. Her stomach became distended and hard and she had great difficulty in standing up. I immediately telephoned my vet and arranged to take Silky to the surgery. By the time we arrived, her stomach had returned to its normal size, but she appeared weak and found it difficult to walk. The pink in her gums had become very pale, almost grey, and examination showed that her spleen was much enlarged. After having been put on a drip, she stabilised sufficiently to undergo surgery. This revealed that her stomach was full of fermenting matter which was removed. During surgery, Silky underwent a gastropexy which attached the stomach to the lining of the abdominal cavity to prevent further twisting. She made a full recovery and lived to a ripe old age. It was only

after all the excitement of the emergency had died down that it became clear what had happened. Silky had helped herself to a very large amount of biscuit meal and had then drunk copious amounts of water. Since that time, all our dog biscuits and meal are stored in a strong feed-bin which the dogs cannot get at.

Case 2: Carnbargus Caleche. (born 5.2.1988). Like many Irish Setters, Minty had an obsession with water and loved to drink from the tap when I filled the water bowls. She thought this was extremely clever and, like a fool, I allowed her to do it! One morning, she refused to get up to eat her breakfast and when I looked at her, her sides were sticking out, making her look like a pack-horse. Minty did not appear to be distressed in any way and kept wagging her tail. I immediately telephoned my vet and raced to the surgery with her. He relieved the condition by sticking a needle into her side which released the accumulated gases and, with the aid of a hypodermic syringe, a dish of almost clear water was withdrawn. This seemed to be the end of the emergency and I was allowed to take her home. She still did not want to eat, but settled down quietly to sleep. In the afternoon she seemed to have recovered completely, but every time she walked past me, I could hear a strange gurgling sound which convinced me that there was air in her system. Back to the vet, who decided to operate while Minty was fit and stable. He got there just in time as her stomach was in the process of twisting. She, too, had a gastropexy and made a speedy recovery.

After this, the management of my dogs was tightened up further and all seemed to be going well. However, on Easter Saturday two years after the first episode, Minty was not quite herself and the strange gurgling sound could be heard again. There were no external signs of bloat, but I was very concerned. Because she was stable, she was referred to the Royal

Veterinary College where we arrived in the late afternoon, probably having broken every speed limit on our journey! I had a call later that night to let me know that Minty was being prepared for surgery as her stomach was in the process of turning. During the operation not a trace of the original gastropexy could be found – the stitches had dissolved before adhesion had taken place. I understand that this is quite common, but I had been living with a false sense of security. Once again, during this episode, Minty had not shown any signs of discomfort or distress. Fortunately, she made a full recovery and is still very well.

Before suffering from bloat, both bitches had been successful in the show ring. Silky had won one CC and three Res. CCs, and Minty had gained her Junior Warrant and four Res. CCs. However, after having survived their operations, I decided not to show them again. Silky had been bred from before bloat, but Minty has never had a litter. I firmly believe that a bitch that has been operated on for GDV should not be bred from for the sake of her welfare. I was just pleased that both my bitches had survived and had regained their health.

CANINE LEUCOCYTE ADHESION PROTEIN DEFICIENCY (CLAPD) or CANINE GRANULOCYTOPATHY (CGS): *What is CLAPD?* This is an inherited disease thought to be specific to the Irish Setter. It is a disorder of the dog's immune system, particularly of the part which controls and combats bacterial infections. Because it is inherited, the disease is present in puppies from birth. Puppies tend to suffer from infections when still in the nest: navels fail to heal, as do scratches and other lesions. Tonsillitis, throat and chest infections are also common. When the pups are about 10 to 14 weeks old, they tend to develop gingivitis and a swelling of the joints and bones, particularly of the knees and

jaws. Attempts to stand up and to eat are very painful. Puppies usually have a high temperature and a greatly increased count of white blood-cells.
Treatment: Initially, most pups will respond to treatment with antibiotics and steroids. However, as soon as treatment is withdrawn, puppies will relapse very quickly and the pattern is repeated.
Prognosis: The outlook for afflicted puppies is very poor and most cases are put to sleep at an early age to prevent further suffering. However, cases that have survived for several months have been known. A test is now available to accurately diagnose the disease. Work is also progressing on a DNA test which, in future, will be able to identify carriers of the disorder.

ENTROPION: A condition in which the corners of the eyelids turn inwards, causing the tiny eyelashes to irritate and inflame the cornea. If it is not treated, the condition can result in ulceration of the cornea and, eventually, in impaired vision.
Symptoms: Any puppy or adult with a continually watering eye should be looked at by a vet. Close examination of the eye will reveal where the lid is turning-in.
Treatment: Entropion can be corrected through surgery to prevent damage to a dog's eye. However, it is considered to be a hereditary condition and afflicted animals should not be bred from; nor should they be shown, as such an operation contravenes Kennel Club Regulations. In some countries, Germany for example, dogs are allowed to be shown, but they are not allowed to be bred from.

ECTROPION: A condition in which the lower eyelid is drooping and turning out.
Treatment: Surgery in severe cases.

FITS: A fit is a convulsive seizure and often occurs when the animal is quiet and relaxed.

Dogs tend to suffer their first fit when they are between two and three years old.

Symptoms: The dog becomes rigid and collapses. This is followed by shaking and muscle spasms and involuntary movement of the legs and feet. During a seizure, dogs are effectively unconscious, but they may kick and bite without being aware of it. Therefore, do not to touch the dog. Try and prevent self-injury during a seizure by removing anything dangerous from near the dog, especially electrical heaters etc. On recovery, place the dog in a quiet, darkened room. Turn off the radio and television.

Treatment: Once the dog has recovered from a seizure, consult your vet in order to obtain a correct diagnosis. There are many diseases which can cause the dog to have fits, epilepsy being one. If epilepsy is diagnosed, it can usually be controlled by medication which allows dogs a good quality of life. Although there is no firm evidence that epilepsy is directly inherited, it seems likely that there is an inherited predisposition to the condition and afflicted Irish Setters should not be bred from.

HIP DYSPLASIA (HD): The hip joint is a ball and socket joint. In cases of hip dysplasia changes occur which prevent the joint from functioning properly. Hip dysplasia is a partly inherited condition and is most common in larger breeds of dogs.

Symptoms: Severe cases of the condition can be extremely painful and can cause the animal to limp. Other signs are a reluctance to run and jump, or showing signs of stiffness when getting up. Dogs with HD also have a tendency to sit down more often.

Diagnosis: Consult your vet who will X-ray the dog. The British Veterinary Association and the Kennel Club operate the official Hip Dysplasia Scheme and scrutineers appointed by the BVA score X-rays which are submitted by the veterinary surgeon. The lower the score, the less evidence of hip dysplasia present. The maximum score is a total of 106 for both hips, 53 on each side; the lowest score is 0. In the USA owners are not required to have their dogs X-rayed. However, if they have been X-rayed and pass the examination they will be given an Orthopaedic Foundation of America (OFA) number which will be recorded on the AKC registration and pedigree.

Prevention: There is no guaranteed way of preventing HD, but the likelihood of dogs developing HD is thought to be reduced by breeding from animals that have been X-rayed and that have good scores.

Treatment: Severe cases can be operated on to relieve pain and suffering.

MEGA-OESOPHAGUS (MO): An abnormality of the oesophagus, which is much enlarged. This prevents the food from being "processed" into the stomach. MO is only one of many swallowing conditions in the dog.

Symptoms: Milk is brought back through the nose. Inability to retain food. Vomiting. In a litter, this can go unnoticed until a puppy shows failure to gain weight. Puppies sometimes make a strange rattling sound, and also cough.

Diagnosis: Mega-oesophagus can be diagnosed when puppies are only a few weeks old. Diagnosis requires an X-ray after barium meal has been administered. If there is an afflicted puppy, the whole litter should be X-rayed to check for further cases. Occasionally, cases of MO can remain undetected in young stock and symptoms are only diagnosed at a much later date. In older animals, MO can also be caused by trauma in later life.

Treatment: There is no realistic treatment or cure for MO and puppies suffering from the condition should be put to sleep. However, very mild cases have been known to survive through dedicated management by the owners.

Prevention: MO is considered to be an inherited

condition and should be avoided in breeding programmes.

PROGRESSIVE RETINAL ATROPHY
(PRA): A hereditary eye disease which is progressive and will eventually lead to blindness in both eyes.
Symptoms: Difficulty in seeing at dusk or in darkness. Bumping into objects in failing light.

In the 1940s and 1950s PRA proved to be the greatest threat to the breed. The condition is hereditary and is carried by a simple autosomal recessive gene which means that both sire and dam of afflicted cases have to be carriers.
DNA TESTING for PRA: The most exciting development in the fight against PRA has been the introduction of DNA testing for RCD-1 (Rod Cone Dysplasia – the correct name for PRA in the Irish Setter). In 1994 the two national breed clubs, The Irish Setter Association, England and The Irish Setter Breeders Club, agreed to co-operate with the University of Edinburgh (and later with Cambridge University) to DNA test 210 Irish Setters which represented the large majority of bloodlines in the breed. In advance, it was agreed that all the test results would be made public, regardless of the outcome. When the results were announced in 1995, of the 210 animals that had been tested, only one Setter was found to be a carrier. Fortunately, the carrier did not have an impact on the breed and, apart from the personal tragedy that this represented to the owner/breeder, RCD-1 can now be considered as a problem of the past. The fact that the breed finds itself in such a fortunate position is very largely due to the action advocated by Mr Rasbridge and demonstrates now just how effective the earlier programme of test-mating had been. PRA was a problem in the USA and, until DNA testing became available, test-matings had been the only way to establish an Irish Setter's status.

Testing your Irish Setter: DNA testing to identify carriers is now available at the Animal Health Trust, and a 5 ml blood-sample taken from an Irish Setter by a vet is all that is required.

Please note that health problems thought to be hereditary should be reported to the breeders of Irish Setters as they would wish to be informed.

COMMON AILMENTS AND DISEASES

ANAL GLANDS: The anal glands are two sacs which lie on either side of the anus. They are normally emptied when the dog is defecating but, occasionally, they can become blocked up and have to be evacuated. A classic sign that this needs doing is when dogs drag their rear ends along the ground. This is *not* a sign that a dog needs worming. Dogs are usually taken to the vet to have their anal glands emptied. However, this is a simple procedure, if rather unpleasant, which can easily be managed by the dog's owner. Ask your vet or a dog expert to show you how it is done.

ARTHRITIS: This condition affects older dogs in the same way that it affects their human counterparts and is 'wear and tear' damage. Joints become inflamed and painful, making the dog less active. There is no known cure, but your vet will be able to prescribe medicine or injections that will not only relieve the pain, but will also slow down the progression of the condition. A warm and comfortable bed away from any draughts should also help.

CANINE DISTEMPER – HARD PAD: This is a highly contagious viral disease, and it is extremely important that all puppies are vaccinated against distemper and that regular boosters are given. Symptoms of the disease are discharge from eyes and nose, raised temperature, loss of appetite, vomiting and diarrhoea. Treatment consists of antibiotics to prevent or control secondary bacterial infections only – drugs cannot kill the virus. Dogs which survive the disease often develop the characteristic thickening of the pads – hence Hard Pad.

CANKER: Canker of the ear is sometimes caused by tiny mites, which are invisible to the naked eye. Usual signs are shaking of the head, scratching of the ear and one ear is often held lower than the other. The ear canal will be red and hot to the touch. Do not poke about inside the ears, but use a powder or drops specially formulated for the treatment of ear mites which are available from your vet. In mature dogs, a major predisposing factor for canker can be a high-protein diet.

CAR SICKNESS: Many Irish Setters are prone to car sickness. However, modern life requires them to be able to cope with car travel. Get youngsters used to the car by not feeding them before journeys and by giving an anti-seasickness tablet well in advance. Once dogs have managed the first few journeys without being sick, they tend to be fine and most will, eventually, learn to enjoy the car.

CUTS, BITES AND ABRASIONS: Allow your dog to lick and cleanse any minor wounds. If the dog does not show any interest in the wound or cannot reach it, clean the wound carefully with dilute salty water, using one level teaspoon per pint. Later apply some antiseptic cream. Repeat the treatment two or three times a day until the wound has healed. Larger cuts may need veterinary attention and suturing. This should not be delayed, as early repair greatly increases the chances of healing quickly. Cut pads are a common problem. Clean the affected area as above and cover with a pad of lint. Then bandage lightly with a crepe bandage. Be careful not to apply the bandage

too tightly and check that there is no swelling below the bandage. To keep a foot bandage clean, put the dog's wrapped paw into an old sock which can be covered with a plastic bag or several layers of cling-film when the dog has to go outside. If your Irish Setter has had a set-to with a cat and has been injured, it is wise to visit the vet for some antibiotic treatment.

DEPRAVED APPETITE: This is the unpleasant habit of eating faeces, which is natural to dogs, but rather offensive to their owners. Puppies learn this by copying their mother who cleans up after them. Prevent the problem by picking up all droppings. However, eating faeces can sometimes reflect a pancreatic insufficiency or a dietary intolerance. If it persists, consult your vet.

DIARRHOEA: Most dogs will suffer from diarrhoea at some time or another during their lives. In most cases it can be put down to something the dog has eaten, such as too much liver, or if the dog has had too much milk to drink. Try and discover if this is the case and then withhold food and milk for 24 hours, but allow the dog plenty of fresh drinking water to which a sachet of lectade can be added. This should normally clear up the problem and the dog can then gradually go back to a normal diet. However, diarrhoea can also be the symptom of more serious conditions and if the problem persists, or if the dog is obviously off colour, do not delay in contacting your vet.

ECLAMPSIA: This is also known as Milk Fever and needs *immediate* veterinary attention. The condition occurs in bitches occasionally in the later stages of pregnancy, but more commonly during lactation when the puppies are making very heavy demands on the bitch. Eclampsia is caused by abnormally low calcium levels in the blood, even when adequate amounts of calcium are given by mouth. The first signs are restlessness and rapid breathing. This is followed by shaking and a loss of co-ordination until the bitch collapses. If left unattended, the bitch will die. Treatment consists of an intravenous injection of calcium by the vet. This will usually lead to rapid improvement.

FLEAS: Even the best kept dogs can pick up fleas. Fleas are difficult to detect and it is usually easier to find the flea dirt on the skin. Typical places to look for the black specks are around the neck and just above the root of the tail. Dogs with fleas tend to scratch frequently and will bite at their coats. Treat the dog or dogs with flea powder or one of the much more efficient sprays or spot-ons, but always follow the instructions carefully. It is also important to treat the dog's bed, and the environment where eggs may have been laid, with an insecticide to prevent immediate re-infestation.

INFECTIOUS CANINE HEPATITIS
A highly contagious virus disease which can attack various organs, but particularly the liver. Symptoms include tonsillitis, high temperature, vomiting and diarrhoea, stomach pain and sometimes symptoms of jaundice. Prevention of the disease is through vaccination in puppyhood, followed by annual boosters.

INTERDIGITAL CYSTS: Small abscesses between the toes. Some Irish Setters seem to be particularly prone to developing interdigital cysts and will lick them continuously. Some are due to grass seeds. Bathe the foot twice a day in warm water to which some sea-salt has been added. Dry carefully and apply some antiseptic cream. Once the cyst has burst, it should heal quickly. A non-healing cyst should always be investigated – or if the dog is lame and off colour.

KENNEL COUGH: A virus disease which is characterised by the dog trying to clear the throat and a dry cough, sometimes accompanied by some frothy mucus. Healthy adults usually shake off kennel cough without any lasting problems. However, it can seriously affect young puppies and old dogs. Treatment is with antibiotics to prevent secondary infections and with cough suppressants. Kennel cough is highly infectious and dogs displaying any symptoms, as well as their kennel mates, should be kept away from shows or similar events for several weeks. Owners who continue to show their dogs, or allow them to mix with others when they have kennel cough, behave in an extremely selfish way as they are helping to spread the condition. Vaccination can be used to prevent the disease and is required by many boarding kennel owners.

LEPTOSPIROSIS: A bacterial disease of the dog which can also affect humans and other species. There are two strains of the disease. One is passed from rats to dogs and the other is passed from dog to dog. The latter, Leptospira canicola, is quite aptly known as "Lamppost Disease" as it is passed from dog to dog via sniffing urine. Vaccination of puppies and regular boosters are necessary to prevent the disease.

LICE: Adult lice feed on the dog's skin and lay eggs in the coat. Dogs with lice usually scratch at the area where lice are to be found, particularly around the neck and ears. Severe infestations can cause anaemia in young puppies. Treat in the same way as fleas.

MASTITIS: Mastitis is an infection of one or more of the mammary glands, usually associated with lactation. It can take some time before a bitch's milk supply becomes adjusted to the demand of her puppies and milk can build up, causing the teats to become inflamed. Check twice a day, by running your hands along a bitch's undercarriage, to make sure that there are no lumps or any inflammation. Ensure that the puppies are feeding from all the nipples, including those between the front legs. If any teats are infected, they will become hard and inflamed and hot to the touch. The condition is extremely painful and this can lead to a vicious circle as the bitch becomes more and more reluctant to feed her puppies and more milk builds up, adding further to the problem. Antibiotic treatment from the vet is required but owners should help their bitch by gently expressing some of the milk, several times a day.

METRITIS: This is a bacterial infection of the uterus, often caused by the retention of an afterbirth. A few days after whelping the bitch becomes restless and develops a temperature. Excessive drinking and a loss of appetite are other clinical signs. There is usually a discharge for several weeks after whelping, which is quite normal. However, the vaginal discharge caused by metritis is usually dark-green, rather copious and foul-smelling. Contact your vet immediately for treatment with antibiotics.

PARVOVIRUS INFECTION: This disease has only been recognised in dogs since 1978. There are two forms of the disease. Canine Parvovirus Myocarditis is a condition where the dam of a litter has not been vaccinated or has not been exposed to the disease to develop antibodies and therefore has no protection to pass on to her puppies. The virus attacks the heart muscle and seemingly healthy puppies can collapse and die. This form of CPV is becoming rarer as most bitches have developed some antibodies through vaccination or exposure to the disease.

The intestinal form of CPV is the most common form and can affect puppies and dogs of all ages. Symptoms are vomiting, abdominal pain, diarrhoea with blood content. Telephone your vet immediately. Keep the dog in isolation to reduce the risk of spreading the virus.

Owners should keep away from other dogs for the same reason. CPV is very difficult to eradicate and domestic bleach and formalin are the only disinfectants that can deal with CPV. Vaccination against CPV is essential.

POISONING: If you suspect that your Irish Setter has been poisoned, make the dog sick as quickly as possible. A mouthful of salt should do the trick. Ring your vet immediately, giving a clear account of what has happened. If you know the source of the poison, take the container with you to the surgery.

PHANTOM PREGNANCY (False pregnancy): This term describes the condition when bitches show signs of pregnancy, nursing or lactation despite the fact that they have not been mated or have failed to conceive. Bitches usually start to display signs about two months after their seasons, i.e. around the time when they would be having their puppies if they had been successfully mated. Bitches start to prepare beds, collect shoes and toys, produce milk and behave in an obviously maternal manner. Some bitches seem to have this problem after every season, but others never develop any signs. Exercise and long walks will usually take a bitch's mind off a "phantom". However, some bitches can become quite distressed and veterinary help has to be sought.

PYOMETRA: Symptoms of pyometra are a loss of appetite, excessive thirst and a raised temperature. It can occur in bitches of all ages, whether they have had a litter or not. The uterus fills up with pus and there is often a foul-smelling discharge from the vagina. This is an Open Pyometra which can be treated with antibiotics and does not necessarily need surgery. If the uterus remains closed, the situation is much more serious and an emergency operation may be needed to remove the uterus and the ovaries to save a bitch's life.

RABIES: A fatal infection which is transmitted through the saliva of many animals, with foxes being the most important carriers of infection in Europe where, for their protection, dogs have to be vaccinated annually. There is no treatment for rabies. To prevent rabies from entering the UK, strict quarantine laws are enforced and dogs and cats have to spend six months in special quarantine kennels before being allowed to be reunited with their owners. In the UK, vaccine is only available for dogs which are due to be exported, and for use in quarantine kennels. At present this law is under review and changes would appear to be on the horizon.

STINGS AND INSECT BITES: Irish Setters can become obsessed with chasing bees and wasps and seem to be completely unaware of the danger that this can involve. If the dog is stung by a bee, the sting is left behind and should be carefully removed with tweezers. Bathe the site with a mild antiseptic solution. Wasps do not leave their sting behind. If the dog was stung or bitten in the mouth, watch out for any swelling that may cause breathing difficulties and apply an ice-pack (a packet of frozen peas is excellent) on the way to the vet. Soluble Aspirin at 10 mg per kg bodyweight is also helpful, unless the dog is on other drugs.

TEMPERATURE: A dog's normal temperature is 38.5 degrees C (101.5 degrees F). Always disinfect the thermometer before and after use. Shake down the mercury, lubricate the thermometer with soap and insert the bulb into the dog's rectum. Keep a firm hold of the thermometer and make sure that the dog does not sit down. Leave the thermometer for at least one minute to get an accurate reading. Electronic thermometers are much easier to read.

TICKS: These are easily picked up when running through long grass, particularly in parts of the country where sheep are reared. Ticks can vary in size and colour, but they all dig their heads into the dog's body and feed off the blood. Do not pull them off, as they leave their heads embedded in the dog, which can cause infections. To remove ticks, soak them in surgical spirit which will make them loosen their grip so that the mouth and head can be removed intact with a twisting action, as if you were unscrewing them.

WORMS: A variety of parasites can infest dogs, but four are particularly common in all breeds of dogs in the UK. They are the following:

The roundworm (Toxocara canis), which has become the topic of concern to humans. A round, white worm varying in length between seven and fifteen centimetres (three to six inches). Treatment and prevention involves routine worming of all your dogs and careful kennel hygiene. Pick up and burn all the droppings and always wash your hands after handling dogs.

The tapeworm – Dipylidium canium. This is a segmented tapeworm and occurs in the small intestine of the dog. Fleas are a necessary part of the life-cycle of the tapeworm. (See advice on flea prevention.) A dog that looks out of condition and is thin and in poor coat despite eating well, may have a tapeworm; small segments of the worm can often be found in the faeces of the dog or on the coat. Dogs can also pick up other types of tapeworm from sheep and rabbits. Effective tapeworm treatment can only be obtained from a vet. Tablets bought in a pet shop are inefficient.

Hookworm and Whipworm: Both are far less common than roundworm and tapeworm. However, if an Irish Setter has been correctly wormed against both, but still remains in poor condition, the dog could be suffering from either hookworm or whipworm or both. It is a

Sh. Ch. Scarletti Cockney Rebel and Sh. Ch. Scarletti Hot Chocolate aged 11 years.

simple matter to have a faeces test done by your vet and treatment against both types of parasites is effective.

Heartworm infection is spread by a mosquito which is not found in the UK. Mosquitoes deposit larvae under the dog's skin which burrow into a vein, from where they travel to the right side of the heart. There they can live for years, blocking the flow of blood, eventually causing heart failure. There may be no symptoms for months or even years. Most frequent signs are a cough, fainting after exercise, lack of energy and bloodstained sputum. A blood test will establish if heartworm is present.

CARE OF THE AGEING DOG

As time marches on Irish Setters, just like their owners, will start to slow down and will want to take life a little easier. The average life-span of an Irish Setter is about twelve years but, if you are fortunate enough, some will stay fit and well for longer. My longest-lived, Dougal, very nearly managed to celebrate his 15th birthday. To some extent longevity is hereditary, but good care and freedom from congenital diseases contribute to it. I usually find that my oldies remain keen on their daily exercise, but then tend to sleep much more between their outings than in their younger days. I do not really like to deprive them of their exercise and I allow them as much freedom as they want. Oldies know how to pace themselves and mine would be desperately disappointed and quite unhappy if they could not join in with the younger Setters. Because we also go out on rainy days, I put a light-weight, waterproof coat on the pensioners, especially on bitches that have been spayed. After such an operation coats often become heavy and woolly and, once wet, they take a very long time to dry out properly. Make sure you dry off the dogs carefully after a wet walk, but most of all, the elderly Irish. Arthritis is a common complaint in the older dog, and the wet and cold do not help the condition.

FEEDING

Older dogs have different nutritional requirements from younger ones and their food should be adjusted accordingly. The amount of protein in their diet should be reduced – they do not need it. There is nothing worse than a stout and overweight Irish Setter, and waistlines should be watched. Some older dogs develop an obsession for food, but it should be remembered that a correctly fed and exercised dog is far less likely to develop heart disease. Most of the major petfood manufacturers have recognised that there is a growing market for

Am. Dual Ch. Kerrycourt's Rose O'Cidermill.

special diets which cater for the senior dog, and some of their products are excellent. They tend to contain more fish oils to maintain good mobility, different calcium and phosphorus levels, as well as extra vitamin B and E to meet the changing needs of older dogs, and all are specially formulated to be easily digestible.

HEALTH CARE

Various ailments can afflict older dogs and many of their conditions are very similar to those of the ageing human! If you have any worries, get your vet to give your Irish Setter a check-up. Teeth can become a problem and excess tartar can quickly build up. This should be removed and if the dog has been used to having the teeth cleaned throughout life, it will be much easier to keep them in good condition in later years. If there is a bad tooth, it is better to have it taken out before the dog gets too old, because of the anaesthetic that will be required.

Do not allow older dogs to lie on concrete or other rough surfaces. Hocks and elbows can easily develop painful calluses. Place the beds in different places for the dogs to go to. This will also stop them from sitting on cold floors and getting a chill. Old Irish Setters have a great capacity for sleeping very soundly and snoring very loudly. They seem to become oblivious to their surroundings and therefore should not be startled and woken up suddenly. Senility can become a problem with old dogs, and some can become extremely intolerant and demanding. I well remember Dougal's behaviour around feeding time. He would bark incessantly until he became so hoarse that his bark was really no more than a squeak. Once he had eaten, he became quite a reasonable old gent again – until the next meal-time! Fortunately, most older Irish Setters just want to be cherished, and they appreciate all the extra little comforts that we can give them.

AT THE END OF THE DAY

The day will come when even your best care and attention will no longer be enough for your old Irish Setter and the decision will have to be made to have your old companion put to sleep. It is very selfish to let dogs go on for too long and it is our responsibility to prevent them from having to suffer. The decision is so very hard to make and does not get any easier but, at the end of the day, it is the very last kind act that we can perform for our dogs. When the day arrives, I always have my vet come to the house where everything is familiar, and I hold the old dog in my arms when the final injection is given. Inevitably, there are tears but they are mixed with a sense of relief that there is no more suffering for a faithful friend. I once read somewhere that it is better to make the final decision rather a day too early than an hour too late – and often, with a very heavy heart, I have had to agree. Our dogs are always laid to rest at home, and we are fortunate to have a very large garden where they can be buried in a favourite spot. For owners without the space, pet cremation provides an excellent alternative.

12 *SHOW CHAMPION KERRYFAIR NIGHT FEVER*

All through the history of the Irish Setter important dogs have left their mark on the breed and have influenced its development. However, in modern times, no other dog has been more influential than Show Champion Kerryfair Night Fever. The fact that this important dog was bred, owned and campaigned by a complete novice should not only give heart to anyone just starting out on a career in dogs, but also demonstrates what an open breed the Irish Setter is. Anyone can make it to the top – provided, of course, that their dog is good enough!

Sandra Chorley bought Night Fever's mother, Cornevon Spring Melody, from Janice Roberts in 1977. She was her second bitch, but the first one that she had bought for show and, according to Sandra, "she made all my dreams come true." She won very well in Puppy and Junior and went on to win a Res. CC. Sandra was keen to breed an Irish Setter that would carry her own prefix, Kerryfair, so Spring Melody was mated to Sh. Ch. Sowerhill Sahib. He was chosen because Sandra felt that his glamour would complement what her beautiful Spring Melody lacked a little. She thought it was as simple as that – and she was right!

The litter was born on September 30th 1979 and a dog puppy named Mack was kept. As a

youngster he was slow to get going and did not set the world alight until he won the Reserve CC under Mr W. Parkinson at Birmingham National in May 1981. He gained two more Res. CCs that year, including one from Mr W. Rasbridge at Leeds who wrote in glowing terms about the dog. This was quite unusual and surprised most people who had been used to his rather more critical show-reports.

Mack started 1982 with CC and Best of Breed at Crufts from Miss Hunt, but did not score again until Manchester 1983 where he was Best of Breed and won the Group. He won his third CC and Best of Breed at the West of England Ladies Kennel Society and won the Group again. Further Groups followed at Manchester and at the Scottish Kennel Club in 1984 and at the same show again in 1985. His great show career lasted until he was eleven years old, when Jim Smith awarded Mack his 26th CC at the Irish Setter Association England Championship Show in October 1990. This was a second CC from this judge, who could find nothing to beat him on that day.

Night Fever's show career was outstanding by any standard, but his career as a stud dog was even more remarkable. He was not line-bred, which made it impossible for any

Sh. Ch. Kerryfair Night Fever   *Photo: R. Willbie.*

		Sh. Ch. Wendover Ballymoss
	Sh. Ch. Wendover Jeeves	
Sh. Ch. Sowerhill Sahib		Wendover Lupina
		Sh. Ch. Stephenshill Gamebird
	Sh. Ch. Sowerhill Sarah	
		Sowerhill Samantha

Sh. Ch. KERRYFAIR NIGHT FEVER

		Sh. Ch. Wynjill Red Robin
	Wynjill Country Woodland	
Cornevon Spring Melody		Sh. Ch. Cornevon Woodsprite
		Sh. Ch. Twoacres Troilus
	Cornevon Tamarind	
		Sh. Ch. Cornevon Primrose

Photo: Oakley.

particular strain or kennel to lay claim to him, but his pedigree contained a string of beautiful Irish Setters. His first litter was born in July 1981 and his last on October 19th, 1990. His time at stud was interrupted by yet another PRA scare, without foundation, in 1988, but he sired a total of 796 puppies, of which 708 were registered at the Kennel Club – a change in the registration system accounts for the discrepancy. From that number came 23 Show Champions, five winners of two CCs, one of which became an Irish Champion, plus a further twelve individual CC winners in the UK.

However, his influence was not restricted to the UK alone, but has been significant in many other countries. These are impressive statistics, but they do not reflect that he was successful on bitches of *all* bloodlines. A prepotent sire, he had the ability to produce a high percentage of

NIGHT FEVER'S PROGENY

Sh. Ch. Fearnley Firecedar.
Born: 10.2.1982.
Dam: Sh. Ch. Fearnley Firegem.
Breeders: Pat and Barry Rhodes.
Owner: Elsa Taylor.

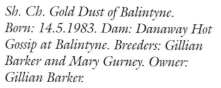

Sh. Ch. Gold Dust of Balintyne.
Born: 14.5.1983. Dam: Danaway Hot Gossip at Balintyne. Breeders: Gillian Barker and Mary Gurney. Owner: Gillian Barker.

Sh. Ch. Wickenberry Knight at Arms.
Born: 15.11.1982.
Dam: Sh. Ch. Wickenberry Baroness. Breeder: Jean Quinn. Owner: Pat Butler.

LEFT: Sh. Ch. Ma Biche of Danaway.
Born: 14.5.1983.
Dam: Danaway Hot Gossip at Balintyne.
Breeders: Gillian Barker and Mary Gurney. Owners: Brian and Mary Gurney.

Sh. Ch. Royal Archer.
Born: 8.10.1983.
Dam: Westerhuy's Red Symphony.
Breeder: Hammond. Owner: Ruth Lewis.
Photo: David Dalton.

Sh. Ch. Amberwave
Moonlight Shadow.
Born: 13.11.1983.
Dam: Sh. Ch. Amberwave
Hera.
Breeders/Owners: John and
Maggie Powis.

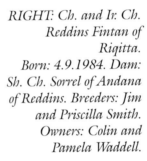

LEFT: Sh. Ch.
Laggan Macbie Lady.
Born: 29.4.1984.
Dam: Laggan Janek's
Jem.
Owner/Breeder:
Norma Marshall.

Sh. Ch. Ballywestow Borealis.
Born: 8.6.1984.
Dam: Sh. Ch. Ballywestow
Pawneese.
Breeder/Owner: Judy Russell.
Photo: Claire Prangle.

RIGHT: Ch. and Ir. Ch.
Reddins Fintan of
Riqitta.
Born: 4.9.1984. Dam:
Sh. Ch. Sorrel of Andana
of Reddins. Breeders: Jim
and Priscilla Smith.
Owners: Colin and
Pamela Waddell.

LEFT: Sh. Ch.
Reddins Ferdinand.
Born: 4.9.1984.
Dam: Sh. Ch. Sorrel
of Andana of
Reddins.
Breeders/Owners: Jim
and Priscilla Smith.

Sh. Ch. Caskeys Justin.
Born: 22.10.1984.
Dam: Caskeys Babette.
Breeders: Bob and Christine
Heron. Owner: Jill Cooke.

Sh. Ch. Bardonhill
Kiss-A-Gram.
Born: 27.4.1985
Dam: Moyna April at
Bardonhill.
Breeder/Owner:
Marita Bott.
Photo: Mike Oakley.

Sh. Ch. Navylark Naiad.
Born: 28.5.1985.
Dam: Navylark Hermione.
Breeders/Owners: Bob and
Win Laurie.

RIGHT: Sh. Ch. and
Ir. Sh. Ch. Glencarron
Macallan.
Born: 1.1.1986.
Dam:Glencarron Lady
of the Lake.
Breeders/Owners:
David and Betty
Laidlaw.

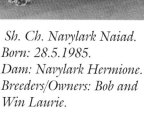

Sh. Ch. Brayville Dynamic
Delegate.
Born: 12.3.1986.
Dam: Brayville Regal Glory.
Breeders/Owners: John and
Ruth Ellis.
Photo: Tracy Vincent.

RIGHT: Sh. Ch.
Brayville Demure
Debutante.
Born:12.3.1986.
Dam: Brayville Regal
Glory.
Breeders/Owners: John
and Ruth Ellis.
Photo: Bob Foyle.

RIGHT: Sh. Ch.
Dunnygask Red
Grouse.
Born: 2.5.1986.
Dam: Sh. Ch.
Dunnygask Spirit of
Spring.
Breeder: Ailsa Harvey.
Owner: Debbie Fryer.

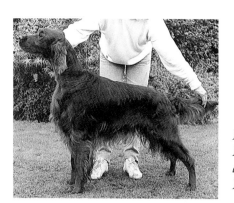

LEFT: Sh. Ch. Danaway Debonair. Born: 27.2.1987.
Dam: Sh. Ch. Disco Dancer of Danaway.Breeders: Brian
and Mary Gurney. Owner: Jackie Lorrimer.
Photo: Anne Roslin-Williams.

Sh. Ch. Bardonhill Splashdown.
Born: 20.3.1987.
Dam: Barleydale Ooh La La It's Bardonhill.
Breeder: Marita Bott. Owners: Peter and
Chantal Walker.

Sh. Ch. Caspians Night Music.
Born: 22.12.1988.
Dam: Wendover Cassidy.
Owners/Breeders: Mike and Sue Oakley.
Photo: Claire Prangle.

winners from most of his bitches. This success won him the Irish Setter Breeders' Club Mars Stud Dog Trophy from 1983 to 1993, but his greatest achievement was to become Top Stud Dog *all breeds* from 1987 to 1991 – an astonishing five years in succession! I spoke to the editor of one of the dog papers after Mack had died and discovered that his staff had laid bets on the number of puppies he had sired. Most of their forecasts had run into thousands and the relatively small number of offspring caused considerable surprise.

When, on April 4th 1994, the day came that Sandra had to say good-bye to the great dog, by now aged fourteen-and-a-half, she was very distressed and telephoned me during her wait

for the vet. As already mentioned, in the late 1980s the breed had experienced a PRA scare which, had it been correct, could have had a disastrous effect. The DNA blood-testing for RCD-1 was just getting under way at the time when I spoke to Sandra, and I discovered that she had earlier allowed a blood sample to be taken from Mack and that it would be tested. She was a concerned owner to the end – but the blood sample was subsequently found to be normal. I am convinced that none of us will see his like again during our life-time, and the extent of Night Fever's enormous influence will become clear when the leading modern kennels are reviewed.

RIGHT: Sh. Ch.
Bardonhill Sea Breeze
over Thendara.
Born: 20.3.1987.
Dam: Barleydale Ooh
La La It's Bardonhill.
Breeder: Marita Bott.
Owner: Dee Milligan.

13 IRISH SETTERS IN BRITAIN & IRELAND

Writing about leading Irish Setter kennels is a large undertaking as the breed is now in the hands of many small but highly successful breeders. In the past, the breeding and showing of successful Irish Setters had mainly been dominated by a few large kennels. Nowadays, breeders tend to keep a small number of dogs, usually in the house, and visitors to famous 'kennels' are surprised to find a few high-quality dogs sharing their owners' settees! When Janice Roberts had the leading kennel and was beating the great establishments, her then husband told a novice exhibitor: "Janice has made it possible for ordinary people to be successful in Irish Setters."

Due to the size of the project, I have concentrated on show kennels that have made up at least three Show Champions. There are many good kennels that produce Irish Setters of quality, but winning three CCs under three different judges in very hot competition is a great achievement. This is confirmed by the very small number of Irish Setters that become Show Champions: in 1994 there were nine, in 1995 there were ten and in 1996 only five made it to the top. During each year, 37 sets of CCs were available.

AMBERWAVE: JOHN AND MAGGIE POWIS
The foundation bitch, Katherine of Audnam, arrived in 1974. She was mated to Dunfarlyne's Peppercorn and Sh. Ch. Amberwave Hera was born in 1978. Hera went to Night Fever and produced Sh. Ch. Amberwave Moonlight Shadow, winner of the Group at Manchester 1989. From Katherine's litter by Sh. Ch. Brinara Inula came Whispering Wind. When Katherine was mated to Sh. Ch. Clonageera Tyrone she produced Sh. Ch. Amberwave Pebbles. The highlight of her career was to win her fourth CC at Crufts in 1997 from the Veteran class for dogs aged seven years or older. Pebbles only had one litter by Sh. Ch. Clonageera Genesis, and their daughter, Lace, born in 1994, is now carrying on the line.

BALINTYNE: GILLIAN BARKER-BELL
Danaway Hot Gossip, one CC, was acquired from the Gurneys and owned in partnership with Mary Gurney. When mated to Night Fever she produced Sh. Ch. Ma Biche of Danaway for Mary, and Sh. Ch. Gold Dust of Balintyne for Gillian. Gold Dust was mated to Free Spirit of Danaway, and Sh. Ch. Balintyne Call Me Madam and her brother Call My Tune, two CCs, three Res. CCs, were retained. Hot

Gossip's daughter, Starduster, won a CC and Res. CC before being exported to New Zealand. Where she became a Champion.

BALLYWESTOW: JUDY RUSSELL

In 1956 Judy persuaded her parents to let her have an Irish Setter. Wendover Romance was bought unseen and has remained Judy's only purchase. She won her first CC in 1961, gaining five in total. At the grand age of eleven she ran for her qualifier and became a Champion. An excellent brood bitch, from her first litter came Ballywestow Sceptre, one CC. However, her most successful litters were all by Sh. Ch. Wendover Vagabond and several matings produced Show Champions Wendover Ballymoss and Brulette, Ballywestow Wendover Beeswing, one CC, three Res. CCs, Dante, Res. CC. and Sh. Ch. Timadon Ballywestow Festoon. Judy retained Frieze, another successful brood, and dam of a CC winner, and Show Champions Kelso and Keyso, whose successful progeny won her the Romance Brood Bitch Trophy, 1980. Her litter to Sh. Ch. Twoacres Wayward Caesar contained Show Champion triplets Ballywestow Persimmon of Oldestone, Petite Etoile and Pawneese. The latter was mated to Night Fever and produced Sh. Ch. Borealis, winner of the Contest of Champions 1988. Pawneese was also mated to Sh. Ch. Sowerhill Satyr of Fearnley and Judy retained Absurdity, who produced the Show

Champion twins Forego and Fleet. A Frieze grand-daughter, Ornament, became the dam of Sh. Ch. The Tetrarch, winner of nine CCs and six Res. CCs. The Ballywestows have always enjoyed life as house-dogs.

BARDONHILL: MARITA BOTT

First established in 1970, all the winning Bardonhills are descended from Moyna April at Bardonhill, born in 1978. From her first litter came Sh. Ch. Bardonhill Supergrass, 11 CCs, two Res.CCs, and Marita acquired his daughter, Barleydale Ooh-La-La It's Bardonhill. Mated to Night Fever, she produced two Show Champions, the Reserve Group winner Bardonhill Seabreeze Over Thendara and Bardonhill Splashdown. Another sister produced a Show Champion and Overboard gained his Ir. Sh. Ch. title. April was also mated to Night Fever, resulting in Sh. Ch. Bardonhill Kiss-A-Gram, Best of Breed, Crufts 1990, as well as the CC winner Bardonhill April Love at Brayville. Kiss-A-Gram was mated to Free Spirit of Danaway and produced Sh. Ch. Bardonhill Team Spirit at Wynjill. The current team includes a litter sister to Team Spirit, Kiss-Me-Quick, dam of Winds of Future and Bardonhill Snow Joke by Sh. Ch. Shenanagin Stockbroker. Marita has now bought in a dog who goes back to two Bardonhill Show Champions, Supergrass and Team Spirit.

Pictured left to right: Sh. Ch. Ballywestow Pawneese, Sh. Ch. Ballywestow Diadem, Sh. Ch. Ballywestow Borealis and Sh. Ch. Ballywestow The Tetrarch.

BARLEYDALE: JOHN AND SHELAGH VANT

In 1968 Twoacres Teresa was bought and she won her title and the CC at Crufts in 1972. Difficult to get into whelp, she was mated to her brother Sh. Ch. Troilus and the CC winner Lucetta was retained. From Teresa's second litter, by Crimbledale Commanchero, Barnadine was kept and mated to Lucetta which provided the Barleydales' basis. Twoacres Triton arrived, aged four, and won two CCs and one Res. CC, but does not figure in the lines. Lucetta was next mated to Sh. Ch. Sowerhill Sahib and produced Mustard Seed, who was put back to Barnadine. Their daughter Mopsa had a litter by Sh. Ch. Bardonhill Supergrass and produced Sh. Ch. Barleydale Pascali, CC at Crufts 1990. He sired Kalymnos, CC, and Sh. Ch. Barleydale Polgara, eight CCs and 11 Res. CCs. Pascali also produced Sh. Ch. Wickenberry Pretty Polly and, when he was mated to Ir. Ch. Wickenberry Nightingale, five litter mates became Irish Champions.

Sh. Ch. Sowerhill Nobleman.

Sh. Ch. Barleydale Polgara.

BONHOMIE: BONNIE ANDREWS

In 1973 Bonnie bought her first Irish Setter, a bitch, from a puppy farm but she was consistently placed at Open Shows. Two Sowerhill bitches arrived, but the real breakthrough came in 1983 with Sowerhill Nobleman. By Sh. Ch. Jason of Andana of Clonageera ex Fearnley Fire Ember of Sowerhill, Nobleman won 10 CCs and five Res. CCs. He was a special dog, and all subsequent stock is descended from him. When used on Clonageera Holly he sired Sh. Ch. Clonageera Forget Me Not, CC at Crufts 1991. She was mated to Sh. Ch. Clonageera Genesis and produced Sh. Ch. Bonhomie Forgotten Dream. In 1988 Bonnie bought Marksway Marquis from Mr and Mrs Martin Russell. A grandson of Nobleman, he won 27 CCs and 26 Res. CCs. The winner of several Groups, he also won Best in Show at Group Championship Shows and Res. BIS at General Championship Shows. Marquis won the CC and BOB from the Veteran class at Crufts in 1997, providing Bonnie with the most emotional moment of her career in dogs.

BRAYVILLE: JOHN AND RUTH ELLIS

John and Ruth acquired an Irish Setter dog in 1974. Moyna Ladybird followed and won well but, due to an injury, was retired early. However, her daughter by Sh. Ch. Brinara Inula provided the foundation for the Brayvilles. Regal Glory, two Res. CCs, was mated to Night Fever and her litter of six puppies contained two Show Champions, Brayville Dynamic Delegate, nine CCs, five Res. CCs, and Demure Debutante, as well as Dynamic Diplomat, one CC, two Res CCs. In 1986 Bardonhill April Love at Brayville, one CC, two Res. CCs, joined the family. By Night Fever ex Moyna April at Bardonhill, she had a litter by Delegate and produced Sh. Ch. Private Affair. Demure Debutante was mated to Sh. Ch. Bardonhill Team Spirit at Wynjill, and Fashion Leader, Res. CC, was retained to carry on the line. Numbers are limited as all the dogs live indoors, and only five litters have been bred to date.

CARNBARGUS: EVE GARDNER
This is my own kennel and all my Irish Setters descend from Sh. Ch. Carnbargus Hartsbourne O'Brady, born in 1966, and his daughter Red Sarah, born in 1970. Another O'Brady daughter, Sh. Ch. Carnbargus Hartsbourne Mattie was made up and her daughter Starlight won a CC and Res. CC. From Red Sarah came Red Silk, the winner of one CC and three Res. CCs. Her daughter, Racing Silk, three Res. CCs, had a litter by Glentarkie Craven-A which contained Champion Cashmere. She gained her qualifier in April 1989 and also ran in two novice stakes. Cashmere was mated to Night Fever and produced Charisma, who went to Sh. Ch. Shenanagin Stockbroker. Their daughter Sh. Ch. Continuity was born in 1994. From Cashmere's second litter came Cordelia, the winner of two CCs. She died tragically young, when aged only three.

CASKEYS: BOB AND CHRISTINE HERON
The first dog was bought in 1965. Bred by

Sh. Ch. Caskeys Zoe.

Miss Besford, of Wendover breeding and registered under that prefix, the puppy was destined to become Sh. Ch. Wendover Caskey, eight CCs and five Res. CCs. Caskeys Cleoni, the foundation bitch, came from a litter by Sh. Ch. Caskey ex Sh. Ch. Joanmas Lottie. Cleoni was mated to her half-brother and produced Sh. Ch. Zoe. The Herons think she was their best bitch and feel that her head was perfection. Her grand-daughter Sh. Ch. Pollyanna of Caskeys won eight CCs and four Res. CCs, which gained her the Quebec Trophy for winning the most CCs during 1979. Her daughter Babette proved to be a great brood bitch and won the Pedigree Chum Top Breeders award for Bob and Christine in 1985. She produced Show Champions Caskeys Pandora and Bo Jo, as well as Pagan, three Res. CCs. The CC winner Burgandy was unfortunately killed in an accident. From Babette's litter by Night Fever came Sh. Ch. Caskeys Justin, Jazzman, one CC, and Jezamy, six Res. CCs. Sh. Ch. Caskeys Humming Bird is the latest title-holder and Caskeys Blarney, Res. CC, is winning well. Dogs owned or bred by Bob and Christine have won 49 CCs.

CASPIANS: MIKE AND SUE OAKLEY
The first dog arrived in 1972 and two bitches, Cornevon Rainbow and Starbright, followed.

Breeding was based on Cornevon/Wendover lines. Caspians Snowdrop was mated to Wendover Washington of Caspians and produced Coppertop Wendy. Her daughter, Wendover Cassidy, was acquired, and mated to Night Fever, which in 1988 produced Night Music. Music's first litter by Free Spirit of Danaway contained Sh. Ch. Caspians The Music Man of Danaway and Finian's Rainbow, two Res. CCs. From her second litter by Sh. Ch. Danaway Debonair came Sh. Ch. Caspians Intrepid, 40 CCs and numerous Group and Best in Show wins; also Caspians Grace, two CCs. A repeat mating in 1995 produced Basilio, one CC. Music won 14 CCs, seven Res. CCs, a Gundog Group and BIS at the Setter & Pointer Ch. Show in 1992. In 1997 she gained the ISBC's Brood Bitch Trophy for the fourth time and has been *Dog World's* Top Irish Setter Brood Bitch for the last three years. Her winning offspring have enabled the Oakleys to become Top Irish Setter Breeders for the last three years.

CLONAGEERA: JIM AND PAT RUTHERFORD
The first bitch, Tralee of Andana, had to be returned to Joan Anderson when the Rutherfords went to live abroad. A new start was made with Bridie of Andana but it was Bella Rosa, born in 1971, who put the Clonageeras on the map. A Gentleman daughter, she won five CCs, two Res. CCs and a Gundog Group. Joan Anderson gave Jim Sh. Ch. Jason of Andana of Clonageera, CC winner Crufts 1981. He has left his mark as the sire of ten Show Champions – a great record for a little-used dog, making his owners Top Breeders in 1983 and 1984. A Bella Rosa daughter, Tamoretta, became the main brood bitch and, when mated to Jason, produced three Show Champions – Clonageera Tarka, Tyrone and Rebecca. Another Tamoretta daughter, Holly, by Westerhuys Dutch

Sh. Ch. Clonageera Stella.
Photo: Libra Photographic / Yvonne Kent.

Impression, produced Sh. Ch. Clonageera Forget Me Not and Friday's Child, one CC. Tamoretta is also the grand-dam of Sh. Ch. Clonageera Samantha. It was decided to mate Bella Rosa to Jason and the result was Sh. Ch. Clonageera Megan, whom the Rutherfords consider to have been their best to date. Her son Sh. Ch. Genesis, by Sh. Ch. Sowerhill Sahib, proved to be prepotent and is the sire of five Show Champions. Germaine was mated to Andana Jake and produced Sh. Ch. Clonageera Stella, dam of several winning youngsters. Pat and Jim have bred or owned 10 Show Champions.

DANAWAY: BRIAN AND MARY GURNEY
In 1972 Wendover Colas was bought as a family pet. By Sh. Ch. Wendover Gentleman, he won seven CCs, including Crufts 1977, a Gundog Group and a Reserve Group. Not extensively used, Colas produced three Show Champions. He was Dog World's Top Irish Setter Sire 1984 and all Danaways are descended from him. Wendover Happy Days was bought and her daughter, Royal Charm, was mated to Free Spirit of Danaway. Their daughter, Danaway Hot Gossip at Balintyne, one CC, was owned by Mary and Gillian Barker. Mated to Night Fever, she produced

Sh. Ch. Disco Dancer of Danaway.

Show Champions Ma Biche of Danaway and Gold Dust of Balintyne. Free Spirit, by Colas ex Westerhuy's Dutch Spirit, won the *Our Dogs* Top Sire Competition for the Breed in 1990. He sired five Show Champions, a dual CC winner and a CC winner. The second Colas/Dutch Spirit mating produced Sh. Ch. Disco Dancer of Danaway: an excellent producer, she won the ISBC Brood Bitch Trophy three times and was *Dog World's* Top Brood Bitch 1991. Her first litter contained Sh. Ch. Danaway Baccante and her second litter, by Night Fever, Sh. Ch. Danaway Debonair. He is the joint breed record holder with 40 CCs, winner of many Groups and Best in Show awards, including Crufts 1993. The Gurneys rate him as their best. His sister Danielle, two CCs, two Res. CCs, was unlucky not to get made up, as was Cornevon Dreamgirl, one CC, seven Res. CCs. The Gurneys were *Our Dogs* Top Breeders in 1991, and dogs owned or bred by them have won 91 CCs.

DELSANTO: CHRIS SHELDON

Chris bought Fondador Martinique in 1979 and she became the foundation bitch for her Delsantos. Bred by Mrs G.G. Follows, Martinique was by Sh. Ch. Shaytell Goldfinch ex Fondador Manyana. As a mate for her second litter Chris chose Sh. Ch. Erinade Scottish Union because "the very famous Sh. Ch. Fondador Charlene had been bred from a Fondador bitch and Scottish Union." The idea worked and produced Sh. Ch. Delsanto Cassandra, five CCs, seven Res. CCs and Best in Show at the Merseyside Gundog Club Championship Show 1989. Cassandra had a fertility problem, but her second litter, of only four puppies, by Bardonhill Fido, contained Sh. Ch. Delsanto Roxanne, CC at Crufts 1996, owned by Chris, and Sh. Ch. Romarna owned by Lynn Muir. Roxanne's first litter to Sh. Ch. Marksway Marquis contained Lucinda, three Res. CCs, and her brother, Luke, one CC and two Res. CCs. to date.

DUNNYGASK: AILSA HARVEY

Ailsa bought her first Irish Setter as a pet but decided to improve her stock. The real turning point came when Ailsa acquired Westerhuy's Dutch Spirit, by Sh. Ch. Cornevon Lovebird ex Sh. Ch. Cornevon Westerhuy's Cloggy. Her two litters by Sh. Ch. Wendover Colas were of considerable importance and all the subsequent Dunnygasks go back to that combination. Sh. Ch. Dunnygask Spirit of Spring was retained from the first mating. Her litter to Fearnley Bucks Fizz produced Dunnygask Vital Spark, CC and BOB Crufts 1992, and sire of a CC winner. His sister Tutti Frutti was mated to Sh. Ch. Shenanagin Stockbroker and produced Sh. Ch. Dunnygask Verbena, owned by David and Sandra Christian. Tutti Frutti's litter by Sh. Ch. Caspians Intrepid contained Gladiator, two

Sh. Ch. Delsanto Roxanne.
Photo: Claire Prangle.

Sh. Ch. Dunnygask Spirit of Spring.
Photo: Rab Munro.

Res. CCs. Spirit of Spring was mated to Night Fever and Dunnygask Red Grouse gained his title for Debbie Fryer. His sister Skylark was mated back to Free Spirit and produced Sh. Ch. Dunnygask New Dawn. Her daughter Allegra, by Sh. Ch. Reddins Ferdinand, is the winner of two CCs. Ailsa is the breeder of five Show Champions.

DUNROON: PETER HEARD
(Field Trial kennel).
Joanma's Adriano was bought as a pet in 1965. By Wendover Game, his dam was of pure Sulhamstead breeding. Adriano was trained for work and was most unlucky not to gain his dual title. Aged five, he went to his first show, the LKA, and won the CC and Best of Breed with further CCs at Crufts and Windsor. Together with his son, FT winner Pheasant of Dunroon, he won the famous English Setter Club Brace Trophy. His grand-daughter Joanma's Una was mated to FT Ch. Glenside Red Hugh and produced FT Jelmara of Dunroon who, unfortunately, died very young. Peter acquired the great bitch FT Ch. Drumshane Agatha and mated her to Jelmara's brother to produce the FT prize winner Dunroon Aurora, the dam of

Dunroon Kestrel, a great shooting bitch. Peter aims, by line-breeding back to the Sulhamsteads, to produce good-looking Irish Setters that can work.

FEARNLEY: PAT RHODES
Brackenfield Sweep arrived in 1963 and two more Brackenfields followed. Flax was mated to Hartsbourne Comet but her daughter Firefly was put to a complete outcross, Sh. Ch. Wendover Racketeer, and produced Sh. Ch. Fearnley Fireflight. The most important bitch, Sh. Ch. Fearnley Firecracker, was bought in 1965 for the princely sum of £5.00 and all the subsequent Fearnleys go back to her. In one of her two litters to Sh. Ch. Wendover Gentleman she produced Firesprite, the dam of Sh. Ch. Fearnley Firecinders of Dallowgill. Elsa Taylor campaigned Sh. Ch. Fearnley Firegem and won the Gundog Group at Manchester 1979 and Reserve Group at the WELKS 1980. One of her sons, Sh. Ch. Fearnley Firecedar, won Best in Show at the Setter & Pointer Club Championship Show, and Platinum won a CC. Sh. Ch. Fearnley Fireflare was made up after being returned to Pat and Barry. By Sowerhill Valentine, the Sowerhills were to play an important role. Sowerhill Satyr of Fearnley was

Sh. Ch. Sowerhill Satyr of Fearnley: Winner of 31 CCs. Photo: Anne Roslin-Wiliams.

bought and with 31 CCs he became the then Breed Record Holder; the winner of several Groups, he retired after Best in Show, Leicester 1984. Fearnley breeding has provided many kennels with their foundation stock. Since Barry's untimely death in March 1996, Pat has made up the Group winner Sh. Ch. Fearnley Firehurricane.

Sh. Ch. Inisheer Falcon.
Photo: Carol Ann Johnson.

GOLDINGS: GORDON AND BIDDY EVANS

The first Irish Setter puppy was bought from the Wendover Kennel in 1966. Pretty Jane, by Wendover Glade ex Wendover Katie was mated to Sh. Ch. Wendover Vagabond, producing the first Goldings litter. Two puppies were retained and Lord Grumpy of Goldings and Wendover Bonnie became the foundation stock for the Goldings. Bonnie was mated to Sh. Ch. Twoacres Troilus and produced the first Show Champion, Goldings Joss Cambier, owned by Mrs Y. Edwards. A Lord Grumpy grand-daughter, Carek Holly at Goldings, was mated to Sh. Ch. Jason of Andana of Clonageera and produced Sh. Ch. Goldings Heike, nine CCs and seven Res. CCs. She was mated to Goldings Oliver and from this litter came Sh. Ch. Goldings Hella.

INISHEER: PETER, YVETTE AND MICHELLE EDWARDS

The Inisheers were established in 1965 with Atlanta of Hedgeway. In 1971, Goldings Joss Cambier joined the Inisheers and was made up in 1975. He was tragically killed within days of gaining his title. In 1981 Rhythm of Andana was obtained from Joan Anderson's Andana Kennel. A good winner, she proved herself an excellent brood bitch and when mated to Joanma's Solo she produced Sh. Ch. Inisheer Flamingo. A great laster, he won a Championship Show Veteran Gundog Group aged eleven. His litter sister Kiwi won two CCs and one Res. CC, and had a litter to Fearnley

Fireflyer. Harmony, one CC and one Res. CC, was retained and when mated back to Flamingo, she produced Show Champion Inisheer Falcon. Flamingo is also the sire of Sh. Ch. Laggan Macbie Lady. Numbers have always been limited to six dogs at a time, and it is hoped that Shana, by Falcon, will continue the line.

JOANMA'S: MRS MARJORIE JAROSZ

The first bitch, of Boyne breeding, was acquired in 1945. Wendover Game was bought in 1963 when aged two-and-a-half years and won two CCs and five Res. CCs. However, his greatest success came as a highly influential

Sh. Ch. Joanma's Scampi.

Four of a kind (pictured left to right): Sh. Ch. Kirkavagh Corejada, Sh. Ch. Fearnley Fireheather of Kirkavagh, Sh. Ch. Kirkavagh Zabara and Sh. Ch. Kirkavagh Musidora.

stud dog. His winning progeny enabled him to become the Breed's leading sire in 1967/68/69. His many winners included Show Champions Scotswood Barabbas, Cornevon Prince Charming and Cinderella, Joanma's Lottie and Joanma's Kayla. Game was also the producer of dual-purpose stock including Ch. Joanma's Adriano, bred by Mrs R. Silverman, and owned by Peter Heard. In 1970 Mrs Eckersley bred Joanma's Saffron, by Dutch Ch. Joanma's Don ex Wendover Chell. He was campaigned by Mrs Jarosz and gained his title. Two of his offspring were made up: Sh. Ch. Joanma's Ranter born in 1972, out of Sh. Ch. Joanma's Rachel, who was a grand-daughter of Joanma's Wendover Yana, two CCs, and Sh. Ch. Joanma's Scampi born in 1973, out of Joanma's Colette. Scampi, won 14 CCs and 17 Res. CCs and was Top Irish Setter in 1976.

KIRKAVAGH: STEVE AND LINDA KING
The prefix was first registered in 1974 and two Sowerhill bitches were bought. However, the foundation bitch, Sh. Ch. Fearnley Fireheather, six CCs, four Res. CCs, came from Pat and Barry Rhodes in 1982. Her first litter, born in 1987, was by her grandsire Sh. Ch. Sowerhill Satyr of Fearnley, and Sh. Ch. Kirkavagh

Corejada was retained. Fireheather had two further litters and her last, by Sh. Ch. Fearnley Firehurricane, contained Sh. Ch. Kirkavagh Musidora, the only bitch in the litter. Her daughter Gazala is the current winning youngster. Sh. Ch. Corejada only had two litters, both by Sh. Ch. Fearnley Firehurricane. Her lasting legacy to the Kirkavaghs has come through her daughter Sh. Ch. Kirkavagh Zabara whom the Kings consider to be their best to date. Born in April 1992, Zabara has won nine CCs, 10 Res. CCs, as well as the Group at WELKS in 1997 – never an easy task for a bitch! Nine litters have been bred since 1987, producing a high percentage of winners. Zabara has had her first litter and her puppies should continue the successful line.

KYLENOE: JOHN AND WENDY MORLEY
The first Irish was bought in 1970 and in 1972 he was joined by Ronnetta Wild Rose of Kylenoe, who became the Morley's first Show Champion. She only had one litter and none of her offspring feature in the kennel's development. In 1979 Bucksett Bonnie of Kylenoe was bought in. By Heathcliffe Tobias ex Pepper of Brackenfield, she won a Res. CC and had three litters. From her second litter, to

Sh. Ch. Kylenoe Chrystal Spirit.

Sh. Ch. Cornhill Pippin, came Sh. Ch. Kylenoe Sun Princess, born in 1983. From Bonnie's third litter, by Carnbargus Star Enterprise, came Dancing Crystal. She was mated to Sh. Ch. and Ir. Sh. Ch. Autumnglow Masquerade and produced Sh. Ch. Kylenoe Chrystal Spirit. Now in training, it is hoped to run her for her qualifier.

LAGGAN: NORMA MARSHALL
In 1978 the foundation bitch Hallglen Celandine, by Sh. Ch. Allsquare Mickey Finn, was mated to Sh. Ch. Wendover Colas and produced Sh. Ch. Laggan Bryan's Boy, nine CCs, 12 Res. CCs, winner of a Gundog Group, and Starshine, one CC. Celandine was next mated to Fetteresk Winter Legend and the only puppy, Janek's Jem, was retained. She was mated to Night Fever and produced Sh. Ch. Laggan Macbie Lady. She was mated back to Bryan's Boy, resulting in Sh. Ch. Laggan Glen Ettrick. During 1991 it was decided to mate Macbie Lady to Sh. Ch. Inisheer Flamingo. The long journey from Scotland to Essex was worthwhile as the litter contained the latest Show Champion, Uptown Girl. Her litter sister, Southern Belle, was exported to the USA where, at the time of writing, she only needs two more points to become an American Champion. Norma had decided to have a litter from Uptown Girl when she was five and sitting on two CCs. Not an easy decision to make, but her daughter Shoshoni Maiden is now carrying on the line.

LOSKERAN: RICHARD AND PAT HIRONS
Show Champion Clonageera Tarka went on to win the Group and Best in Show after being awarded his first CC and Best of Breed at Midland Counties in 1980. His CC-winning daughter Lorelli was mated to Jennison Phantom twice and produced in 1985 Sh. Ch. Loskeran Oleander, owned by Gerald and Kate Condron, and in 1987 Sh. Ch. Loskeran Gold Crown, owned by the Stanleys.

MOYNA: BARBARA BIRCH
The Moynas were founded by Sh. Ch. Morningstar Melanie. The highlight of her career was winning the CC at Crufts in 1969 under Mr F. Warner-Hill. Melanie was mated to Sh. Ch. Twoacres Troilus and produced Sh. Ch. Moyna Mr O'Hara. The mating was repeated and, this time, the litter contained Sh. Ch. Moyna Michelle, nine CCs, five Res. CCs and a Reserve Gundog Group. Barbara was able to acquire Rickerscott Bridget Maguire, by the influential sire Sh. Ch. Scotswood Barabbas; she gained her title, and had the distinction of winning Best in Show at the ISAE Championship Show in 1973, at the ISBC Championship Show in 1974, and again at the ISAE in 1977 – by that time aged eight. The combination of the Troilus/Melanie lines with stock from Bridget Maguire by Moyna Jamie produced excellent bitches, providing foundations for several successful kennels.

REDDINS: JIM AND PRISCILLA SMITH
The first bitch was acquired in 1972. She was of Wendover breeding and during the 1970s was joined by further stock bred from similar lines. Sorrel of Andana of Reddins won the first CC in 1980 and gained her title in 1981, winning five CCs and two Res. CCs. An excellent brood bitch, in her litter to Sh. Ch. Jason of Andana of Clonageera, born in May 1983, she produced two Show Champions:

Reddins Jonah and Reddins Justin of Stylersetts. In 1984 Sorrel was mated to Night Fever and from this litter came the Waddell's Ir. Ch. and Ch. Fintan, CC at Crufts 1988, who had also gained his qualifier, and Sh. Ch. Ferdinand, 21 CCs, 13 Res. CCs, Gundog Group at Crufts 1989 and further Groups at WELKS, Richmond and the LKA. He was twice Best in Show at the ISBC. The latest title-holder, bred by Jim and Priscilla in 1991, is Sh. Ch. Reddins Myrna out of the CC winner Harriet. She is owned and campaigned by John Hall. Her sire, Sh. Ch. Barnaby of Wesbere at Cressway was bred by Priscilla in partnership with Sheilah Gutsell. Jim and Priscilla keep a large kennel of Irish Setters and were Pedigree Chum Top Irish Setter Breeders in 1989, 90, 92, 93 and 94.

RUA: MARY TUITE
PORSCHET: COLETTE TUITE
(Dual purpose kennels).
Mary is determined to keep the breed's working ability alive and Rua Affluent Shannon and Rua Damian's Dandy Avanti feature in show and field trial pedigrees. Via Dandy, and through the introduction of pure field trial lines, came FT Ch. Rua Connemara of Porschet. Her sister is the dam of FT Ch. Rua Marta, making Mary the breeder of two FT Champions. Sirrah's sister, Syllabub, won the KC Non Winners Stake and produced Errigal, one CC, three Res. CCs, 50 Green Stars, and Golden Bough, three Res. CCs and Green Stars. Dandy's most famous offspring is Ch. Astley's Portia of Rua, the winner of eight CCs, two Res. CCs. She was Best of Breed Crufts 1980 and 1981, when she went on to win the Group and Best in Show. She gained her qualifier in 1980 and her daughter Celtic Romance provided the foundation for the Porschets. Portia was mated to Night Fever and produced Mary's Flame of Tara at Rua, two CCs, one Res. CC. Colette's Flame of the Forest Porschet also won two CCs. She was tragically killed when aged only 26 months. Colette acquired Rua Connemara of Porschet from her mother, and she became her first Field Trial Champion.

Ch. Astley's Portia of Rua: Best in Show Crufts 1981.

Sh. Ch. Shenanagin Stockbroker.

SCARLETTI: RITA PIKE

The foundation bitch Margaretwoods Conductress, by Sh. Ch. Scotswood Barabbas ex Bridget of Castleoak, won a Res. CC. From her only litter by Sh. Ch. Cornevon Stargem came the twins, Sh. Ch. Scarletti Cockney Rebel and Sh. Ch. Hot Chocolate. Both won Res. CCs at Crufts 1982. Another sister, Tangerine Dream, also won a Res. CC. Cockney Rebel sired Sh. Ch. Suteresett Hot Rumour and Sh. Ch. Bardonhill Supergrass, and Hot Chocolate had a litter by Sh. Ch. Zorosean Agvamarina which produced Scarletti Silver Sprint. She was mated to Bardonhill Crafty Cockney by Scarletti, full brother to Supergrass. From her "Pink" litter came Lily the Pink who went to Sh. Ch. Royal Archer and produced Sh. Ch. Scarletti Hill Street Blues, born in 1987. Tickled Pink won a CC and two Res. CCs. and Pink Panther sired Sh. Ch. Suteresett Coconut Capers and the CC winner Artful Almond. So far, Rita has only bred nine litters.

SHANDWICK: PAT BUTLER

In her first litter, the foundation bitch Palelsa Boadicea produced Sh. Ch. Shandwick Silver Spray, born in 1980. In 1983 Boadicea was mated to Sh. Ch. Twoacres Gold Eagle and from that litter came the two Show Champion bitches Shandwick Golden Spray, 18 CCs, 15 Res. CCs, and Golden Rose, owned by Will Brown and Chris Sones. Silver Spray was also mated to Gold Eagle and in 1985 produced Sh. Ch. Shandwick Starcarrier. Pat is now showing the Res. CC winner Withersdale Crystal Maze. She is out of Withersdale Livia, a Golden Rose daughter by Pat's Night Fever son, the Group winner Sh. Ch. Wickenberry Knight at Arms.

SHENANAGIN: ALISTER AND CATHERINE WATT

Alister's first Cornevon died tragically and Sh. Ch. Cornevon Lovebird, 15 CCs, 10 Res. CCs, was acquired. He was Top Irish Setter in 1974 and won the CC at Crufts. He won Best in Show at the Setter & Pointer Club Championship Show and at the ISAE in 1975 and won Res. CCs at Crufts in 1976 and 1977. He sired four title holders and a further five CC winners, making him the Breed's Top Stud Dog in 1977 and 1978 and runner-up twice. A Lovebird grand-daughter, Dunnygask Enchanting Spirit, Res. CC, became the foundation bitch and was mated to Sh. Ch. Bardonhill Supergrass. Shilling was retained and mated to Wendover Raffles, by Night Fever. This combination produced Sh. Ch. Sugar and Spice, who won her second CC at Crufts 1993. She was mated to Sh. Ch. Bardonhill Team Spirit at Wynjill and from this litter came Sh. Ch. Stockbroker, 14 CCs, 17 Res. CCs and a Reserve Gundog Group. Stockbroker was Top Irish Setter Puppy 1992 and Top Irish Setter 1994. Three of his daughters have gained their titles. Another daughter, Fetteresk Take That to Shenanagin, Res. CC, was acquired and is the mother of promising stock. Only seven litters have been bred so far.

SOWERHILL: OLWEN HUNT

Miss Hunt owned her first Irish Setter before the war and her foundation bitch Norlan Tessie Belle was bred from test-mated stock. Unshown, she proved to be an important brood bitch. From her second litter to Maydorwill Happy Lad came S. Winsford Robert, three Res. CCs, and S. Jilinda; and

Sh. Ch. Sowerhill Sarah: Winner of the Romance Brood Bitch Trophy 1979, 1981, 1982 and 1983.
Bred and owned by Olwen Hunt.
Dam of Sh. Ch. Sowerhill Sahib (sire of Night Fever), Sh. Ch. Sowerhill Sarong of Kingscott, Sh. Ch. Sowerhill Satyr of Fearnley (winner of 31 CCs), and Sowerhill Sailor of Wendover (a top sire in Sweden).

from her third litter, to Ch. Boisdale Boggit, came Sowerhill Red Mist. From these three a high percentage of present-day Irish Setters is descended. In 1968 Sowerhill Red Colleen of Kitewood was acquired and won six CCs, one Res. CC and a Gundog Group. Mated to Sh. Ch. Stephenshill Gamebird twice, she first produced Sh. Ch. Storm, 18 CCs and Top Irish Setter in 1977. From the second litter came Valentine, Res. CC. In 1973 Sowerhill Sarah, (Gamebird ex Sowerhill Samantha) was born. She gained her title and has had a considerable impact on the breed. From her two litters to Sh. Ch. Wendover Jeeves came Sh. Ch. Sowerhill Sahib, Sh. Ch. S. Sarong of Kingscott and Sh. Ch. S. Satyr of Fearnley, S. Sarabelle who won a Res. CC and S. Sailor of Wendover who went to Sweden. Sahib has left his mark as the sire of Night Fever. The combined success of her progeny enabled Sarah to win the Brood Bitch Trophy in 1979, 81, 82 and 83. A Satyr daughter, Fearnley Fire Ember, was acquired and produced Sh. Ch. Nobleman. The three Best in Show winning Irish Setters at Crufts all go back to Norlan Tessie Belle.

TATTERSLEE: JENNIE REED

Jennie bought her first Irish Setter in 1974, which was followed by the foundation bitch Brackenfield Tatters in 1975. She was joined by a dog puppy, Brackenfield Fagus, and, when mated together later, they started the Tatterslee Kennel. Fagus also sired the first title holder to be made up by Jennie, Sh. Ch. Coralmist

Country Cotswold at Tatterslee. A Fagus/Tatters grand-daughter, Topham's Trophy, the result of an outcross, was mated to Sh. Ch. Erinade Scottish Union and a single puppy was born in 1984. Sh. Ch. Tatterslee Toute Seule gained her title at the age of nine-and-a-half. She was mated to Rhuwind Special Edition and Special Effect was kept. Born in 1992, he was made up in 1997. To date, he has won six CCs and three Res. CCs.

THENDARA: DEE MILLIGAN AND JEREMY BOTT

The Thendaras are based on three Bardonhill bitches: the litter sisters Bardonhill Bikini and Sea Breeze, by Night Fever, born in 1987, and Bardonhill Eeny Meeny of Thendara, CC at Crufts 1992, born in 1988, by Sh. Ch. Shandwick Starcarrier. Sh. Ch. Bardonhill Sea Breeze over Thendara, nine CCs, six Res. CCs, won a Reserve Gundog Group and was Best in Show at two Breed Club Championship Shows. A good brood, her litter to Sh. Ch. Clonageera Genesis contained Sh. Ch. Thendara Okay Yaa, Best of Breed at Crufts 1995. Popular with overseas breeders, his semen has been exported to Sweden and Australia. His three litters to the Res. CC-winning Bikini have been successful and winners have gone all over Europe. Sh. Ch. Kennedy was retained and is the winner of 10 CCs and six Res. CCs, the Group at Bournemouth 1995 and Bath 1996.

Sh. Ch. Timadon Debs Delight.

TIMADON: GEOFF AND ALICIA COUPE

Gaelge Gariona, the foundation bitch, was born in 1962, by Ch. Brackenfield Hartsbourne Bronze ex Sh. Ch. Gaelge Gertina, a Ch. Wendover Beggar daughter. Her Wendover lines were concentrated on and Gariona was mated to Sh. Ch. Wendover Ballymoss. Bilby and Forever Amber were retained. Gariona's next litter was by Sh. Ch. Wendover Gentleman, incidentally his first. The litter contained Sh. Ch. Wendover Herald of Cuprea who later went to Canada, and Aust. Ch. Timadon Jaunty. Forever Amber was also mated to Gentleman and produced Dorianne. She was mated to Sh. Ch. Wendover Royalist, and produced the first title-holder with the Timadon prefix, Sh. Ch. Kendel. He was the sire of four Show Champions and a dual CC winner. In 1966 Ballywestow Festoon was acquired. She gained her title and won Best in Show at the ISAE in 1971. When she was mated to Gentleman, the CC winner Ballina was retained. In 1973 Tallulah of Timadon, the litter sister to the important Sh. Ch. Wendover Jeeves, was bought in. When mated to Kendel, she produced Sh. Ch. Timadon Concorde. Ballina was mated to him and produced Ch. and Ir. Ch. Timadon Exclusive Edition who gained her qualifier in 1982. Ballina was also mated to Sh. Ch. Kendel and produced Sh. Ch. Timadon Charlies Angel and Whimsical. Her daughter, Brulette, is the dam of the latest Show Champion, Timadon Debs Delight, and his CC-winning sister Airs and Graces.

TWOACRES: JUNE COATES

The first bitch was bought as a family pet, but had some success in the show ring. In 1965 Musbury Melisande of Twoacres was acquired. Her first litter, to Sh. Ch. Wendover Gentleman, turned out to be highly successful and Melisande still holds the record for producing the most CC winners in one litter: The "T" litter contained four Show Champions plus a dual CC winner. Teresa became the foundation for the Barleydales, and Traviata did the same for the Wickenberrys. Tamburlaine won Best in Show at Windsor 1970 and Troilus was Best in Show at Belfast 1971, after having won Groups at Leeds and Blackpool in 1970. Troilus was Top Irish Setter in 1971, winning a total of 21 CCs, replacing his sire as the top CC winner. Troilus turned out to be prepotent, producing six Show Champions as well as 14 other CC winners. His winning offspring won him the Mars Stud Dog Trophy in 1974, 75 and 76. His sister Tosca was mated to Sh. Ch. Timadon Kendel and Francesca was retained and became

Pictured left to right: Sh. Ch. Twoacres Troilus, Sh. Ch. Twoacres Teresa (foundation bitch of the Barleydales), Sh. Ch. Twoacres Traviata (foundation bitch of the Wickenberrys) and Sh. Ch. Twoacres Tamburlaine.

Sh. Ch. Bardonhill Team Spirit at Wynjill.

the first to be test-mated when the PRA scare started in the 1970s. Troilus mated Sh. Ch. Cornevon Cinderella and Solace of Twoacres was acquired, winning a CC as a Junior. Mated to Wendover Treasurer, she produced Sh. Ch. Twoacres Gold Eagle, the sire of four Show Champions. Wendover Sportsgirl, born in 1978 by Baron of Wendover ex Wendover Lupina, was bought in; she won a CC and Res. CC but disliked showing. She was test-mated and the three current bitches are descended from her, including Jade, two CCs, three Res. CCs.

WICKENBERRY: JEAN QUINN
Jean's foundation bitch, Sh. Ch. Twoacres Traviata, was born in 1968, a member of the famous "T" litter mentioned above, bred by June Coates. Mated to Baron of Wendover, she produced Sh. Ch. Wickenberry Baroness, the winner of 10 CCs, 11 Res. CCs, a Reserve Gundog Group and Best in Show at the National Gundogs Championship Show 1981. Baroness was mated to Sh. Ch. Twoacres Wayward Caesar and from that litter came two Show Champions, Clansman and Countess, born in 1980. In her litter by Night Fever, Baroness produced Sh. Ch. Wickenberry Knight at Arms and the dual CC winner Ir. Ch.

Nightingale. Her winning children won her the Romance Brood Bitch Trophy in 1982. Countess was also mated to Night Fever and from her litter also came a Show Champion, Nebbiolo, and a dual CC winner, Nearco. The latest title holder was Sh. Ch. Pretty Polly, born in 1986. She won her first Res. CC at Leeds in 1987, when only a few days out of puppy, and her last Res. CC at Crufts in 1996 from Veteran. Jean was *Our Dogs'* Top Breeder in 1986 – a great achievement for her small kennel, where only an occasional litter is bred.

WYNJILL: JILL HOLLEY
In 1971 Cornevon Tranquil was bought, primarily as a family pet, but Jill's parents thought that showing her would be a nice interest for their daughter! In 1972 Janice Roberts bred a litter by Sh. Ch. Cornevon Snowstorm ex Sh. Ch. Cornevon Violet and Jill went to see the puppies every week. Eventually, Woodsprite was chosen and became Jill's first CC winner at Leeds in 1974, where she also won Best of Breed under Joe Braddon, going on to win seven CCs and six Res. CCs. On Janice's advice, Tranquil was mated to Margaretwoods Caretaker of Scotswood, and Wynjill Red Robin was retained. He won his

first CC in 1975, gaining five more in 1978 as well as Best of Breed at Crufts in 1979. He still remains Jill's favourite Irish Setter. Two litter sisters were also successful, winning a CC and Res. CCs. In 1975 Robin and Woodsprite were mated and produced Sh. Ch. Wynjill Country Fragrance. At that time Jill owned four Irish Setters – three of them Show Champions. In 1990 Bardonhill Team Spirit at Wynjill was bought in. By Free Spirit of Danaway, he gained his title and is proving himself a successful sire.

OTHER KENNELS OF NOTE

There are many kennels that consistently produce winning stock and will always have to be reckoned with. Mary Bowman has bred two BONAHAIRD title holders, Show Champions Snowboots and her granddaughter White Diamonds. Brenda Levick's CORRIECAS Kennel enjoyed great success with Sh. Ch. Baron, the winner of two Groups and Reserve Best in Show, Manchester 1972. His son, Sh. Ch. Fagan, won his third CC at Crufts in 1983 and went on to win the Group and Reserve Best in Show. Viveca Vamplew's ERINADE Kennel turns out consistently high quality stock. Sh. Ch. Erinade Scottish Union was made up and sired five Show Champions – all bitches. Viveca also piloted Sh. Ch. Erinade Neulah to her title and won a CC with her son, and Exotic has won two CCs. Lynne Dale campaigned Sh. Ch. Wendover Royal Justice to his title and made up her homebred HARTSFELL Aida.

Lynne Muir is well known for handling Sh. Ch. Melody Minet and Sh. Ch. Fondador Charlane, 21 CCs, a Group and Reserve Group winner, all owned by Mrs Follows. Lynne made up her own Sh. Ch. Delsanto Romarne and is now breeding successfully under her own prefix ROMARNE. In recent years Jackie Lorrimer has enjoyed phenomenal success with Sh. Ch. Danaway Debonair, the winner of 40 CCs and numerous Group and Best in Shows, including Crufts 1993. Other commitments prevent Jackie from breeding under her OAKCHASE prefix, but she is now successfully campaigning a Debonair son, Sh. Ch. Caspians Intrepid. Rachel Shaw has gone to the top and won Best in Show at Crufts in 1995 with her homebred Sh. Ch. STARCHELLE Chicago Bear. He had already won a Group and Best in Show at the Setter and Pointer Championship Show in 1993 before his Crufts win. Chicago Bear won 13 CCs and 12 Res. CCs, and was *Dog World's* Top Irish Setter in 1995. His sister Sh. Ch. Starchelle The Blue Angel also gained her title.

The successful mother and daughter partnership of Sue Hockley and Teresa Gisby bred Sh. Ch. SUTERESETT Hot Rumour, 13 CCs, two Groups, Reserve Best in Show National Gundogs 1986 and Best in Show 1987 at the same event. Sh. Ch. Coconut Capers gained her title and her brother has won a CC, as has her daughter Cuddly Connie. The partnership of Will Brown and Chris Sones made up Sh. Ch. Shandwick Golden Rose and bred Sh. Ch. WITHERSDALE Songbird of Serrula and Withersdale Evergreen, the winner of two CCs. Some well-known names are no longer actively involved with breeding and showing, but continue to serve the breed. Rita Bryden bred and campaigned the influential Sh. Ch. SCOTSWOOD Barabbas and Sh. Ch. Scotswood Fara. Barabbas' contribution to the breed, through his successful offspring, has been considerable, both at home and abroad. Rita is now President Elect of the Irish Setter Association, England, having served as Treasurer for many years. Maureen Hurll made up a Barabbas son, Sh. Ch. Hurricane of CARRAMORE, as well as Sh. Ch. Carramore Irish Moonshine and was most unlucky not to make up her brother, Irish Piper, the winner of two CCs and and two Res. CCs. Maureen is concerned for the welfare of the Breed and runs the Eastern Irish Setter Rescue.

THE REPUBLIC OF IRELAND

In its native land, the Irish Setter is a popular breed and approximately 400 are registered annually with the Irish Kennel Club Ltd. The Irish Red Setter Club is more than a hundred years old and mainly orientated towards Field Trials. However, the Show Committee organises the annual Championship Show. It is only since 1990 that the title of Show Champion has come into existence but just as many dogs are running for their Qualifiers as ever. Most of the successful show stock has been imported from the UK and, due to the relative ease of access, British stud dogs have been used to good effect. Irish dogs have made their presence felt at British Shows and have gone home with top honours.

IR. Ch. Ardbraccan Everglade.

ARDBRACCAN: TRUDY WALSH

Ch. Ardbraccan Aristocrat proved himself to be a dog of all-round excellence. He was Irish Setter of the Year 1978, 1979, 1980, 1981 and 1985 and topped this by becoming Show Dog of the Year All Breeds 1979-1980. Many times Best in Show at All Breeds and Club Championship Shows, he won over 50 Green Stars and a Reserve CC. A first prize winner at Obedience, he was an excellent Gundog. Mainly of Wendover breeding, he produced Champions Ardbraccan Celtic Charm and Everglade. Celtic Charm was Irish Setter of the Year 1993 and Everglade is the sire of Icelandic Ch. Ardbraccan Famous Grouse. The Group winner Brandy Beau would have been a Show Champion, had the award been recognized in his time.

DUNSWOOD: JEAN AND MARTYN TURNER

Ir. Ch. Wickenberry Nightingale, born in 1982, by Night Fever ex Sh. Ch. Wickenberry Baroness, won 20 Green Stars with 145 points and two CCs and three Res.

CCs and was unlucky not to have gained her UK title as well. She was Best in Show at an All Breeds Championship Show and Reserve Best in Show at two UK Breed Club Championship Shows. She was also a Finalist at the Top Irish Show Dog of the Year Competition 1987. Nightingale gained her qualifier at the Wicklow and Wexford Field Trial in October 1986. A highly successful brood bitch, she produced five Irish Champions to Sh. Ch. Barleydale Pascali. Birdsong was retained and the other four gained their titles in different ownerships. From her litter by Ir. Ch. Dunswood Little Owl (Sh. Ch. Twoacres Gold Eagle ex Wendover Maeve) came another Irish Champion, Night Owl, and the Res. CC winner Ir. Sh. Ch. Dunswood Florence.

LOUGHANTARVE: MAE AND RODNEY TRENWITH

Ch. and Irish Ch. Timadon Exclusive Edition put the Loughantarve Setters on the map on both sides of the Irish Sea. She won Best in Show at the Irish Red Setter Club Championship Show twice and Best in Show

Ir. Ch. Wickenberry Nightingale: Dam of five Irish Champions.

at the Irish Breeds Society Championship Show. She gained her qualifier at the Wexford Gundog Club Trial in 1982. In Britain she won seven CCs and five Res. CCs and was Best of Breed at Crufts in 1985 and 1986. Mated to Sh. Ch. Corriecas Fagan she produced Ir. Ch. Loughantarve Fagan, winner of two Best in Shows at All Breed Championship Shows. His sister, Ir. Ch. Kerry Lynn, had won one CC and one Res. CC. when illness ended her show career. Her sister Sally also gained her Irish Champion title. When mated to Sh. Ch. Sowerhill Satyr of Fearnley, Exclusive Edition produced Ir. Sh. Ch. Kerry Erin, Res. CC.

RANALEEN: BRIAN GRACE
Brian campaigned Ch. Dunswood Thunderbird to his title and qualifier. His Ir.

Sh. Ch. Reddins Declan won a CC and Best of Breed. He acquired Fearnley Firesheen of Ranaleen, and won two Res. CCs. She was Best in Show at the Irish Red Setter Club Championship Show and became an Ir. Sh. Ch. when aged only 20 months.

OTHER KENNELS OF NOTE
Michael and Maire McCarthy have campaigned several Dunswoods to their titles, including Ch. Little Owl, Res. CC., Ch. Stormbird, All Breeds Show Dog of the Year 1989-1990, and Ch. Night Owl. Both are out of Ch. Wickenberry Nightingale. They have also made up Ch. Wickenberry Double Trouble. Other breeders had success with Dunswood stock, and Sheila Hughes, CLOONMINDA, made up Ch. Dunswood Ladybird, while Bernie McGrath campaigned Ch. Dunswood Chorus and her daughter Ch. Lisronagh LASSARINA. Sylvie Crossen showed and qualified her homebred Ch. RENCROSS Busy Lee.

NORTHERN IRELAND
ROHANMOR: CATHY LOUGHLIN
A frequent visitor to the UK and to shows south of the border, she has made up Ir. Sh. Ch. Bardonhill Overboard. He also won four Res. CCs and was Northern Ireland's Show Dog of the Year 1989 and Gundog of the Year 1992. Bonahaird Black Magic also became an Ir. Sh. Ch. as did her son, by Overboard, Ir. Sh. Ch. Rohanmor the Real McCoy.

14 THE IRISH SETTER IN NORTH AMERICA

By Connie Vanacore

The last quarter of the twentieth century was marked by a enormous surge in popularity of the Irish Setter in America, followed by a precipitous drop. In 1974 Irish Setters were the third most popular breed in the country with more than 58,000 registered. By the mid-1980s registration figures had plummeted, to find the Irish Setter in the mid-50s in the popularity list. Their numbers continued to drop until by 1998 they had stabilized at approximately 2,000 registrations per year, putting them at between 58th and 60th in popularity among all registerable breeds with the American Kennel Club.

The interest in Irish Setters which began in the late 1960s and early 1970s introduced the breed to fanciers who have become the mainstay of breeders in the United States. Mixed in with the huge population of pet owners were a small coterie of breeders who built on bloodlines of the past to continue and define the Irish Setter to this day. As numbers declined, these breeders found that by combining bloodlines that were well established in the 1950s they were able to produce Setters of quality. Today, almost all the Irish Setters which are seen in the show ring derive from the dominant sires of those earlier years. The use of chilled and frozen semen has enabled breeders to cross regional boundaries more freely and to use dogs which might otherwise not have been available to them. This has been a two-edged sword: while it has enabled bitches to be bred to top sires, it has also narrowed the gene pool, so that there are a few dogs which can be found in the majority of pedigrees in the United States today.

Recently some breeders have recognized the danger in breeding too closely over many generations and have reached out to Australia to import dogs and semen to incorporate into their breeding programs. It is also difficult to overestimate the importance of the Meadowlark-Indeed crosses to breeding stock in the United States today. Even a cursory look at some of the breeders profiled here can testify to their influence on the future of the breed in the US. The following are some of the breeders who began their involvement with Irish Setters over the past twenty-five years.

AVON FARM: LESLIE RUSSELL
Oregon City, Oregon.
Leslie purchased a male of Tirvelda bloodlines in 1973, Ch. Niebline Streamliner, and another male, Ch. Zodiac's Arista Extremist. Two Niebline-bred bitches arrived next, both of Tirvelda stock. From combining these dogs

143

Am. Ch. Avon Farm Miss Chevious. Photo: Kohler.

Leslie produced Ch. Avon Farm's Applause, her foundation bitch. She stayed within the Tirvelda bloodlines, but bred Applause initially to Ch. Scarlly's Red Hot. Her current generations trace back to Ch. Avon Farm Miss Kitty and her recent offspring, Ch. Avon Farm Miss Chevious, Miss Kathleen and Miss Conduct. She looks to Miss Chevious to be her next key producer.

BALLYCROY: FRED AND CONNIE VANACORE
Mendham, New Jersey.
Along with a home in the country in 1956 came Fred and Connie's first Irish Setter, Phantom Brooks Ballycroy, from Brooks and Dodie Emory, a kennel no longer in existence. Breeding occasionally, in 1972 they bred their bitch, Ballycroy Rua Catlin to Ch. Tirvelda Nor'Wester to produce Ch. Ballycroy Northern Sunset, the foundation sire for Santera Irish Setters. They purchased a bitch, who became Ch. Fieldstone Trace of Burgundy (Ch. McCamon Marquis ex Glen Cree Merriment). Descendants of this bitch carry on the Ballycroy line through her grand-daughter, Ch. Ballycroy Royal Burgundy and her daughter Ballycroy St. Clare (Ch. Ballymera's Stormin' Norman ex Ch. Ballycroy Royal Burgundy).

BALLYMERA: PATRICE CLAWSON
Avon, New York.
As with so many Irish Setter fanciers, Patty found her first Irish Setter by chance. Hooked on the breed, she determined to obtain the best breeding stock she could, and found her way to the Meadowlark Kennels of Rose Ross. From Rose she purchased two puppies within a few months of one another. The first became Ch. Meadowlark's Whispering Breeze (Breezy) (Ch. Meadowlark's Masterful ex Meadowlark's Wyndchimes). The second was Am. Can. Ch. Meadowlark's Rainbow 'N Roses (Molly). Breezy was bred four times, three of them to Ch. Quailfield Mak'n Business. Those three litters produced twelve Champions, with several more pointed. Two of these are Best in Show dogs – Am. Can Ch. Ballymera's Stormin' Norman and Ch. Jewelset's Made For You. Breezy's fourth litter is by the Mak'n

Am. Can. Ch. Ballymera's Stormin' Norman.
Ashbey Photography.

Business grandson, Ch. Quailfield's Successful Business. This litter is just getting started. Molly was bred twice, first to Ch. Meadowlark's Vindicator and then to Ch. Quailfield Mak'n Business. Several Champions have ensued from these breedings. Offspring of both of these bitches have been closely line bred to carry on the Meadowlark bloodlines.

DC/AFC Cordon Bleu Bright Star JH

BRIGHT STAR SETTERS: WENDY REED CZARNECKI
Petaluma, California.
Wendy's foundation bitch and her first Irish Setter was purchased as a pet in 1972. She became Field Ch. Lady Ribbon Bright Star CD. By chance Ribbon was noticed by a hunter who bred and trialed Gordon Setters and he noticed Ribbon's potential as a good bird dog. Norm Sorby worked with Ribbon and eventually sent her on to a more accomplished field trialer. Wendy became convinced that her goal was to produce dual field and show Champions. With Ribbon as her foundation she worked through subsequent generations, always attempting to find dogs which were capable of working in the field as well as shining in the show ring. After 25 years and five generations she produced the 17th AKC Dual Champion, Cordon Bleu Bright Star JH (Tempe), bred from Am. Can. Ch. Lyn Erin Midnight Blue ex Am. Can. Ch. Scarlet Victory Bright Star, Am.Can. CD, JH, VC.

BROPHY: KEN AND LINDA RUFF
Sycamore, Illinois.
Ken and Linda bought their first Irish in 1972 and bred their first litter in 1976. Their Irish Setters come from field lines and Brophy Irish Setters dominate field trials in the United States today. Their early dogs came from the Norab Kennels of Tony Baron and from a male which they purchased from Ed McIvor of Ivor

ABOVE: NFC, 2 x NAFC, FCC, AFC Ivor Glen Ruben.

RIGHT: NAFC, AFC, FC Brophys Center Fielder.

Glen Kennels. The Ivor Glen background has played a dominant role in their breeding program. NFC, twice NAFC, FC & AFC Ivor Glen Ruben ROM is their main foundation dog. He was bred seven times and produced seven field champions and four offspring which won seven National Championships. A son of Ruben, NFC, NAFC, FC & AFC Brophy's Mahogany Fielder, carries on the line. His daughter, NFC, FC & AFC Brophy's Pumpernickel, defeated most AKC dogs in a single year in all breed competition.

Brophy's Red Storm Rising, owned by Bob Geddeis, proved to be an important sire, although he died at an early age. A full brother,

145

NAFC, AFC, FC Brophy's Center Fielder, owned by Ray and Jackie Marshall, is producing excellent dogs, while a Ruben grand-daughter, NFC, FC & AFC Hazelwood's Speedy Gonzales, owned by Robin Baker and Marion Pahy, has produced three field Champions to date and several more that have the potential to make her the all-time best-producing field dam.

CAIRNCROSS: RENETTE BERGGREN
Longmont, Colorado.
Renette, as with so many fanciers today, began her love affair with Irish Setters after seeing the Walt Disney movie *Big Red* in 1963, but it was not until 1968, while working for a professional handler, Larry Downey, that she fell in love with one of their puppies. She bought the dog and, with the guidance of the Downeys, finished him. She was hooked and in 1971 purchased Ch. Kilgary Aman from the Wisconsin kennels of Michael Johnson. He became the foundation stud for Cairncross kennels and was also instrumental in the kennels of O'Kerrie, Rossan and Tramore. From Cheryl Mika (O'Kerrie) Renette purchased O'Kerrie's Autumn Ecstasy (a Kilgary Aman grand-daughter) and Rossan's Xanadu (a Kilgary Aman daughter). These two bitches became her foundation and the combination of their offspring has proved to be the most successful in her breeding program. Xanadu was a product of Aman bred to a Beaverbrook bitch. This combined the Draherin influence on the sire's side with Tirvelda on the dam's side. Ecstasy brought the Aman influence on both sides of the pedigree. Xanadu was bred to Ch. O'Kerrie's Armagh, which strengthened the Tirvelda line on the sire's side. This mating produced Ch. Cairncross Second Wind, who is proving to be a successful sire. Bred to Autumn Ecstasy he produced three Champions, one of which, Ch. Cairncross Deja Voodoo, has produced four

Champions. His influence outside of Renette's kennel is just beginning to be felt.

CAMELOT: NORBERT AND NENA DEE
Lucketts, Virginia.
The Dees purchased their first Irish Setter in 1973 and their foundation bitch, Shane's Irish Taradee, CD in 1975. Tara's bloodlines were a combination of Draherin and Knockross and from those beginnings, combinations of Meadowlark and Scarlly dogs were added. One of their bitches, Ch. Camelot's Stardust (a Taradee grand-daughter) was a top winner in 1987 and 1988. A young dog, Ch. Camelot's City Slicker, is making his mark as a show dog and producer, and a young bitch obtained from the Johnstone's Kintyre kennel, Ch. Kintyre's Debutante, finished her championship at 15 months of age and will be bred to City Slicker.

Am. Ch. Camelot's Stardust.

CASTLEBAR: CRAIG AND PAT HACKENBERG
Park Ridge, New Jersey.
Craig started in Obedience in the 1970s and purchased his first show Irish from Ted Eldredge – Ch. Tirvelda Final Ruling. Then,

Am. Ch. Castlebar Country Statesman.

again from Ted, Craig and Pat received Ch. Tirvelda Skylark and bred her to Am. Can. Ch. McCamon Marquis. They leased a Canadian bitch, Ch. Sardonyx Canadiana (a Ch. Candia Indeed daughter) and bred her to Ch. McCamon Marquis (a Tirvelda-Rockherin combination) to produce Ch. Castlebar Sardonyx Witsend (Petals). She became their foundation bitch and, when bred to Ch. Meadowlark's Vindicator, produced Ch. Castlebar Command Presence (Opie). He has produced 11 Champions, two tracking dogs, seven junior hunters, three CD titlists, one CDX and two working towards their agility titles. Opie's sister, co-owned by Craig and Dale Hood (Ruxton) of Towson, Maryland, Ch. Castlebar Garden Party (Tulip), has produced two Champions and one junior hunter. Opie, bred to his half-sister Ch. Castlebar Forever Yours, has produced Ch. Castlebar Country Statesman. Tulip, when bred first to Ch. Quailfield's Mak'n Business, produced Ch. Ruxton's Larkspur, and when bred to his son Ch. Ballymera's Stormin' Norman, produced the young bitch Castlebar's Ruxton Olympia. Both of these bitches will be the future breeding stock for Castlebar and Ruxton.

CHALLENGER: BOB AND PAT ROBINSON
Phoenix, Arizona.
The Robinsons purchased their first Irish in 1962. He became Ch. Portrait O'King's Challenge (Ch. Draherin King's Ransom ex Ch. Bryfield Portrait O'Eve). A few years later they acquired Ch. Courtwood Spring Breeze, one of nine Champions from Ch. Candia Indeed's first litter by Susan Hahnen's Ch. Kelly Shannon O'Green. Another Indeed daughter, this one bred by Shirley and Dick Farrington (Shawnee) and a sister to Ch. Shawnee Pipedream O'Charlton, became their second important foundation bitch; she was Ch. Shawnee Prairie Challenge. All Challenger dogs descend from these two bitches.

CHAMBERLAYNE: CRAIG C. COOPER
Lynnwood, Washington.
Craig received his first Irish Setter as a gift from his parents in 1976. His foundation bitch, Ch. Charlton's Thistledown, was heavily linebred on Ch. Candia Indeed, still the top sire in the breed. She produced two litters, including Am. Brazilian Ch. Chamberlayne's Masquerade and a bitch he kept, Ch. Chamberlayne's Think of Me. Her breeding to Ch. Kinvale Evergreen Destiny produced Ch. Chamberlayne's Big Easy and Ch. Chamberlayne's Echo of Kinvale. Bred to Ch. Kinvale Send In The Clowns she produced Am. Can. Ch. Chamberlayne's Sassafrass, owned by Michael Sicora.

Am. Can. Ch. Chamberlayne's Big Easy.

COURTWOOD: SUSAN HAHREN
St Paul, Minnesota.

Susan acquired her first Irish Setter in 1955, but it was not until 1971 when she purchased Kelly Shannon 'O Green as a hand-me-down dog from the first owner, that she began breeding and exhibiting. Kelly finished her Championship easily, but her great contribution to the breed came through four litters, all of which were sired by Ch. Candia Indeed, who retains his title to this day as the top sire in the breed. The four litters were named for the seasons of the year. Notable for their impact on the breed were Ch. Courtwood Spring Son, who was sent east and used by Mary Merlo's Evergreen kennel and others, and Ch. Courtwood Summer Forecast who became a prominent sire.

Sue and others used bitches from these four litters to carry on the Courtwood line. Ch. Courtwood Summer Magic was bred to Ch. Charlton's Moon Lover to produce the extremely important Ch. Courtwood Marxman and Manuscript. Marxman was the most heavily used and is behind many of the Meadowlark dogs of today.

In the early 1990s Ch. Courtwood Golden Gate (Ch. Rossan's Raz Ma Tazz ex Ch. Courtwood Bright Ruby) was used to good advantage by several kennels and is the sire of 19 Champions. Ruby was bred to Ch. Charlton's London Fog to produce two litters, 'silver' and 'gold'. She is an ROM with nine Champions. One of the silver litter, Ch. Courtwood Silver Slippers was bred back to Golden Gate to produce Ch. Courtwood Bandanna who is now an ROM dam with seven Champions to date.

Her current stock includes the combination of Bandanna bred to Ch. Courtwood Grand Hotel to produce the 'rains' litter, including Ch. Courtwood Heavy Rains making his mark on the east coast. Several of this litter are being shown and bred.

CUCUHULLAIN: M. CATHERINE SEYMOUR
Brookfield Center, Connecticut.

Kate's first Irish Setter was bought in Somerset, England in 1969 from a breeding combining Brendower and Halstock lines. After moving to the United States she bred this bitch to Ch. Bayberry Kinkaide (a Tirvelda-bred dog). Her influential early producer was Am. Can. Ch. Cucuhullain Chelsea Morning. The 'Diamond' litter resulted from a mating to Am. Can. Ch. Courtwood Summer Forecast (a Ch. Candia Indeed son). One of that litter, Am. Can. Cucuhullain Diamond Morning, was the dam of Ch. Cucuhullain Good Fortune, when bred to Ch. Cucuhullain Eternal Prince (Can. Ch. Cucuhullain Diamond Summer ex Ramblin'Red Iaslinn, leased from Anne Marie Kubacz). Recent litters are descended from these combinations.

Am. Ch. Cucuhullain Good Fortune.

ESTRELLA: JEANETTE HOLMES
Paradise, California.

Jeanette began her association with Irish Setters in 1969 and eventually became a professional handler. She no longer shows dogs as a full-time livelihood, but continues in this capacity part-time, while maintaining a small kennel. Jeanette acquired her foundation stock from Winy Arland, Charlton Kennels. Her foundation bitch was Ch. Charlton's Indeed I

Do, a daughter of Ch. Candia Indeed and a Tirvelda-bred bitch, Ch. Bayberry Happy Time. When bred to Candy K's Redford, an Indeed son, she produced the influential sire, Ch. Charlton's London Fog. Jeanette has tried to maintain those lines in her breeding program.

EVERGREEN: MARY MERLO
Mastic Beach, New York.
The founding brood bitch for Evergreen kennels was purchased in 1978 from Joan and Ernie Viola and Dana Haskell (Kinvale). She was the show bitch Ch. Kinvale Royal Irish (Am. Can. Courtwood Spring Son ex Ch. Kinvale Majorette of Kendel CD). Mary bred Royal Irish to Ch. Charlton's Moon Lover (Ch. Courtwood Summer Forecast ex Can. Ch. Kinvale's Charlton). This was a very successful combination, producing several National Specialty class winners, including Ch. Evergreen Personal Best. Personal Best was bred twice, producing several Champions, including Am. Can. Ch. Evergreen Chase the Clouds JH, CGC. A breeding of Royal Irish to Ch. Courtwood Manuscript (Ch. Charlton's Moon Lover ex Ch. Courtwood Summer Magic) produced a notable sire for Evergreen and for the Kinvale kennels. He was Ch. Kinvale Evergreen Destiny ROM. Most of the dogs in both Kinvale and Evergreen trace back to this dog. Mary considers Susan Hahnen (Courtwood) to be an important mentor for her foundation stock.

Am. Ch. Evergreen Chase The Clouds.

GABHANTYR: CELESTE AND JACK GAVIN
Morriston, Florida.
Celeste and Jack became involved with Irish Setters with the purchase of a foundation bitch, Tirvelda Brengwain, from E.I. Eldredge of Tirvelda Farms. Their foundation dog, who became the sire of 20 Champions, was Am. Can. Ch. Tirvelda Hunter's Moon (Treve), also from Ted Eldredge. Celeste preferred campaigning dogs to breeding, and after Treve was retired from a successful show career she purchased Ch. Shawnee Pipedream O'Charlton ROM, winner of two consecutive National Specialties and Number 1 Irish Setter in 1981. He was the sire of 40 Champions, grandsire of Ch. Meadowlark's Vindicator ROM and great-grandsire of Ch. Meadowlark's Wyndjammer ROM. Celeste also owned Wyndjammer (Rhett) who was the Number 1 Irish Setter in 1987 and the sire of 67 Champions.

Her last dog was Ch. Meadowlark's Vindicator ROM (Jamie). He was the Number 1 Irish Setter in 1988, owned by his breeder, Rose Ross and Nick Theodose. Celeste acquired him in 1989 and he became Number 1 Irish in 1990. He is the sire of 81 Champions to date, with others still being shown. He is the number 2 sire, behind Ch. Candia Indeed, in the history of the breed. Both Vindicator and Wyndjammer are behind almost all of the top dogs in the country today, often in combinations of the two.

JAMOND: DUANE AND JACKIE DRUMMOND
Carthage, Indiana.
The Drummonds acquired their first Irish Setter in 1973 from Charlene Legan of Charnel Kennels in Illinois. He became Ch. Charnel's Chuker D. Indeed (a Candia Indeed son). Their foundation bitches were Mandolin Star Struck and Ch. Mandolin Tough Enough. Two important dogs came out of these bitches or

Am. Ch. Jamond Call The Play.

their offspring – Ch. Jamond's Bostonian and Ch. Jamond's Call the Play. All the Drummonds' dogs trace back to Ch. Candia Indeed through several generations.

JEWELSET: JULIANNE WATERS AND KIM VELLETRI
West Greenwich, Rhode Island.
Jewelset began in 1973 with the purchase of their first Irish Setter, Celou's Tiffany Macrory from the late Louis Iacobucci. Their first show dog was Ch. Dutch Valley Sundance Kid, from

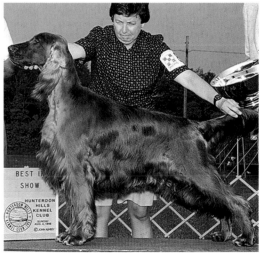

Am. Ch. Jewelset's Made For You.
Ashbey Photography.

Marion Mullet. He was their first Champion. The next dogs also carried the Dutch Valley prefix. They continued to produce dogs using Meadowlark lines and, when they saw Ch. Meadowlark's Whisperin' Breeze, owned by Patty Clawson, they purchased a Ch. Meadowlark's Vindicator daughter, Ballymera's First Encounter. They then co-bred a litter of Whisperin' Breeze to Ch. Quailfield's Mak'n Business. Six in this litter completed their Championships. It was the "Made" litter. Ch. Jewelset's Made 'N the Shade was bred to Ballymera's First Encounter to produce several Champions and other dogs pointed. The main influences on Jewelset lie in the combinations of Ch. Meadowlark's Vindicator, Wyndjammer, and the Vindicator son, Mak'n Business. A 1997 breeding of their Best in Show bitch, Ch. Jewelset's Made For You, to Ch. Rusticwood's Running Mate will carry on those lines.

KERRYCOURT: JEANNIE AND MICHAEL WAGNER
Wellington, Ohio.
The Wagners purchased their first dog in 1971 as a personal hunting dog. Committed to the dual dog, they found it difficult to find a dog who had the appearance of the traditional Irish Setter combined with good hunting ability. Ultimately, a dog who became important in their breeding program was a bitch they rescued from a garage sale. She was inbred on some old and valuable lines. They bred her to Dual Champion Shane's Irish High Noon to produce Karrycourt's Royal Flush, who became their foundation bitch. She, in turn, was bred to Fld & AFC Cidermill's Gonna Fly Now. This breeding produced Dual & AFC Karrycourt's Rose O'Cidermill ROM. Rose was bred twice, first to NFC, NAFC, FC, AFC Brophy's Mahogany Fielder and then to Karrycourt's Teddy Bear CD, VC. Several field Champions have ensued from these offspring, many of whom are already pointed in the field.

KERRY EIRE: SUSAN R. GRIFFITHS
Derby, New York.
Sue's foundation bitch was Ch. Danalee Cover
Girl, bred in 1976 to Ch. Candia Indeed. This
breeding produced Ch. Kerry-Eire Little Rebel,
CD, VC, who was a successful show bitch as
well as an important producer for Sue and for
the Sunshine Kennels of Kathy Whiteis and the
Rusticwoods Kennels of Carolyn Roche. Her
brother, Ch. Kerry-Eire Revolutionary, was
Number 1 Irish in 1980, but he has made his
mark on posterity through his daughter, Ch.
Kerry-Eire Coral Charm. Charm, bred to Ch.
Meadowlark's Vindicator ROM, produced the
Quailfield litter which included Ch. Quailfield
Mak'n Business and his siblings. Charm's
offspring from three litters carry on the Kerry-
Eire tradition.

KENOBI: JOE AND GERRY LEE
Gibsonia, Pennsylvania.
Gerry acquired her first show Irish Setter in
1982. He became Ch. Villa-Dan Darth Vader
and most of their dogs descend from him. They
bought their foundation bitch from the
Rockherin Kennels of Frank and Katharine
Wheatley. She became Ch. Rockherin Neesa of
Kenobi ROM, and, when bred to Darth Vader,
produced seven Champions from her one litter.
His background is mostly Tirvelda. Neesa was
a Ch. Meadowlark's Wyndjammer daughter
and her dam combined Ch. Indeed with
Tirvelda lines. They continue to work with
those bloodlines.

Ballacroy Kimberlin Autumn

KIMBERLIN: CLAIRE ANDREWS
North Scituate, Rhode Island.
Claire acquired her first Irish Setter in 1947. At
that time she showed actively in both
conformation and Obedience with her dogs
and in limited breeding has consistently
produced winning stock over the years. Her
foundation bitch, Ch. Shawnlea's Gayla, was
purchased from Miss May Hanley. She was the
dam of Am. Can. Bda. Ch. Kimberlin Encore.
In 1971 Ch. Kimberlin Cara, a top producing
dam, was bred to Ch. Tirvelda Sportin' Life to
produce her most influential bitch of the time,
Am. Bda. Ch. Kimberlin Kyrie. Kyrie, bred to a
West Coast dog, Ch. Thenderin William
Muldoon produced Ch. Kimberlin O'Killea of
Top'O, who is found behind most of Claire's
dogs and was an important sire for Karolynne
McAteer and Marion Neville's Red Barn
kennels. A son of O'Killea, Ch. Tioga Tegan to
Kimberlin, was bred to a McCamon bitch,
which brought back some of the old Tirvelda
lines. Tegan, when bred to Ch. Fieldstone Trace
of Burgundy, owned by Connie Vanacore, gave
Claire her most important brood bitch so far,
Ballycroy Kimberlin Autumn. Claire's current
show dog is a double grandson of Ballycroy
Kimberlin Autumn bred to Ch. Regalaire
Royal Majesty, tracing back to
McCamon/Tirvelda lines.

*Am. Ch. Kenobi Awesome
Design.*

KINLOCH: BOB AND PATTY COWIE
Chesapeake, Maryland.

The Cowies' first two show bitches were acquired from the Scarlly Kennels of Penny Nunnally in 1979. These half-sisters, Ch. Scarlly's Fiddle DeeDee and Ch. Scarlly's Sailing Silhouette plus a male acquired from Tom and Barbara Johnstone, Ch. Kintyre Midnight Flyer, were the basis for their breeding program. The Cowies then purchased Ch. Trendsetter's Steppin' Out as a puppy from Mike and Kathy Landon. This bitch took their breeding program in a slightly different direction when she was bred to Ch. Meadowlark's Vindicator. Five Champions resulted from that breeding. Two subsequent breedings of Ch. Kinloch's Ruby Tuesday (a Scarlly-Meadowlark cross) to Ch. Tramore Simply Smashing and Ch. Scarlly's Evening Reflections strengthened that cross. They have continued this bloodline with the purchase of Kintyre's Diva of Kinloch (Ch. Quailfield's Mak'n Business ex Ch. Scarlly's Love Potion No. Nine) co-owned with Barbara Johnstone.

KINVALE: ERNIE AND JOAN VIOLA
Huntington, New York.

Ernie purchased his first Irish Setter in 1964 from the Kilkara kennels of Kelly Fox. This male became Ch. Kilkara Firebrand CD. In 1966 he acquired Ch. Kilkara Fireflame CD and in 1969 Flame was bred to Ch. Tirvelda Nor'Wester to produce the first Kinvale litter. Ch. Kinvale Majorette of Kendal CD was the result of a second breeding of Flame to Ch. Tirvelda Middle Brother, co-owned with Dana Haskell. This became the foundation of the lasting friendship and co-ownership of the Violas and Dana. Majorette was the dam of Mary Merlo's foundation bitch, Ch. Kinvale Royal Irish, the start of another long-term relationship. The purchase of a Meadowlark bitch, Meadowlark Mystique, solidified the Tirvelda lines. When combined with the Courtwood influence, brought in through Evergreen, it produced Ch. Kinvale Evergreen Destiny and more recently, Ch. Chamberlayne's Echo of Kinvale.

LYN ERIN: LINDA ACQUAVELLA
Manorville, New York.

Linda started in 1974 with a dog obtained from Lucy Jane Myers of Draherin Kennels. Ch. Draherin Leading Man was her foundation sire. He was bred to a Draherin-bred bitch, Ch. Lyn Erin Trace of Thunder, which Linda purchased from Dr Robert Helferty and Ruth Cordes, to produce Ch. Lyn Erin Rhythm 'N Blues, Ch. Lyn Erin Diamonds Are Forever and Ch. Kimberlin Katydid. He was also bred to another Draherin bitch, Draherin Niadh, also purchased from Lucy Jane Myers. From that union came Ch. Lyn Erin Chances Are and Ch. Lyn Erin Memory. Tracy and Niadh are the foundation of Linda's line and all subsequent generations come from those two bitches.

McDERRY: CAREN McWEENY
Plympton, Massachusetts.

McDerry Irish Setters was established in 1967 as the family effort of Mary, Arlie and Susan Dash. Their strongest foundation bitch proved to be Ch. Redwhiskey Kiss Me Kate. She was bred three times, always to dogs with Thenderin bloodlines (a strongly line-bred kennel in California). Caren acquired Ch. McDerry's Jaimie Girl, the second important bitch in their line and the one which cemented the long-term partnership of the Dash family and Caren. Jaimie Girl was bred to Ch. Courtwood Manuscript, producing Ch. McDerry's National Jubilee JH. This bitch was bred to Ch. Courtwood Golden Gate to produce Ch. McDerry's Becky Thatcher JH. In 1990 Mary and Caren purchased from Kate Seymour the dog who is now a leading sire in the breed, Ch. Cucuhullain Good Fortune ROM. He is the sire of the top-winning bitch

Am. Ch. Lyn Erin Rhythm 'N Blues.

Am. Ch. Chamberlayne Echo of Kinvale.
Photo: Alverson.

Am. Ch. McDery's Becky Thatcher.

Am. Ch. Meadowlark's Wyndjammer ROM.

Am. Ch.
Meadowlark's
Shazam.

Ch. McDerry's Lil Misunderstood, National Specialty winner Ch. Ramblin'Red Fortune Teller and Ch. Ramblin'Red Nightn'gael Kian. In 1997 they acquired Australian Ch. Quailmoor Jamacan Rum and plan to incorporate his bloodlines into their breeding program.

MEADOWLARK: ROSE MARY ROSS
Midland, Virginia.
No recent history of the Irish Setter in America would be complete without noting the influence of Meadowlark on almost every breeding line in the United States today. Rose, and her husband F. Allen Ross, obtained their first Irish Setters from the Tirvelda kennels of Ted Eldredge in 1970. Their foundation stock consisted of Tirvelda Samaria and Tirvelda Fortune Teller. Samaria was killed in an automobile accident, but not before she produced one significant litter when bred to Ch. Draherin King's Ransom. This litter contained Ch. Tirvelda Meadowlark Ebbtide, among others. At the same time Rose acquired Glen Crec Merriment, who never completed her Championship, but was an important producer for Rose and for Mary Ann Alston, when bred to Ch. McCamon Marquis. Merry, when bred to Ch. Rendition Erin of Sunny Hills, produced the "I" litter, which included Interlude and Impossible Dream, both top producers themselves. Ebbtide produced three Champions when bred to Meadowlark's Honor Guard. Ch. Meadowlark's Masterpiece was sold as a puppy to Penny Nunnally (Scarlly) and was her foundation sire. Madrigal and Moonlight Magic were incorporated into Rose's breeding program. Ebbtide, when bred to Ch. Candia Indeed, produced Ch. Meadowlark's Anticipation, a top show dog, twice winner of the National Specialty.

Two dogs of particular importance to the breed were produced in 1984. Ch. Meadowlark's Intrepid (Ch. Meadowlark's Masterpiece ex Ch. Meadowlark's Interlude) was bred to Meadowlark's Magical Mirage (Ch. Shawnee Pipedream O'Charlton ex Ch. Meadowlark's Moonlight Magic). The result of that breeding was Ch. Meadowlark's Vindicator, the most influential sire of today. A repeat breeding of that combination produced Ch. Meadowlark's Equalizer, born in 1988. A brother to Equalizer, Ch. Meadowlark's Energizer, was sent to Australia, where he is being used extensively at stud. The second dog of immense importance was Ch. Meadowlark's Wyndjammer, a son of Ch. Courtwood Marxman ex Meadowlark's Aviance. Aviance was an Interlude daughter. Both Vindicator and Wyndjammer were co-owned by Celeste Gavin. Both are featured prominently in today's Irish Setters in the United States and Canada.

MORRIGAN: ROBERT AND MARGE McKAY
Mahwah, New Jersey.
Bob and Marge purchased their first dog as a pet. He had Red Barn bloodlines and became Ch. McKay's Red Baron CD. Robert and Marge were persuaded to show him and he finished his Championship and went on to win the first Irish Setter Club National Specialty in 1973 under the renowned British judge, J. W. Rasbridge. Their foundation bitch was

Morrigan's Red Star at Night.

purchased from Anne Marie Kubacz, Ch. Summerset Special Deal. A group-winning bitch, Katie was bred twice, producing Champions in her litters, first from Ch. Ramblin'Red Verran and then from Ch. Courtwood Heavy Rains. Two from the Heavy Rains litter are pointed.

NIGHTN'GAEL: DR EILEEN McDONALD
New Rochelle, New York.
Eileen has had two separate periods of involvement with Irish Setters, beginning in 1975 when she bought a young dog from Claire Andrews (Kimberlin.). He became Ch. Kimberlin Brian's Song, but, although he was bred, circumstances prevented Eileen from continuing to breed and show for several years. Then, in 1992 Eileen purchased another Kimberlin dog and a bitch from the Kubaczes, Ramblin'Red Exhilaration (a Ch. Castlebar Command Presence daughter). She was a successful show bitch and, when bred to Ch. Cucuhullain Good Fortune, produced the youngest Irish Setter ever to finish – Am. Can. Ch. Nightn'gael Ramblin'Red Kian, finished at seven-and-a-half months. Littermates to this dog are also pointed. Eileen plans to continue with combinations of these dogs to produce occasional litters.

O'KERRIE: CHERYL MIKA
Monee, Illinois.
Cheryl's first Irish Setter was purchased in 1969, although she credits her mother with having given her a love and respect for dogs before that time. Her mentors in the breed were Larry Downey, the Irish Setter breeder and professional handler, and Bernard Baron, who was President of the Irish Setter Club of America. Her most influential dog was Ch. O'Kerrie's Armagh (Ch. Tirvelda Distant Thunder ex Ch. O'Kerrie's Cherry Cherry CDX) and her foundation bitch was O'Kerrie's Kismet. Kismet was bred twice to Ch. Kilgary's

Am. Ch. O'Kerrie's Armagh.

Aman. She was the dam of Cherry and also of Ch. O'Kerrie's Sweet Surrender. Both of these bitches are behind all of Cheryl's stock. Armagh and Cherry are also important in other kennels, among them being Cairncross.

PATERJAY: ANNA JONES
Pittstown, New Jersey.
Anna began in Obedience in 1971 and successfully competed in that arena until she decided to enter the show ring in 1979. She purchased Ch. Rendition Peppermint Patti from Pat Haigler and Ch. Meadowlark's Honesty O'Padian from Rose Ross. The Rendition-Meadowlark cross has been very successful for Paterjay and continues through a co-owned dog, Ch. Meadowlark's FireNRain . This dog has also produced well in Australia through the use of frozen semen.

PAUNCEFOOT: STEPHEN AND PATRICIA SALT
Berea, Kentucky.
Pauncefoot was founded in the Worcestershire parish of Bentley Pauncefoot, England in 1965. Since leaving England in 1969, the Salts travelled extensively with their dogs until moving to Kentucky in 1989. Starting in 1975 the Salts produced a show line descending from Canadian Ch. Marrona Mystic Star of

Pauncefoot FD, who was acquired from the late Mrs Peg Stokes of Sussex. This line continues strongly in the Fairline kennels of Vicky and Patrick Hunt of North Gower, Ontario. Starting in 1987, a field line was based on the field trial winner Carlysle Emerald Jewel, with later infusions of Brophy and Damika. The foundation for this line was FC AFC Kopper Key Ms. Nellie, who was acquired from the late Faunt Ekey when he retired from field trialing. Three of Nellie's grandchildren are carrying on the Pauncefoot line.

PENDRAGON: LORRAINE BISSO
Metairie, Louisiana.
Lorraine grew up around an Irish Setter that was part of her family and she purchased her first Irish in 1964 when she was still a junior handler. After she finished college she purchased a bitch of Tirvelda and Rockherin breeding, Tara Hill Reflection. Bred twice, she produced both field and bench Show Champions. She has tried to work within a combination of the old lines of Tirvelda and Rockherin when she can find them.

PIN OAK: JIM AND NANCY GODBEY
West Swanzey, New Hampshire.
The Godbey's foundation bitch was purchased from Lynne Mehring. She was Ch. Shangrila Wyndchime, a Wyndjammer daughter. Bred to Ch. Rossan's Raz-Ma-Taz she produced the top-winning Ch. Pin Oak Vicksburg JH. Bred to Ch. Orchard Farm Kelsey (a Vindicator son), she produced Ch. Pin Oak Robert E. Lee JH. Their young stock is descended from these three dogs.

Am. Ch. Quailfield Successful Magic.

QUAILFIELD: PATRICIA NAGEL
Angola, New York.
Patty bought her first Irish as a pet for the children and as a learning experience for the family. In 1984 she bought her first show bitch from Sue Griffiths (Kerry-Eire). She became Ch. Kerry Eire Special Treasure and, when bred to Ch. Sunshine's First Rate (a Ch. Kerry-Eire Revolutionary son), produced Ch. Quailfield McCalls. At about the same time she leased Ch. Kerry-Eire Coral Charm ROM from Sue Griffiths and bred her to the influential Ch. Meadowlark's Vindicator. This line produced the dogs that define Quailfield, the most important of which is Ch. Quailfield Mak'n Business. A bitch from that litter, Am. Can. Ch. Red Hot Business, co-owned with Joan Staby, has produced several individuals in the "Successful" litter. Offspring from Mak'n Business are currently important in several kennels throughout the United States.

Am. Ch. Pin Oak Vicksburg JH.

QUINNIVER: PAMELA SCHAAR
Warrenton, Virginia.
Pam's first litter was whelped in 1972 from a bitch of Harmony Lane breeding and the Killagay kennels of Connie Christie. She

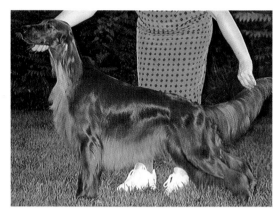

Am. Ch. Quinniver's Premiere.

continued to look for a strong foundation and eventually purchased a dog, Tara Hill's Harvest Moon (Ch. Tirvelda Telstar ex Ch. Rockherin Rebecca). He was bred to several outstanding bitches, one of which produced Ch. Shangrila Moon Shadow for Lynne Mehring. Harvest Moon is also behind Ch. Pin Oak Vicksburg and Ch. Pin Oak's Robert E. Lee. In the early 1980s Pam purchased Rockherin Quinn from the Wheatleys who has featured predominantly in subsequent generations. Her litter by Ch. Rossan's Raz-Ma-Taz produced Ch. Qinniver's Intermezzo, Arabesque and Premiere. Pam has used Intermezzo as a sire for her recent litters. Premiere, owned by Amy Maxwell, when bred to Ch. Meadowlark's Vindicator, produced three Champions. Pam continues to blend Rockherin and Tirvelda lines.

RAMBLIN'RED: ANNE MARIE, RANDY AND PETER KUBACZ
Jackson, New Jersey.
Anne Marie and her brothers and sisters bought an Irish Setter as a Christmas present for their parents in 1968. She trained Shannon's Kerry of Windsor UD herself and showed in breed and Junior Showmanship. Meanwhile, Randy bought his first Irish and became involved in field work, trialing his dog to become Field and Amateur Field Ch. Galway's Red Disappointment. Anne Marie and Randy met through their involvement with the breed and were married in 1975. They remained active in the field and won the Irish Setter Club of America's first National Field Trial Championship with National Red Setter Champion, Field and Amateur Field Ch. Ramblin'Red Banshee.

Anne became more interested in the show ring and bred her first Champion, Ramblin'Red Avelle CD VC to Ch. Draherin King's Ransom, producing two Champions. Ch. Ramblin'Red Guinevere was a successful show dog but Ch. Ramblin'Red Glingael proved to be a better producer. Her son, Ch. Ramblin'Red Kildavan was a top winner and producer, and another brother, Ch. Ramblin'Red Phaegan, in limited use also, was instrumental in establishing Ramblin'Red Kennels. Another Avelle daughter, Ramblin'Red Iaslinn produced 10 champions when leased to Kate Seymour of Cucuhullain Irish Setters.

Line breeding on Kildavan and Phaegan produced other important dogs for Ramblin'Red, including Ch. Ramblin'Red Verran and Vanara. Vanara, when bred to Ch.

Am. Ch. Ramblin' Red Quincidence.

157

Cucuhaillan Good Fortune, produced the National Specialty and Group winning bitch Ch. Ramblin'Red Fortune Teller, co-owned with Mariette O'Malley. Dogs who have had a major influence on Ramblin'Red are Ch. Shannon's Erin, Ch. Draherin King's Ransom, Ch. Shawnee Pipedream O'Charlton and Ch. Meadowlark's Vindicator.

REGALAIRE: BARBARA RIEGLE
Okemos, Michigan.
Barbara's association with Irish Setters began in 1972 with the purchase of her foundation bitch, Am. Can. Ch. McCamon Northern Star, from Susan McCamon (McCamon Kennels). McCamon is directly line-bred from Tirvelda and Rockherin lines. She produced a number of Champions, the most significant of which, Regalaire Blush With Pride, produced Ch. Regalaire Music Man, winner of the Irish Setter Club of America Centennial show and the sire of many Regalaire Champions. Also in that litter was the influential bitch Ch. Regalaire Sound of Music. In 1992 Ch. Gwyndara Southern Cross was imported to the States from Australia and his get in that country are just beginning to be seen.

ROCKHERIN: FRANK AND KATHERINE WHEATLEY
S. Redwood, Michigan.
The Wheatleys purchased their first Irish Setter in 1953, making their line one of the oldest still active in the United States. From the late Dr Jay Calhoun the Wheatleys purchased Ch. Caldene Ailene. When bred to Rockherin Flynn

in the 1960s she produced one of their finest litters, including Ch. Rockherin Race, who finished undefeated in five straight shows, and Ch. Rockherin Rebecca who finished in 1971. Rebecca was the foundation for many important kennels, including that of McCamon, Regalaire and Quinniver. The Wheatleys have continued to breed on those lines, incorporating Meadowlark and Indeed, through a breeding of Ch. Meadowlark's Anticipation to Rockherin Carrie. This litter contained Ch. Rockherin Sheena ROM, bred twice, once to Vindicator and once to Wyndjammer. Several current breeders have foundation stock from these two litters.

Am. Ch. Rumraisin Sorcerer.

RUMRAISIN: DEBRA HAMILTON
Armonk, New York.
Rumraisin Irish Setters began in 1986 with the acquisition of Ch. Ramblin'Red Quincidence from Anne Marie and Randy Kubacz. The daughter of Ch. Ramblin'Red Kildavan ex Ch. Ramblin'Red Lorelle, Quincy was bred to Ch. Red Barn Top O'The Line in 1991 to produce Ch. Rumraisin On The Q.T. (Violet), and her sister, Rumraisin On The Run (Bonnie), co-owned with Sandra Smith. Bonnie was bred to Ch. Cuchullain Good Fortune to produce Ch. Rumraisin Sorcerer. Debra acquired Ch.

Am. Ch. Rockherin Shangrila At Last.

O'Dandy's Caitlin O'Balcaire, a Good Fortune daughter. In 1997 she was bred to Ch. Courtwood Heavy Rains. These young dogs trace back to Ch. Candia Indeed.

SANTERA: NORBERT AND SANDRA NOVICIN
Mt. Airy, Maryland.
Sandy obtained her first Irish from the Wilson Farms Kennels of Dave and Ruth Wilson. Heavily line-bred on Tirvelda Wilson Farm, Scarlet Tirvelda CD was bred to Ch. Ballycroy Northern Sunset (Ch. Tirvelda Nor'Wester ex Ballycroy's Rua Catlin). This produced two males, the most important of which was Ch. Santera Tamberluck. Tamber was the tenth in a direct line of Best in Show dogs through Northern Sunset. He produced a son, Ch. Villa Dan Vallejo, that also went Best in Show. Tamber produced 16 champions, several of which have been influential in other kennels. In 1986 an outcross to Ch. Ramblin'Red Kildavan has successfully combined the old Tirvelda lines with Ramblin'Red lines. Several of these offspring are either Champions or pointed, and so carry on the Santera tradition.

SAXONY: JEAN ROCHE
Versailles, Kentucky.
The first Irish came to Jean Roche in 1974 with the purchase of a bitch, Serandida Saxony Sunflower, from Susan St. John Brown. From this bitch and her offspring, primarily Ch. Saxony's Midnite Forgetmenot (sired by Ch. Marquis Midnight Special) and Ch. Saxony's Wildwood Flower (sired by Ch. Scarlly's Red Hot), have come the most important of the Saxony dogs, Ch. Saxony's Uptown Tangerine and Ch. Saxony's Evening Reflections, line-bred on Scarlly dogs. In the most recent generations Jean has combined Meadowlark and Scarlly lines, intensifying the attributes of both.

Am. Ch. Saxony's Evening Reflections.

SHANGRILA: LYNNE AND BILL MEHRING
Highland, Michigan.
Shangrila setters was established in 1967 with a combination of show and field dogs. They worked their dogs in show, field and obedience, producing some field champions and obedience-titled dogs. In 1973 they purchased a bitch puppy from Betty Crawford (Shannon) and she became Ch. Shannon's Scarlet Urchin. Bred to Tirvelda Eamon of Gabhantyr she produced Ch. Shangrila Scarlet O'Hara ROM. Scarlet was bred to Tara Hill's Harvest Moon to produce Ch. Shangrila Moon Shadow and several other notable dogs and bitches which have had an influence in the breed. Moonshadow's daughter by Ch. Shangrila Southern Crown CD produced Ch. Shangrila Wyndchime ROM, the foundation for Pin Oak kennel. In 1989 she purchased Rockherin Shana of Shangrila from Frank and Katherine Wheatley. She has produced several Champions for them and in 1992 Ch. Rockherin Shangrila At Last was acquired from the Wheatleys. The combination of these two animals and their offspring are the basis for the Shangrila dogs of today.

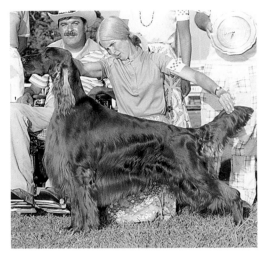

Am. Ch. Shawnee Pipedream O'Hara ROM.

SHAWNEE: RICHARD AND SHIRLEY FARRINGTON

Riverside, California.
Although their first Irish Setter arrived in 1969, it was not until 1971, when they purchased a show bitch from Pat Haigler of Rendition Irish Setters, that the Farringtons became seriously involved with the breed. This bitch, Am. Can. Ch. Rendition's Indian Summer ROM, became one of the top producing bitches in the breed. She was bred three times to Ch. Candia Indeed. One of those offspring was Ch. Shawnee Pipedream O'Charlton ROM, a National Specialty winner twice and the sire of many Champion get. A grand-daughter of Indian Summer, Am. Can. Ch. Shawnee Night Lace ROM, produced 13 champions out of 29 puppies, including five from one litter when she was bred to Draherin Pied Piper. The Farringtons have stayed within the Candia Indeed, Draherin blood lines for most of their breeding stock.

TAINARON: NANCY AND W. CURTIS CONNER, JR.

Montague, Massachusetts.
Nancy received her first Irish Setter as a gift from her husband Curt in 1969. Ch. Tainaron Saffron Replica CD was purchased from the Tirvelda Kennels of E.I. Eldredge and all dogs of their breeding come down through the Tirvelda bloodlines. All the dogs currently owned trace back to Ch. Tirvelda Michaelson and Ch. Tainaron Masterstroke, a product of Meadowlark breeding which, in turn, was founded on Tirvelda lines.

TOKEN: KAREN(KAY) AND BILL BEDEAU

Hot Springs, South Dakota.
Kay and Bill started in 1970 with Irish Setters which she rescued. She and her children trained their dogs in Obedience and tracking and she became increasingly involved with Obedience, both as an exhibitor and as a teacher. In 1985 they bought their first show dog, Ch. OTCH Bluewin's Fancy O'Shaughnessy UD, JH, VC (Sean). Sean's titles represent both conformation and Obedience Championships and also junior hunter and versatility titles. Sean's pedigree is heavy on Charlton lines, which go back to Draherin. Kay's mentor in Irish Setters is Jeanette Holmes, from whom she leased a bitch, Ch. Fancy Free Peg O'My Dreams CD. Peggy was bred to Ch. Sunshine First Rate to produce Ch. U-UD Token's Talk of the Town CDX (Sally) and U-CDX Token's Unsinkable Molly B, UDT (Molly.) Every Irish Setter bred at Token has Peggy's dam, Ch. Charlton Indeed I Do, in its pedigree. This bitch is a daughter of Ch. Candia Indeed, the top sire in the history of the breed to this day.

TRAMORE: GINNY SWANSON

Evergreen, Colorado.
Tramore began in 1972 with the purchase of a pet, but it was not until 1977 that Ginny began to breed and show, with the success that has resulted in more than 60 champions to date. From her original bitch she has a tail bitch line of five to seven generations. Most of her

Am. Ch. Tramore Kiandra.

WINDNTIDE: PAT AND CAROL McGARRY

Normandy Park, Washington.

The McGarrys bought their first Irish Setter in 1970, a puppy from Jay and Kellie Zirkle, who became Am. Can. Ch. Dunbrook Enchantment. She was bred to Am. Can. Ch. Tirvelda Hunter's Moon and from her came the first of a succession of outstanding bitches. Ch. Windntide Sophistication, a top-winning bitch, was bred to Ch. Dunbrook Love Is Blue to produce Ch. Windntide Hot Cross Buns. Sophistication was bred again, this time to Ch. Meadowlark's Masterpiece, producing Ch. Windntide Cordial on the Rox, who is the dam of Ch. Windntide Sandcastle when bred back to a Dunbrook foundation line dog, Ch. Dunbrook Once in a Blue Moon (Ch. Dunbrook Love is Blue ex Ch. Tirvelda Sarsfield Cameo). Sandcastle is carrying on the strong bitch line, with her litter currently being shown.

current stock comes down through Ch. Tramore Kiandra ROM. She has combined offspring of Kiandra, a line-bred bitch on Ch. Candia Indeed, with Meadowlark lines through Ch. Meadowlark Vindicator and Vindicator's brother, Ch. Meadowlark's Equalizer.

VERMILION: BRUCE AND MARY FOOTE

Magnolia, Texas.

Bruce and Mary acquired their most successful breeding stock in 1991 with the purchase of Ch. Rusticwood's Song of Hawaii from Carolyn Roche. Song of Hawaii (Riley) is a son of Ch. Quailfield's Mak'n Business ex Ch. Rusticwood's Made in Heaven (a Meadowlark-Candia Indeed cross). Subsequently they added Ch. Meadowlark's Irish Lace and Ch. Meadowlark's Eyecatcher, Ch. Meadowlark's Renaissance, Ch. Meadowlark's Curtain Call, Meadowlark's Impetuous and Ch. Meadowlark's Quartermaster. They have continued to breed within those lines.

Am. Ch. Windntide Sandcastle.

Can. Am. Ch. Lyn Erin Midnight Blue.

IRISH SETTERS IN CANADA

The population of Irish Setters in Canada nowhere approximates that of the United States. In 1997, 27 litters with 214 puppies were registered. Even in the 1970s when population rose commensurate with that of the States, the numbers were quite low.

Several dogs in the 1970s and 1980s made their mark as prepotent producers. Can. Am. Ch. McCamon Marquis, Can. Am. Ch. McCamon Royal Burgundy (the dam of Marquis), Can. Am. Ch. O'Irish Dangerman, Ch. Wyndfield's Olav Olympia, Can. Am. Ch. Dunholm Finn McCool, Ch. Renegade Of Lenair and Can. Am. Ch. Rebecca's Irish Lace. Can. Am. Ch. McCamon's Impresario (Am. Ch. Kimberlin Killea O'Top O ex Can. Am. Ch. McCamon's Grande Dame (Marquis' sister) was Number One Irish Setter for three years and Number One all breeds in 1987. He was owned by Dave Carey and shown throughout his career by Mr Carey's son, William Alexander.

Current winners in the 1990s in Canada are Can. Am. Ch. Quailfield's Mak'n Business (Ch. Meadowlark's Vindicator ex Ch. Kerry-Eire Coral Charm – a sister of Mak'n Business); Can. Am. Ch. Quailfield Stylish Success (a grand-daughter of Vindicator and Coral Charm); Can. Am. Ch. Meadowlark's Muir Woods (Vindicator ex Meadowlark's Solitaire); Can. Am. Ch. Orchard Farm Dream Girl (Am. Ch. Meadowlark's Masterful ex Ch. Orchard Farm Kayla).

Here are brief biographies of the owners of these and other dogs of prominence currently active in the breed.

TEALWOOD: DAVE CAREY
Moffat, Ontario.
Dave was a professional handler of all breeds and a breeder/owner of Irish Setters since 1972. In the 1970s he handled his dog Ch. Wyndfield's Olav Olympia to the top Irish Setter for two years and Number two sporting dog. He was the owner of Can. Am. Ch. McCamon's Impresario. His foundation bitch was purchased from Mary Klinck (Orchard Farm). She was Can. Am. Ch. Orchard Farm Dream Girl (Am. Ch. Meadowlark's Masterful ex Ch. Orchard Farm Kayla).

KULANA: VALERIE AND HEIDI GERVAIS
Cobble Hill, British Columbia.
The Gervais' first Irish Setter was purchased as a pet in 1966. After a couple of false starts they acquired from Lorne and Avis Mackie (O'Leprechaun) Am. Can. Ch. O'Leprechaun Bangor Boy in 1970. Through the Mackies they contacted Lucy Jane Myers of Draherin Kennels in the United States. From her they purchased their foundation bitch Can. Ch. Draherin Will O' the Wisp. They bred her to Ch. McCamon Jesse James, owned by Sue McCamon, and have maintained that line to the present with Ch. Kulana Noble Lad of Kenerin and Ch. Kulana Never Ending Story CD.

In 1984 Lucy Jane sent them Am. Can. Ch. Lyn Erin Memory and in 1989 they acquired her brother, Am. Can. Ch. Lyn Erin Midnight Blue. He is the sire of one of the few American Dual Champions, Cordon Bleu Bright Star, and of several other titled dogs. His sister was bred to Am. Ch. Meadowlark's Wyndjammer. To introduce another bloodline they bought Am. Can. Ch. MiJean's Court Jester, who traces back to Tramore and O'Kerrie lines in the United States. Kulana Irish Setters have been honored with the Pedigree Breeder of the Year Award for 1995, 1996 and 1997.

ORCHARD FARM: MARY KLINCK
Cottam, Ontario.
Orchard Farm began in 1938 when Mary Klinck's parents purchased their foundation bitch from the great American breeder, Jack Spear of Tyronne Farm Kennels. They produced several Champions from combinations of of Tyronne Farm dogs. In 1971 Mary and her mother decided to bring in another line as the remaining foundation dogs were too old. From the Brewbakers in Wisconsin they purchased a puppy who became Can. Am. Ch. Rebecca's Irish Lace (Am. Ch. Tirvelda Michaelson ex Am. Ch. Rockherin Rebecca). All Orchard Farm dogs today can be traced directly back to Irish Lace.

The best producer from Orchard Farm has been Can. Am. Ch. Orchard Farm Close Encounter (Am. Ch. Rockherin Royal Ragen ex Can. Am. Ch. Orchard Farm Julianne). All the foundation stock traces back to Rockherin, Tirvelda and through them to Meadowlark.

McCAMON: SUSAN McCAMON
Vancouver, British Columbia.
Sue McCamon, known during her most active years with Irish Setters as Sue Korpan through marriage, started in Irish Setters in Saskatoon with two pet Irish from the Ardee Kennels of Lorraine Weick. Although of pet quality they were excellent hunting dogs. The third addition was a Champion Shannon's Erin daughter, who finished her Championship in Canada. She was Ch. Pacesetter Morgan McCamon.

In 1971, realizing that they would not recognize their goal of producing show quality Irish unless they started with the best pedigrees they could find, the Korpans took a 4,000 mile journey to find the right bitch. On the advice of Ted Eldredge of Tirvelda Farms they ended up at the kennels of Beurmann and Elizabeth Brewbaker and bought from them a daughter of Ch. Tirvelda Michaelson ex Ch. Rockerin Rebecca. She became Am. Can. Ch. McCamon's Royal Burgundy. She was a magnificent bitch, a top winner, number one Irish in Canada and the dam of 23 CKC Champions and seven AKC Champions.

One of the most successful combinations was the mating of Burgundy to Ch. Tirvelda Telstar, a combination that was repeated three times. From the first litter came the most influential show dogs and producers, Am. Can. Ch. McCamon Marquis and his sister, Am. Can.

Littermates (pictured left to right): Can. Am. Ch. Orchard Farm Sarcanda. Can. Am. Ch. Orchard Farm Fay, Can. Am. Ch. Orchard Farm Devon (Am. Ch. Meadowlark's Wyndjammer – Orchard Farm Close Endeavour).

Am. Can. Ch. McCamon Marquis.

Ch.McCamon Grande Dame. Marquis was top Irish Setter in the United States in 1977 and 1979 and in Canada in 1981. Although Sue is no longer showing and breeding Irish Setters, these two dogs, plus others produced from these lines have had a major influence on the breed on both sides of the border.

ALLEGRO FARM: ARLENE SKENE
Langley, British Columbia.
Although Irish Setters have been a lifelong love for Arlene, it was not until the late 1980s that she was able to purchase a puppy from Meadowlark. She became Can. Am. Ch Meadowlark's Allegro (Ch. Meadowlark's Vindicator ex Meadowlark's Wyndsong, a Wyndjammer sister), and their foundation bitch. She was joined later by Am. Can. Ch. Meadowlark's Inspiration, another bitch who has contributed to Allegro Farm's success. Their foundation sire is Can. Am. Ch.

Meadowlark's Muir Woods (Ch. Meadowlark's Vindicator ex Meadowlark's Solitaire), a top winning dog in both the United States and Canada. His daughter out of Inspiration, Can. Am. Ch. Allegro Farm Dance 'Til Dawn, is the current winner and producer for Allegro Farm.

CAPTIVA: JILL TAYLOR
Cambridge, Ontario.
Jill has been involved with Irish Setters for her entire life, as her mother and father bred and showed them professionally. Her foundation bitch was purchased from Quailfield Kennels in 1992. She is Can. Am. Ch. Quailfield Stylish Success (Hazelhill Sugar Shack ex Am.Ch. Quailfield Red Hot Business, a sister of Mak'n Business). Her first litter was by Can. Am. Ch. McCamon's Impresario. Four Canadian and three American Championships resulted from that litter, among them Can. Am. Ch. Captiva's Ride With The Wind. Her second litter by Am. Mex. Ch. Sunshine's First Rate is now being shown.

To bring in another line Jill imported Shannonlee Aubrieta from Joyce Webb in England. She was lost to cancer early, but produced two litters by Ride With The Wind. These contained her future breeding stock, Captiva In Living Colour and Captiva Ready To Rock And Roll. She also bred an Impresario daughter, Lordlarry's Spice Of Life to Can. Am.Ch. Quailfield Risky Business (a Mak'n Business brother).

It is obvious from these brief biographical histories that the bloodlines of Canadian and American dogs are intimately intertwined. Although others have made their mark on the Irish Setter in Canada, currently, and for the forseeable future, the invisible border between the two countries extends to the dog world.

15 THE IRISH SETTER WORLDWIDE

AUSTRALIA

There is little documentation about Irish Setters in Australia until the late 1800s. Champion Garry (Imp. UK) won a first at the Royal Melbourne Show in 1899 and a number of dogs from well-known kennels were imported from the British Isles. Foundations were laid and the breed gained in popularity. Later, more stock arrived from England, including English Champion Marksman of Ide, as well as a number of Hartsbournes and Wendovers, many of them gaining their Australian titles.

By the 1960s the breed had become popular, competing at field trials, obedience and shows. During the 1970s and early 1980s increased popularity led to large numbers being bred, resulting in many strays. The situation improved, and quality, once again, has become the prime objective. In the Eastern States, the population of Irish Setters is much larger than on the west coast, and the vast distances involved tend to restrict competition between the two. Undoubtedly the most significant development in the breed has been the introduction of American bloodlines, either through imported frozen semen or through imported dogs and bitches, and there is now a very strong presence of American lines in the show stock. However, more English blood-lines have also arrived and future developments should be very interesting.

To gain the title of Australian Champion, dogs must win a total of 100 Challenge points under at least four different judges. Points are awarded on the basis of five points for the challenge and one point for each dog of the breed being exhibited that day, to a maximum of 25 points. A Group win earns 25 points, but the challenge points cannot be added to the Group points. If no other dog or bitch is exhibited, a minimum of six points is gained. Judges have the right to refuse a challenge.

AMHURST: MYRA RHODES THOMAS and MARGARET THOMAS

Established in 1972, the locally-bred foundation bitch was mated to the imported Wendover Crofter in 1974 and three Champions were produced. The next import, Wendover Jaquetta, was also mated to Crofter and breeding was based on pure UK lines, which is still maintained. Apart from some Clonageera and Sowerhill blood, breeding is pure Wendover, making the Amhurst Kennel their biggest representative in the Southern Hemisphere. Crofter had arrived with Ch. Sowerhill Keelta, owned by Jenny Scott. Mated together they started the Jarrador Kennel and produced Ch. Jarrador Gamekeeper, Best in Show at the Irish Setter Club of Victoria's Championship Show under Kitty Edmondson. He sired the top winner Ch. Amhurst Jarasaigh, Best in Show at Western Australia's Royal Show in 1986. When David Wong imported Wendover Fitzwillie, Amhurst Bronya was mated to him and produced Ch. Amhurst Hitchhiker. Another outstanding Amhurst dog of English breeding, via New Zealand, was Ch. Counta Espionage, Best in Show winner under two British judges.

BAIYAI: ROBERT AND HELENE GRATION
Established in 1967 – and their first dog became a Champion. Only an occasional litter has been bred and some of the dogs were not shown. Nevertheless, five Champions were made up. In 1993 Wendover Cane Sugar was acquired and is close to gaining her title. She took maternity leave to produce a litter, by AI, to Sh. Ch. Caspians Intrepid. Although this does not claim to be a high profile kennel, successes include Challenges and Best of Breed at Royal Shows, Group Awards and Best in Shows.

BRODRUGGAN: JAYNE STEWART
Graeme Lack started breeding in 1942 under the Ben-Lac prefix which, in 1967, changed to Brodruggan, and daughter Jayne became involved. Their foundation bitch, Ch. Colclough Portia, produced four Champions. The decreasing gene pool led to the first Irish Setter being imported from the USA – and Robalee Yank sired 47 champions. His sister, Ch. Robalee Velvet, produced three Champions, including Ch. Firewater who had a great career, culminating in Top Dog of the Year, Irish Setter Club of Victoria 1981-1982, and the Group at Royal Melbourne 1981. Another US import produced two further Champions, Roxy and Page Wun. From Roxy

came Titian Tarah, Runner-up Bitch of the Year 1994, ISCV. Page Wun produced three Champions. Her son Far And Away won the Group at Hobart Royal 1994 and Best of Breed, Sydney Royal 1995. When run in field trials, Broadway Jo gained a field trial certificate and points towards a Dual Championship. Since Graeme's death, Jayne has continued, and has imported Timadon Pride and Prejudice from England.

COLCLOUGH: WILLIAM AND MARY WALDRON
The prefix was registered in 1956 and many Champions have been owned and bred. The first great winning dog was the Best in Show and Challenge winner Ch. Colclough Cavalier, a grandson of Aust. Ch. Hartsbourne Brutus. A Cavalier son, Ch. Colclough Copperplate, may not have matched his sire's illustrious show career but was Best Exhibit at the Irish Setter Championship Show in 1970 and sired 20 Champions.

EIREANNMADA: GREG BROWNE
The prefix was first registered in 1968, but Aust. Ch. Ballina of Irishflame, imported from South Africa in 1973, provided the important foundation for the kennel. She introduced the American Kinvarra, Tirvelda and Bayberry bloodlines to Australia and, by combining her breeding with existing Australian stock based on Hartsbourne/Wendover lines, she produced Aust. Ch. Eireannmada Arizona. A highly influential sire, he was followed by his equally successful son, Aust. NZ Ch. Eireannmada Montana. Three stud dogs were brought in from New Zealand – NZ Ch. Redstone Oakley, Aust. NZ Ch. Ballymoss O'Dougal and NZ Ch. Ballymoss O'Carrig. They can be found in the pedigrees of some of the most successful kennels. Greg imported Charltons Marigold from the USA, and her mating with Montana produced Wells Fargo, the sire of a string of

Aust. Ch. Gwyndara Montpelier.

Champions, and of the influential sire Quailmoor Defiance. The current top male, Ch. Eireannmada At Tulane, is by Ch. Meadowlarks Energizer (Imp. USA) whose influence on the development of the breed cannot be over estimated. Earlier imports from the UK had included Timadon Aclare and Aust. Ch. Timadon Jaunty and, more recently, frozen semen by Eng. Sh. Ch. Thendara Okay Yaa has been used, as has semen from Am. Ch. Sunnyhills Wings of the Wind. The stud team has produced over 100 Champions and, with such an international background, it is not surprising that Eireannmada stock can be found in many countries.

GWYNDARA: TREVOR AND LEEANNE JONES

Ch. Taraglen Juturna was bought in 1979 and, with her nephew Ch. Taraglen Plantaganet and his son Ch. Kelibri Carbon Copy, provided the foundation. From Tara's only litter came Ch. Gwyndara Georgie Girl. Mated back to her grandsire, Plantagenet, she produced four Champions. Open To Offers won the challenge at the Irish Setter Club of Victoria and sired an Amercian Champion by AI. The Bitch Is Back is the dam of Am. Ch. Gwyndara Southern Cross who has produced several American Champions. Who's That Girl has 10 Australian Champions to her credit, and one nearing her championship in the USA. Her first litter by her grandsire, Carbon Copy, produced five Champions and her second litter, by frozen semen, was to American Champion Dunholm Windsor and included, among others, Champions Montpelier, Go It Alone and Wear It Well. 20 Australian Champions, one American Champion and a Champion in Singapore have been bred.

PENDORIC: L.G. AND A.M. HEARN

This kennel was established in 1971and the foundation bitch arrived in 1981. Ch. Taraglen

Aust. NZ Ch. Eireannmada Montana: a top sire, like his father, Arizona.

Opus One was mated to Aust. NZ Ch. Eireannmada Montana and three Champions resulted. Ch. Taraglen Flair, with a line to Fondador Eleanor (UK), had a litter to NZ Aust. Ch. Ballymoss O'Dougall, and daughter Pendoric Prim and Proper was mated to a Montana son ex an American dam. Champion brothers Izy For Real and Parade, BOB at Melbourne Royal 1987, resulted. A second prefix, Marigold, was started together with Greg Brown, and Marigold Aphrodite was mated to Quailmoor Defiance. They produced Aust. NZ Ch. Marigold Mad About Men and Ch. By The Way, Top Dog in South Australia for many years. Many Champions followed and in 1992 frozen semen was imported from American Ch. Meadowlarks Fire 'N Rain and put to Eireannmada Red Echo, which produced Ch. Pendoric Fire 'N Ice and Pandemonium; both multiple Best in Show winners. The semen was also used on a Marigold bitch to produce Ch. Pendoric Annie Laurie.

Aust. Ch. Quailmoor Indian Summer: 29 BIS wins, No. 1 All Breeds 1992.

QUAILMOOR: NORMA & GRAHAM HAMILTON AND SIMON BRIGGS.

This kennel was established in the 1960s with Ch. Parr Leyn Symphone. She had a successful show career and, when mated to Ch. Greglyn Red Radience, produced Champions Royal Leason, Royal Rogue and Royal Gem. Gem was mated to Eireannmada Arizona, and Ch. Outrageous, Best in Show at Brisbane Royal 1980, was born, making her the start of a long line of top winning bitches. Ch. Tarraglen All Aglow and Ch. Parr Leyn Sonata O'Erin were acquired. All Aglow produced 13 champions and, when Sonata was mated to Quailmoor Fireball, an All Aglow son, she produced Chs. Periwinkle, Pepper Prelude and Premonition. From Periwinkle came Ch. Zee who produced Ch. Kiss Me Kate – all top winning bitches. American bloodlines were introduced and Ch. Aria, a Prelude daughter, was mated to Ch. Seregon Second Coming and Ch. Georga Brown, whom the Hamiltons consider to have been their best bitch, was born. Her daughter, Indian Summer, holds the Breed Record with 29 Best in Shows and was No.1 All Breeds in 1992. Georga Brown had a second litter, by American import Meadowlarks Energizer. Nightlark went to Finland and won Best in Show at Helsinki International twice. Indian Summer produced Champions Jumping Jack Flash and Jamacan Rum, who also went to Finland and equalled Nightlark's record. No other kennel has ever won Helsinki International four times.

TARAGLEN: KEITH McCARTHY.

Established in 1967 with Mavang Amber Glow and Greglyn Giselle. Both bitches won well and Amber produced eleven Champions, including Best in Show winners Troilus, Achilles, Aurora and Toccata, Victorian Gundog of the Year, 1974. From Giselle's first litter came Timandra, Best in Show winner, and Best Opposite to her son, Ch. Hyperion, at the Specialty 1974. Another son, Ch. Tannhauser, sired 15 Champions. When he was mated to Fondador Eleanore, three Champions were born: Zodiac, Zabriski and Zenith who won three Melbourne Royal Challenges and two Specialties in 1982. A repeat mating produced three further Champions. A litter by Zenith ex Toumanova produced two Best in Show winners including Ch. Ultimate, winner of the first Top Irish Setter of Australia Competition. In 1980 two important litters were born. From the first came Ch. Plantagenet, owned by the Gwyndara Kennel, and Ch. Tamsin, a prolific winner. The second litter produced Toccason, Top Irish Setter Dog in Victoria for four years and sire of 26 Champions, including the outstanding Spellbinder, Top Irish Setter in Victoria for three years, and Spectre De La Rose. A dog puppy by the American import Ch. Seregon Second Coming was bought in. He proved to be outstanding in the ring and sired two great winners: Champion Maria, three times Top

Aust. Ch. Taraglen Spellbinder.

Pictured from left to right: NZ Ch. Fieldworthy Double Top, NZ Ch. Fieldworthy Dare Devil, NZ Ch. Fieldworthy Copyright, NZ Ch. Fieldworthy Double Pick and NZ Ch. Fieldworthy Double Star.

Irish Setter bitch in Victoria, and Champion Xtravaganza, Best in Show Hobart Royal. To date 104 Champions have been produced.

NEW ZEALAND

The key kennel during the 1950s and 1960s was Rose Cumming's Red River Kennel. Two of her dogs won Best in Show at the National Dog Show. During the 1960s Frank Cantwell's Ballymoss Kennel started to come to the fore with imported Wendover stock and achieved a pre-eminence which was to last until the late 1980s. Imports included Ch. Wendover Sonata and Wendover Old Fellow and many breeders owe their success to Ballymoss foundation stock or to the kennel's stud dogs. Frank Cantwell was instrumental in establishing the Southern Irish Setter Club in 1975, serving as President for seven years. Irish Setters reached their peak of popularity during the 1970s and 1980s when interest in the breed was high, particularly for show and obedience. In the 1990s the interest has dwindled and only a few key breeders for show remain. However, there has been a stabilisation in the use of the Irish Setter in the field.

FIELDWORTHY: LIONEL AND GAIL SHERIDAN

This kennel was first established in 1975; Ch. Ballymoss O'Tullyconna was acquired and from her first litter, by Aust. Ch. Timadon Jaunty, came Jannah. O'Tullyconna was next mated to Aust. Ch. Eireanamada Arizona, and Aristocrat and Ch. Aquarius were retained. When mated to Ch. Ballymoss Kerriemuir, Jannah produced Ch. Kinvarra, a multiple Best in Show and Group winner. The Sheridans' most successful dog, he was the Irish Setter Club's Top Stud Dog 1989. Mated to Aquarius he sired Champions Double Top, Double Pick, Best in Show at the Irish Setter Club Championship Show 1989, and Double Star. Their successes won Gail and Lionel the Irish Setter Club's Breeder's Trophy three times.

Jannah was next mated to Grand Ch. Clanfarrah Counter Spy and produced Ch. Copyright. She was mated to Double Top, and produced Ch. Dare Devil, a third generation Group and Best in Show winner. In 1990 Balintyne Starduster via Chugerra, one CC, one Res. CC, was imported in whelp to Sh. Ch. Bardonhill Supergrass. Stock from her litter joined kennels in NZ and Australia. Margate and Holyroyd were retained. The latter gained her title and produced three Champions for Kelvan Lean's Merryfield kennel. In 1991, semen was imported from Wendover Raffles and Ch. Raffleson was born. Starduster won her NZ title and was Best in Show at the Southern Irish Setter Club in 1992. In 1993 the Fieldworthy Kennel won the prestigious All Breeds Pal Breeder Sweepstakes.

KILSHEELAN: JOHN AND ROBYN GASKIN (Field Trial Kennel)

Initially, their involvement began with show and obedience, but now the Gaskins only

169

concentrate on the working side. In 1979 Samdonne Shanandoah CDX became John's first FT Champion. Imported from Australia, he won the National Pointer and Setter Championship. His daughter, FT Ch. K. Flirt produced FT Champions K. Airdrie and K. Arabella who won the NZ National in 1989 and 1990. The most influential dog was the first UK import NZ FT Ch. Erinvale Captain. Bought as a two-year-old in 1985, he had already won the UK KC Derby Stake in the hands of Billy Darragh. With his progeny, he dominated field trials throughout the late 1980s. He is the sire or grandsire of all the current top winning field trial dogs in Australia and New Zealand, producing six FT Champions. FT Ch. Carrbridge Lady Stacia was imported from Australia and won the three biggest Point and Setter Field Trials ever held in NZ, in 1986. The current top winner Field Ch. and FT Ch. Kilsheelan Gingersnap is Lady Stacia's grand-daughter, by the second UK import Erinvale Clancy of Kilsheelan. A third import, in association with Brazenwinds in Australia, arrived in 1996. UK FT Ch. Jonsmae Startime of Erinvale is the sire of a FT Ch. in the UK. John and Robyn are senior field trial judges and have officiated in many countries. They helped in the creation of the new title Field Champion, as opposed to Field Trial Champion. A Field Champion can only be made up by working with wild game such as pheasant and quail, instead of working with pigeons etc.

LANASCOL: CAROLYN CEDERMAN

The kennel was established in 1970 and the acquisition of Ch. Redcrest Symphony (out of Aust. NZ Ch. Quailmoor Humouresque) started a breeding programme based mainly on Australian lines. Symphony was mated to Aust. NZ Ch. Quailmoore Kracker Jack and produced three Champions. Her daughter, Red Reflection, also produced several Champions. Imports from Norma Hamilton's Quailmoor Kennel followed, including Champions Premonition, Tell Tale and Notorious. From Peter Mangos came Aust. NZ Ch. Tarralain Triumph (by Aust. Ch. Timadon Jaunty). A multiple Best in Show winner, he sired Grand Ch. Cheer Leader, the first Irish to become a Grand Champion. The title is based on three Best in Show wins and 100 CCs. Cheer Leader also sired many Champions including Ch. Gladrags. She was mated back to Triumph and produced Grand Ch. Keepsake. Sent to Australia to be mated to US import Aust. Ch. Meadowlarks Energizer, she produced Ch. Work Of Art, already a Best in Show winnner. Carolyn has also imported stock from Eireannmada and is currently campaigning Aust. NZ Ch. Eireannmada Seqoia.

MARINDALLAS: DON AND LESLEY EMMS

The kennel was started in 1970 with a bitch of Wendover/Hartsbourne breeding and gained her title. Ch. Lady Sarah of Clonakilty was mated to the UK import Wendover Hornblower and Marindallas Clandeboy became the first home-bred Champion. It was

Pictured left to right: NZ Ch. Marindallas The Legacy, NZ Ch. Marindallas John Henry, NZ Ch. Marindallas Look A Like, NZ Ch. Marindallas O' So Smart, NZ Ch. Marindallas Saucy Sue and NZ Ch. Marindallas Love Potion.

decided to concentrate on Wendover lines and Frank Cantwell managed to buy Wendover Country Boy for the Emms. He became a highly successful showdog, winning Best in Show All Breeds and Best in Show at the Southern Irish Setter Club Championship Show under the late Janice Roberts. Country Boy left his mark by producing a string of Marindallas Champions including Sea Jade, Meredith, Masterpiece and Grand Ch. Gayton Boy. One of his daughters, Grand Ch. Sapphire, was mated to Don and Lesley's son Stephen's Ch. Farrahway of Redstone and from this litter came Grand Ch. Clanfarrah Counterspy, almost a legend in his lifetime. His influence continues through his stored semen and, two years after his death, an exciting litter to NZ Ch. Fearnley Firewisp (Imp. UK) has been born. Wendover Wise and Wendover Country Royale were imported and more recently Firewisp and NZ Ch. Caspians Regard. The last two are co-owned with Stephen who has his own successful Clanfarrah Kennels.

REDCREST: GARRY AND SHELLEY WALKER

Redcrest was established in 1970, and the first of two Quailmoor bitches arrived from Australia in 1975. Aust. NZ Ch. Humouresque became a multiple All Breeds and Specialty Best in Show winner and a great brood bitch, producing four Champions and foundation stock for several kennels. The second import was out of Aust. Ch. Tarraglen All Aglow, one of Australia's most illustrious bitches, and Ch. Quailmoor Interlude became the dam of three Champions. Further imports from Australia included Ch. Pendoric Priscilla and Aust. NZ Ch. Wilangi Straitsman. Two others joined the Redcrests for a time and were campaigned to their titles – Aust. NZ Ch. Quailmoor Royal Rogue and Aust. NZ Ch. Fieldmark Lee O'Erin, both owned by Pam Wilde. In the late 1980s Ch. Clonageera Summer Magic was imported from the UK. A Best in Show winner at the Irish Setter Club Championship Show from the Veteran Class in 1997, his record as a stud dog is outstanding and his gets include Ch. Redcrest Magic Moment, Best in Show at the 1995 Irish Setter Club Championship Show.

SWEDEN

During the early 1970s, a number of dogs and bitches were imported from the Wendover kennel. Some of the imports proved to be influential and can still be found in many Swedish pedigrees. Kennel Profils imported Wendover Marie, Griddle and Gangster, a widely used stud dog. One of the breeders to make use of him was Anette Bjorken of the Chesterton Kennel. She mated Profils Bijou to him and kept Anjou-Bisset. She was mated to Wendover Jarvis and produced the winner Kilroy. Jarvis was a winner himself and features in the pedigrees of most of the leading kennels.

KENNEL BONBON: AGNETA PAMP

Bonbons Irish Electra was mated to Dino of Wendover and produced outstanding offspring. Bonbons Irish Eagle became a a top winner, and his sister Irish Ever So Nice gained a Field Trial Certificate and became an Italian Champion. She returned to Sweden and won her qualifying CACIB to become an International Champion and Swedish and Norwegian Champion. Wendover Touch Line was imported, a big winner and producer. His son, Tactic's Chianti, was Top Irish Setter in 1985 and 1986. More recently, stock has been imported from the Reddins kennel, which is blended with existing lines.

KENNEL COPPER: CAMILLA OSTMAN

The kennel was started with Övre Lövhöjdens Regina who was mated to Wendover Touch Line. This established a strong female line through Copper's My Heart Belongs to Daddy who was mated to Sowerhill Sailor of Wendover and produced Just One Of Those Things. She, in turn, went to Danaway Diplomat and gave An Affair To Remember and All Over The Place. Regina's son, The Man I Love, and another daughter, The Lady Is A Tramp, did some useful winning. However, her daughter My Wild Irish Rose, by Tactic's Great Gatsby, is one of the top winning bitches ever. She was mated to Wickenberry Kestrel, and Matters Of The Heart and My Rebellion Son were retained.

KENNEL DISCOVERY: BARBRO CARLSSON AND BO LJUNGGREN.

This is a top winning kennel that has come to the fore during the last ten years and is based on Citadel's The Temptress, by Wendover Touch Line. She was mated to Buccaneer of Clonageera and produced the winners Danilo and Dusty. Another, Donna, has had a litter by Clonageera Fortuneteller which produced Keep Up With Me. When mated to Fearnley Warlord, Not For Sale was kept. Number One Only went to Kennel Ember and won, as has Clonageera Miracle. Both have had several litters. Thendara Guilt Edged was imported and, when mated to Not For Sale, they produced Secret Wish, Star Light and Star Dust, the winners of Groups for Setters and Pointers in 1997.

Fearnley Warlord: Sweden's most successful Irish Setter in the show ring.

KENNEL EEL GARDEN: BIRGITTA SCHELE

The foundation bitch Lövhöjdens Josefine was mated to the two Wendover dogs Jarvis and Touch Line and produced winning offspring to both. However, Candy Carmine and Coppercoat Cissy, by Sowerhill Sailor and Happy Heather, by Danaway Diplomat, now feature in the pedigrees. Fearnley Fireduchess was imported and, together with Fearnley Warlord and Fearnley Fire Monarch, they provide the basis for the kennel today. Candy Carmine was mated to Warlord, which resulted in Kiss Me Kate, Top Irish Setter 1995. Happy Heather also had a litter to Warlord and their daughter, Pearls Of Passion, went to Fire Monarch. Their youngsters, Tattle Tail, Tea For Two and Trick Or Treat are already winning well. Warlord and Monarch have been top winners, with high placings in the Swedish Kennel Club's All Breeds List, and Warlord is the Top Irish Setter show dog ever.

KENNEL RED TAILS: TOMMY EISGÅRD

Tommy started with two Wendover bitches, Venus and Verity. Two of their top winning offspring were Cinderella, by Wendover Gangster ex Verity, and Red Tails Donna, by Cinderella's full brother ex Venus. They were successful under Scandinavian and British judges and are among the top winning bitches. Cinderella was mated to Wendover Jarvis and their daughter, Red Tails Irish Witch, produced an outstanding litter to Sailor. Marion and My Melody and the dog Mr Magoo won extremely well, with Marion and My Melody each becoming Top Irish Setter twice – Marion in 1987 and 1988, My Melody in 1989 and 1990. Another sister, Mireille, provided the foundation for the Sunny Pride's. Sowerhill Sailor of Wendover greatly influenced Tommy's breeding and holds the record for winning most progeny groups. His son Irish Admiral is the kennel's most recent top winner and when

Sowerhill Sailor of Wendover with his winning Progeny Group. Sailor holds the record for winning the most progeny classes.

mated to My Melody, they produced the current brood bitches Roberta and Romance. My Melody was also mated to Corriecas Alexander, resulting in Viceroy, sire of the winning bitch Yes I'm Irish, and another bitch, Lordly Sweetlove, was imported from Belgium.

BELGIUM
By the end of the 1960s the fortunes of Irish Setters in Belgium had reached an all-time low but, fortunately, Piet Jacobs was charmed by the breed and undertook its rescue from near-obscurity with imported stock. The foundation bitch for his famous Lowfield Kennel, Hanke van Wolmerum, came from Mr van Gemert in Holland. She was followed by a number of influential dogs from Britain, including Joanma's Don, Guildwich Gulliver and his sister Gen (by Sh. Ch. Scotswood Barabbas) Scotswood Hotspur. Cornevon Quiet Gentleman (by Sh. Ch. Twoacres Troilus ex Sh. Ch. Cornevon Cinderella) was probably the most successful of his imports, both at shows and at stud. The imported dogs and their offspring set a very high standard and enjoyed great success in Belgium and abroad, and the Lowfield Kennel provided many new breeders with their foundation stock. Piet was instrumental in the creation of the Irish Setter Club which came into existence in 1973 and is part of the Setter Club of Belgium, which caters for all varieties.

Between 1975 and 1984, 23 new kennels were registered but only the kennel "Of the Chicken Farm", owned by Kees and Jozefa Geysen-Cox, which was founded by Cinderella

of the Hunter's Home, is still active now; Midnight Danser and Mis Fiona are among their most successful Setters. Between 1985 and 1997, 16 kennels were registered and the current leading kennels started to make their presence felt in the 1980s. Ronny and Carine Blomme imported Wynjill Topaz in 1983. His influence can still be found in current pedigrees. More recently they imported Sh. Ch. Crimbledale Hello Dolly.

LORDLY: JEAN AND RITA STRUYF-DE GROOF
This kennel was started in 1985 with Westerhuy's Dutch Pearl. Her sons, Sh. Ch. Jilian and James, Dog of the Year 1988/89/90, were retained. Sh. Ch. Tenderlove Kizzy van de Westerhuy was acquired and became the real foundation bitch. Mated to Sh. Ch. Harvey of the Hunter's Home, she produced Show Champions – Lordly Loverboy, Lovey Dovey, Love Touch, and also M'Buster, by Sh. Ch. Danaway Dante. Lovey Dovey was a successful brood and produced Show Champions Our

Pictured left to right: Sh. Ch. Tenderlove Kizzy. v.d. Westerhuy, Sh. Ch. Lordly Lovey Dovey, Sh. Ch. Lordly Our Pride and Sh. Ch. Lordly Scrappydoo.

Pride, Pomerol, Promise and Rumpypumpy. Our Pride whelped Sh. Ch. Uptodate and Sh. Ch. Scrappydoo, a fourth generation Show Champion by If Newgay. Aged only two-and-a-half she became Dutch Irish Setter of the Year in 1996. Lordly have won four Best in Show awards at Club Championship Shows in Belgium, Luxembourg and in the Netherlands. Until now, Jean and Rita have bred 11 litters, producing 11 Show Champions.

OF THE GOLDEN VALE: SONJA RIJKERS
Sonja started with Sh. Ch. Snowhite van de Westerhuy and produced Sh. Ch. Most Mangonel of the Golden Vale, by Camelotshof Yri. Another bitch was acquired, Sh. Ch. Lordly Love-Touch, who became the main foundation. Mated to Sh. Ch. Hotwave v.d. Westerhuy, she produced Orthoclaes, Best in Show at the Belgium Club Championship Show 1996, and Sh. Ch. Otavite. From her litter by Sh. Ch. Explosion of the Hunter's Home came Sh. Ch. Redlight, Dog of the Year 1995-1996-1997.

VICARY'S: YVONNE HILL–DECOSTER.
This kennel has become one of the most successful on the Continent, largely due to the foundation bitch Ch. Handy Hunt of Huize Comtessa, bred by Tiny Koster-Houten. Probably the most successful show bitch of the 1980s, she also proved herself to be a good brood. From her first litter by Ch. Hunter van het Adelaarsvaren came Show Champions Kingfisher, Keyless Girl and Kissing Kindly. Next she had a litter to Wynjill Topaz, resulting in two more Champions, Little Lolly and Look Out. Keyless Girl was mated to Revival Morning Mist and produced Ch. Noble Son. From her second litter by Ch. Harvey of the Hunter's Home came Ch. Vicary's Powerfield. A mating between Noble Son and Little Lolly produced four Champions, including Ch. Pipepiper. Born in 1991, he won a string of

Sh. Ch. Handy Hunt van Huize Comtessa, aged ten years. One of the most successful show bitches of the 1980s.

titles and ended his active show career by becoming Supreme Champion of Champions in Basle in 1997. From Little Lolly's litter by Vicary's Principal came another Champion, Soloist. Yvonne puts her success down to the exceptional female line started by Handy Hunt.

THE NETHERLANDS

Holland has always played an important role in the development of the Irish Setter. The fact that Mrs Ingle Bepler was prepared to buy Castor, a third prize winner in a class of four at Arnhem in 1904, indicates the high quality of Irish Setter that was being bred in Holland in the early 1900s. Castor may not have impressed the Dutch but in England, renamed Clancarty Rhu, he won, and sired large numbers of winners. In Castor's day, Irish Setters were owned by the Dutch Royal family and Princess Wilhelmina, later Queen, kept a large kennel, with her favourite being Swell. Successful kennels such as Rhienderstein were descended from stock bred by Irishman Robert O'Callaghan and Dutch breeders produced winners in many countries. There was no divergence between show and working Irish Setters, and shows and trials were organised by the Dutch Setter Club, which catered for all varieties.

The Irish Setter Club of the Netherlands was founded in 1915 and a change in direction took place. Dogs were starting to be bred mainly for show but members were still concerned to preserve their working ability. English bloodlines became more important, especially the Rheolas, via the Henriado dogs. In the 1930s Hartsbournes started to make their influence felt through Jan Hesterman's O'Cuchulains as well as through G. J. Verweij's Sutherlands and, in the post-war period, Nel van der Sijde's Irish Setters came to the fore under her Goldwyn prefix. Up until the end of the 1960s Hartsbourne-bred stock maintained a winning edge and Shandon O'Cuchulain and his litter sister Bessy became International Champions in Germany and had considerable influence. During the 1970s, interest in the Irish Setter bred purely for show increased and, for a time, Wim van Gemert's Van Wolmerums kennel, based on Wendover lines, excelled. Imports from Janice Roberts' Cornevon Kennel

started to dominate the show scene and three famous breeders shaped the development of the breed. Tiny Koster-Houten's van Huize Comtessa was based on Sandra, by Brackenfield Tartar, and was bred from mainly Hartsbourne lines. Sandra produced Champions and winners to several sires and is the direct ancestor of the important Handy Hunt v. Huize Comtessa. Tiny is no longer involved with the breed, but other influential breeders still own the leading kennels.

OF THE HUNTER'S HOME: PIET AND MARGA ROKS

The kennel was founded by two Cornevon bitches – Ch. Starlight, by Sh. Ch. Twoacres Troilus ex Sh. Ch. Cornevon Primrose, imported in 1973, and Ch. West Whirligig, by Margaretwoods Caretaker of Scotswood ex Cornevon Stargazer. West Whirligig was Top Irish Setter in the Netherlands in 1979. Starlight's litters produced many Show Champions and winners. Another import from Janice Roberts was Cornevon the Conqueror. There have been many Champions over the years, not only in the Netherlands, but all over Europe. During the mid-1980s the influential Ch. Hunter v.h. Adelaarsvaren, by Ch. Echo of

Aust. Ch. Eireannmada Mustafa, bred by Greg Browne in Australia, based with Piet Roks.

*Netherlands Ch.
Hotwave v.d.
Westerhuy*

the Hunter's Home, was campaigned and produced a string of Champions. The litter brothers Dutch Champions Harvey and Humphrey of the Hunter's Home were important winners, with Harvey also proving himself to be a successful stud dog. An exciting development is the loan of Aust. Ch. Eireannmada Mustafa from Greg Browne in Australia. Widely used at stud, it is hoped that his bloodlines will increase the gene-pool in the Netherlands.

WESTERHUY: WILLY DUYNKERKE.
Willy Duynkerke has been an influential figure in Holland and in Britain. She was already successful and had imported several Cornevons before she came to live in England in 1976, where she campaigned Sh. Ch. Cornevon Westerhuy's Dream and Sh. Ch. Cornevon Westerhuy's Cloggy, bred by Janice Roberts. Eventually, both went back with Willy to the Netherlands, but not before leaving top winning progeny. They continued their successful careers and produced Champions on both sides of the Channel. From Cloggy came Dutch Little Flirt v.d. Westerhuy, and Cloggy's

daughter, Westerhuy's Dutch Appeal, proved to be an excellent brood and produced a number of Show Champions including Westerhuy's Sea Minstrel, Hotwave and Windcatcher v.d. Westerhuy. Dream was also responsible for many winners, including Carrig Maid's Harriet in Germany. Over the years, Willy has continued to import stock from Britain to keep up the high standard of her kennel.

FIELD TRIAL DOGS IN THE
NETHERLANDS
For a time the Irish Setter almost disappeared from competition in the Netherlands. There had been an attempt to revive the interest in the 1970s, but Dutch show dogs could not compete satisfactorily in field trials. Stock was imported from John Nash's Moanruad Kennel in Ireland but without lasting success. However, some Dutch triallers were successful with German-bred stock based on Moanruad lines, and in 1995 Gerard Mirck won the European Championship with Ullah von Royal. This rekindled interest and in 1997 the Irish Setter Club decided to give support to the working dogs.